Science in the New Age

SCIENCE AND LITERATURE

A series edited by George Levine

Science in the New Age

The Paranormal, Its Defenders and Debunkers,
and American Culture

DAVID J. HESS

The University of Wisconsin Press

The University of Wisconsin Press
114 North Murray Street
Madison, Wisconsin 53715

3 Henrietta Street
London WC2E 8LU, England

Library of Congress Cataloging-in-Publication Data
Hess, David J.
    Science in the new age : the paranormal, its defenders and
debunkers, and American culture / David J. Hess.
    256 p.   cm. — (Science and literature)
    Includes bibliographic references and index.
    ISBN 0-299-13820-8 (cloth)   ISBN 0-299-13824-0 (pbk.)
    1. New Age movement—United States—History.   2. New Age movement—
United States—Controversial literature.   3. Parapsychology—United
States—History.   4. Parapsychology—United States—Controversial
literature.   5. Skepticism.   I. Title.   II. Series.
BP605.N48H47   1993
306.4 2—dc20   93-18890

To Joanne Wagner:
critical theory reading group colleague;
a brilliant, skeptically minded graduate student;
lost to leukemia

Contents

Preface

SCIENCE can answer many questions, but when faced with death and other ultimate problems of meaning, the scientific world view either responds with silence or suggests skepticism. The alternative, religion and various otherworldly philosophies, remains a force in contemporary society if for no other reason than because death and the other problems of meaning remain part of the human condition. In one sense, then, the topic of this book is the universal problem of the dialogue between science and religion, knowledge and faith, skepticism and otherworldly experience.

My road to understanding the universal, however, is through a critical inspection of the particular. I focus on the debate in one society, the United States, and on the segment of its population that contests the reality of phenomena known as "paranormal": the psychic, mental, or spiritual phenomena that are believed to fall outside the range of the "normal," as defined by current scientific knowledge (a definition I adapt from *Webster's New World Dictionary*, Guralnik 1986). Although I make no attempt to answer the ultimate questions of meaning, I will show how the range of positions that have appeared in the debate—from skeptical materialism to otherworldly spirituality—are not the product of purely intellectual or spiritual processes, but instead are part of an ongoing cultural dialogue.

I consider three main communities: New Agers, who accept the paranormal in the context of a broader quest for spiritual knowledge; parapsychologists, who define paranormal phenomena to include a narrow range of phenomena for which they seek a scientific basis; and skeptics, who adamantly oppose all paranormal beliefs and claims. I also examine Hollywood movies that portray skepticism and paranormal experience, for those cultural texts provide a commentary on the other three communities and constitute an important aspect of the dialogue on the paranormal in the United States. I begin with the obvious: New Agers, parapsychologists, and skeptics disagree, and often vehemently, about what constitutes valid and invalid knowledge. However, I show that beyond the surface of charges and countercharges of pseudoscience, of positions staked out and defended as more or less "true" knowledge, and of orthodoxies and heterodoxies, they are also forging a shared culture. It is not political and self-conscious enough to be called a counterculture, but this emergent paranormal culture is enough "beyond" (para) the mainstream that I think of it as a "paraculture."

To interpret culturally the dialogue between defenders and debunkers of the paranormal, I take as my point of reference "American culture." More a useful heuristic than a superorganic thing, American culture is only meaningful when contrasted with something it is not: non-Western cultures, other national cultures, regional American cultures, transnational scientific cultures, and so on. I therefore write from the "distant view" of the comparativist, to borrow the phrase of the anthropologist Claude Lévi-Strauss (1985). My understanding of American culture is derived from the comparative tradition of anthropology and sociology, and, more specifically, from my own experience as an anthropologist who did fieldwork on science, religion, and popular culture in Brazil (1991b). Although I do not mention Brazil very frequently in the pages that follow, that country and its culture remain a fundamental point of reference. Only after I had spent time among what would be the equivalent of Brazilian skeptics, parapsychologists, and New Agers (although such categories do not exist in the same way there) was it possible for me to see how deeply the three communities in the United States articulate the conflicts, dilemmas, and assumptions of American culture. As for many other cultural anthropologists, my native culture now appears slightly foreign to me, and consequently connections that others probably have not noticed have become for me not only visible, but salient.

I have written this book so that it is accessible to interested nonexperts, including people struggling to understand better their own involvement in New Age groups or skeptical alternatives, but I write primarily for other scholars situated at the intersection of disciplines known as "cultural studies": anthropology, literary studies, cultural history, the sociology of knowledge, and other related fields. As a scholarly book, *Science in the New Age* has gone through a number of drafts and versions, and along the way many people have contributed their insights and comments. The series editor George Levine and the press editor Barbara Hanrahan deserve first thanks for their support and encouragement. The sociologist Tom Gieryn and the anthropologists Gary Downey and Sharon Traweek provided helpful criticisms, encouragement, and suggestions, as did the anthropologist Patric Giesler, who took time out from fieldwork in Bahia to write up some very helpful comments.

Conversations with many of my colleagues at Rensselaer helped me to conceptualize various parts of the book; among them are Carol Colatrella, Deborah Coon, Shirley Gorenstein, Linda Layne, Roxanne Mountford, Alan Nadel, David Porush, Langdon Winner, and Ned Woodhouse. I also benefited greatly from discussions with the sociologist Sal Restivo, who has helped me to orient myself in the field of science and technology studies and has read and commented on earlier versions of the manuscript, particularly chapter 7. Many other people read earlier versions of the manuscript (or sections of it) and provided helpful comments and bibliographic references. They include Carlos Alvarado, Michael F. Brown, Deborah J. Coon, George Hansen, Stanley Krippner, Brian Martin, James Matlock, G. Gordon Melton, and Trevor Pinch. My former teachers—the anthropologists James A. Boon, Roberto DaMatta, and David Holmberg, and the historian Thomas Holloway—will recognize their influence in the pages that follow, and I hope no other acknowledgement is necessary. Finally, my brother Phil spent several late nights with me one holiday vacation watching old horror movies, and I thank him once again for putting up with me.

Prior to embarking on this journey into the symbolic world of the borderlands and frontiers of science and popular culture, I wish to answer one question that has frequently been raised: what is your own position? I have, at different phases of my life and to varying degrees, found myself immersed in each of the three cultures discussed in the pages that follow. I find it possible to understand why members of each culture find their world so compelling, just as I am suspicious of those who readily take sides with one position or another. As I move back and forth from fieldwork among Brazilian Spiritists to schoolwork among American academics, I watch my own mixes of belief and skepticism shift, although often in ways that are contrary to the dominant beliefs of the group with whom I am engaged at the time. I therefore find dogmatic skepticism as much a type of true belief as religious dogmatism; both seem, in William James's apt phrase, to be "two opposite sentimentalisms" that "divid[e] opinion between them" (1960:315). I do not presume to judge one or the other viewpoint as the most "truthful"; instead, my fragmented and contradictory experience have led to a personal position of reflexive skepticism, that is, a skepticism that is skeptical of its own skepticism.

Part I

Introduction

1

The Three Cultures:
New Age, Parapsychology, Skepticism

[I]f the anthropological study of religious commitment is underdeveloped, the anthropological study of religious noncommitment is nonexistent.
— Clifford Geertz (1973:109n)

From the sociological point of view there is little more to be said about the boundary of science in general. The boundary is a convention . . .
— Barry Barnes (1982:93)

The New Age Movement

Past lives therapists and crystal healers, earth goddesses and lost civilizations, mantras and gurus, Harmonic Convergence and shamanic voyages, Hollywood ghosts and California channelers, natural medicine and pagan rituals, Shirley MacLaine and Marilyn Ferguson: the list of manifestations of what is sometimes called the New Age movement goes on and on. A great deal *is* being said, and much more remains to be said, both by and about those who defend, debunk, practice, and most of all write about the skeptical spirituality or credulous scientificity of unconventional otherworldliness and paranormal belief in the United States. An integral part of the landscape of a country where a third of the population is unchurched, the New Age movement represents a deep interest in alternatives to conventional knowledge and faith that future scholars may well find crucial to understanding American culture in the last decades of the millennium.[1]

The "New Age movement" may be most easily and vividly defined by a list of beliefs and practices such as the one just given; but it is possible to be somewhat more precise and, in the process, to take the first step toward a cultural analysis of the movement. J. Gordon Melton, a United Methodist minister and religious studies scholar who has specialized in new and al-

3

ternative religions, locates the origins of the New Age movement in "the distinctive synthesis" of Eastern religion and transpersonal psychology that emerged out of the 1960s counterculture and the government's rescision of the Asian Exclusion Act in 1965 (Melton 1988:36–43; see also Melton, Clark, and Kelly 1990). He dates the origins of the New Age movement at "around 1971," but he also notes that its roots can be traced back to the Enlightenment's scientific critique of official religion in the eighteenth century and to the Spiritualist movement of the nineteenth century (1988: 36–41). In a sense, then, the New Age movement is not very new, for Americans have been trying to bridge the gap between science and religion for a long time, just as they have been turning for inspiration to the ancient wisdom of Asia – "turning East" (Cox 1977) – since at least the days of Emerson and Thoreau.

The followers of occult and metaphysical traditions of the past were not antiscientific, and today New Agers have a penchant for bringing together the technical and the spiritual, the scientific and the religious. The anthropologist Loring Danforth, who studied New Age fire walkers, finds an important aspect of contemporary New Age thought in this crossing of secular and sacred boundaries: "Where the New Age movement does differ from other more clearly religious movements is the degree to which it draws on areas of American culture that would be considered not only secular but scientific as well. In characteristically eclectic fashion, people involved in the New Age movement have made full use of recent scientific developments in the fields of psychology and biology. Paradoxically, then, although much New Age thinking is characterized by a lack of faith in science, it would not be an exaggeration to say that in the New Age science has become a sacred symbol, psychology a religion" (1989:254).

I will explore that paradox in more detail later; at this point I wish only to emphasize how difficult it is to accommodate the New Age movement to conventional analytical categories such as religion. An interest in modern science is one of the key "elements" of New Age discourse and practice, along with an interest in Eastern philosophies and the psychology of human potential. To these three elements I would add four others: Native American religion, goddess religion and primitive matriarchy, therapies that integrate body and mind (and "spirit" when it is a separate category from mind), and all things understood to be "natural" (e.g., organic food, natural healing, and ecology). Together, these elements locate New Age discourse and practice in an arena of debate and dialogue that takes place with reference to science, religion, feminism, biomedicine, psychotherapy, environmentalism, and non-Western philosophies.

A list of features serves as one concise way of getting a handle on the idea of a New Age movement, but I would like to balance that approach with a second definition that focuses on social structure and cultural context. Just as one might question how new the New Age movement is, one could also question its nature as a cohesive social movement. It is a "movement" more in the sense of that other "movement" from which it derives: the late sixties "Movement" of students, antiwar protestors, black power advocates, feminists, hippies, and communalists. Both movements shared a vague goal of changing the "establishment" and bringing about a better society, and New Agers today might be seen as heirs to the side of the sixties counterculture that opted for spiritual transformation rather than direct social change.[2]

Indeed, heirs to the hippies might be the best sociological description of the people sometimes known as "New Agers." Although the New Age movement is only a loose amalgam of various interlocking social groups and organizations, it is nevertheless rooted in a shared generational experience. Several scholars have associated the New Age movement with the baby-boom generation, the seventy-five-million Americans born between 1946 and 1964 (e.g., Brown 1989).[3] Susan Love Brown, an anthropologist who did fieldwork in the Onanda World Village of northern California, found that the mean age of her New Age community in 1986 was 37.7: thirtysomething rapidly turning fortysomething (1987:120; 1989). Likewise, Danforth described a similar demographic group: "people who came of age in the 1960s, people who are now well into their thirties and trying to make their way as adults in the very difficult world of the 1980s" (1989:254). In short, the New Age movement might be described as one aspect of the graying of the greening.

Describing New Agers as graying baby boomers should not imply reducing them to yuppies. The latter term implies a class dimension that may not be an entirely accurate description of New Age demographics. Although the New Agers discussed here are predominantly middle class, significant sociological divisions also play themselves out within the New Age movement. For example, my own observations of groups in upstate New York suggest that people drawn to Spiritualist churches and psychic development groups have less formal education than those drawn to meditation groups.[4] More important, the overall picture is one of diversity; in visiting holistic health fairs, meditation centers, Spiritualist churches, and so on, I have been struck by the number of attendees who were either too old or too young to be baby boomers, just as I have been impressed by the diversity of the ethnic, class, and occupational backgrounds of the people whom I observed or with whom I spoke. Perhaps the New Age movement is best defined by who is missing: in addition to the large segment of the population drawn to conventional religions (what could be called the "churched" majority), there is probably a disproportionately smaller number of people who have advanced graduate education in the social sciences and humanities and/or are active in progressive politics — that is, two other paths often taken by baby boomers who were touched by the other Movement of the 1960s.

Who, then, are some representative examples of New Agers? The answer is far from straightforward. The New Age movement is defined around interests, products, and participation in local voluntary organizations rather than by a national umbrella organization. As a national movement, it is an amorphous series of converging tendencies, groups, and ideas. It is difficult to say, "Take me to your leader." There isn't one. However, at the national level there are important writers, thinkers, and spokespersons to whom we can turn for examples of what New Agers believe. Marilyn Ferguson has often been mentioned. The editor of the *Brain/Mind Bulletin*, a newsletter that reports on new research in psychology and the neurosciences, Ferguson is best known as the author of the *Aquarian Conspiracy*. The book's cover advertisement announces it as "the New Age watershed classic," and, in a comparison that most Americans would probably not find flattering, the skeptic Carl Raschke argues that "Ferguson's book is for New Agers what *The Communist Manifesto* was for the First International" (1988:330).

There are dozens of other prominent spokespersons and authors, and I have chosen only to discuss a few carefully selected examples who represent some of the important tendencies within the New Age movement (see the Appendix for a discussion of my selection criteria and methodology):

Lynn Andrews, a Los Angeles–based writer who in some ways is the feminist answer to Carlos Castaneda. She describes the ceremonies and spiritual beliefs of Native Americans and other native peoples, one important area of New Age spirituality.

José Argüelles, the Mexican-American art historian who is best known as the architect of Harmonic Convergence, a national New Age celebration that occurred in 1987.

Shirley MacLaine, the actress turned New Age guru. She is the author of several popular books, including the book (and movie) *Out on a Limb*.

Ruth Montgomery, a journalist who achieved some fame for her book on Jeane Dixon (Montgomery 1965), the psychic who is said to have predicted President Kennedy's death. Montgomery later became the medium for the spirit of the well-known medium Arthur Ford, and therefore she provides one example of the world of trance channelers.

Katrina Raphaell, the author of the well-known "crystal trilogy" (1985, 1987, 1990), whose work opens a door to the world of crystal healing.

Diane Stein, a feminist activist who is probably best known for the book *The Kwan Yin Book of Changes* (1985), the "first women's I Ching." She provides an example of the world of goddess religion, neopaganism, and ecofeminism.

Parapsychology

Because the New Age movement is so close historically and culturally, it is difficult to gain critical distance on its beliefs and practices. One starting point is academic parapsychologists, who study paranormal phenomena such as psychokinesis (anomalous "mind-matter" interactions) and extrasensory perception, which includes telepathy, clairvoyance, and precognition. Parapsychologists call these phenomena "psychic," "psi," or "paranormal," and they would define their field as the systematic study of patterns of organism-environment interaction that appear to be anomalous with respect to known physical laws. Thus, when parapsychologists use the term "paranormal," they intend for it a considerably narrower scope than do the skeptics and much of the media and general public, for whom "the paranormal" is sometimes synonymous with the "occult" or the "supernatural" (e.g., Frazier 1981, 1986). I shall also use the term "paranormal" in the broader sense, particularly when discussing skeptics and Hollywood movies; however, when discussing the "paranormal" in the context of the parapsychologists, I will be using the word in their more restricted sense.

Although many cities have psychics and popular healers who call themselves "parapsychologists," I will be discussing only the community of research-oriented scientists and scholars. Academic parapsychologists generally have graduate training, and they view parapsychology as a scientific discipline, albeit one that is not generally accepted by the broader scientific community (see McClenon 1984). Sociologically, then, parapsychology is a heterodox science and therefore quite the opposite of the New Age movement, which is a popular social movement. To generalize, parapsychologists are neither wholly opposed to nor wholly supportive of the claims of New Agers and related spiritual or occult groups. Instead, they believe that scientific methods should separate the wheat from the chaff, the credible from the incredible.

In the English-speaking world, parapsychological research is generally traced back to the last decades of the nineteenth century and the founding of the British Society for Psychical Research, whose members included leading scientists and intellectuals. The American Society for Psychical

Research was a spin-off from the British organization, and the American branch owes much of its early existence to the support of the psychologist and philosopher William James. The first psychical researchers in Britain and the United States attempted to document and assess the evidence of claims of paranormal phenomena. In Britain, for example, they gathered case histories of apparitions and other reports of psychic experiences, and in the United States they focused a great deal of attention on the medium Leonora Piper, whose spirit communications purportedly provided evidence for either life after death or telepathy and clairvoyance. Although the psychical researchers found the study of telepathy and clairvoyance interesting in itself, many were drawn to the research area because it promised to shed light on the "survival" question, that is, whether or not the human personality survives death.

Over the years an increasing number of mediums were exposed as fraudulent, and psychical researchers began to realize that lay reports of subjective experiences could never substitute for direct observation. Consequently, they became increasingly uncertain of the case-history method and more interested in experimental alternatives. In the 1930s, the botanist couple Joseph Banks Rhine and Louisa Rhine led the transformation of American psychical research into an experimental field. J. B. Rhine used the term "parapsychology" in place of psychical research to signal his newer laboratory-based, experimental methodology, and he popularized the controversial science in both academic and popular forums from his base at Duke University. In 1937, for example, J. B. Rhine founded the *Journal of Parapsychology*, and in subsequent decades both he and Louisa Rhine wrote numerous books on parapsychology for general public consumption (e.g., J. B. Rhine 1934, 1953; L. Rhine 1961, 1975).

The Rhines had a tremendous influence on the development of the field in the United States, and many of the leading experimentalists in American parapsychology today received at least some training in J. B. Rhine's laboratory. It would not be an exaggeration to say that for many years the words *parapsychology, Duke University*, and *J. B.* and *Louisa Rhine* were all closely linked in the American popular imagination. Their writings interested the general public in part because they articulated a vision of how parapsychology could help bridge the gap between science and religion, as well as contribute to solving society's pressing problems. As a result, the Rhines' work will be an important point of reference for my cultural analysis.

Although the Rhines exerted a tremendous influence on the development of academic parapsychology in the United States, they were not the only major force. The psychologist Gardner Murphy, for example, was also influential, notably in the New York area, where he helped defend a vision of psychical research that was more closely linked to psychology and philosophy. Some parapsychologists today also part from the Rhines by remaining interested in the question of life after death and the older research problems of the psychical researchers. At the other extreme, a larger group would eschew the linkages the Rhines attempted to build between parapsychology and religion. There are even some "parapsychologists" who would prefer to go by the more sanitized name of "psi researchers" or "anomalies researchers." Thus, while the parapsychology of the Rhines has been extremely influential in the United States, it remains only one current among others.

Most of the different schools and tendencies are represented in the Parapsychological Association, an international organization whose membership consists primarily of Anglophone researchers and whose annual meetings serve as the principal event of the calendar year for academic parapsychology. Although the organization has grown since its inception in 1957, the meetings remain small today; of the ones I attended during the 1980s, the number of participants was low enough that all sessions were plenary. Nevertheless, the Parapsychological Association has included among its members some well-known psychologists and psychiatrists, such as Irvin Child, Jan Ehrenwald, Jules Eisenbud, Gardner Murphy, Stanley Krippner, Gertrude Schmeidler, and Charles Tart. The organization has also attracted a number of philosophers, physicists, biologists, historians, and social scientists.

The views of parapsychologists are important in the arena of debate and dialogue on paranormal beliefs and New Age spirituality because New Agers and others interested in paranormal experiences can point to parapsychology and say, "Yes, science does legitimate at least some of our beliefs." Thus, while parapsychologists are numerically a small community, they have a disproportionately important position because they occupy a crucial middle ground between the strongly proparanormal beliefs of the New Agers and the strongly antiparanormal beliefs of the skeptics and most of the scientific community.

Although parapsychologists occupy an important cultural space, they tend to shy away from popular claims about the place of their field in American culture or in debates about science and religion. A perusal of the pages of *The Journal of Parapsychology* and *The Journal of the American Society for Psychical Research* — the two major American parapsychology journals — quickly reveals that the vast majority of the literature of academic parapsychology in the United States consists of rather dry laboratory reports, theoretical discussions, and, less frequently, case studies of psychic experiences. As a result, from this extensive literature I focus on only a few publications in which parapsychologists issue somewhat broader statements. Frequently, these publications include presidential addresses or programmatic statements delivered to the Parapsychological Association: for example, addresses or papers by the psychiatrist Ian Stevenson, the editor Rhea White, the engineer and psychologist Dean Radin, the philosopher Hoyt Edge, the engineer Robert Jahn, and the anthropologist Michael Winkelman.

In addition to the presidential addresses and programmatic statements, parapsychologists occasionally discuss cultural and social issues in popular books addressed to the general public. The Rhines provide an important starting point, and in the chapters that follow I will discuss in more detail books such as J. B. Rhine's *New World of the Mind* and Louisa Rhine's *ESP in Life and Lab* and *Psi, What Is It?*[5] After the Rhines left the public spotlight, a number of other people occupied the position of interpreters of parapsychology to the general public. They include the following:

> Stanley Krippner, a leading humanistic psychologist who is perhaps best known in parapsychological circles for his work at the Maimonides Dream Laboratory. He is also known as a kind of ambassador of parapsychology; over the years he has built bridges between American parapsychologists and other groups, both in the United States and abroad.
>
> Robert McConnell, who until his retirement was a professor of biological sciences at the University of Pittsburgh. In the 1980s he published several books on parapsychology that to some extent provide a counterbalance to the anthologies published by skeptics during the same period (see McConnell 1983a, 1983b, 1987).
>
> Janet Lee Mitchell, a psychologist at Yavatai College in Arizona who authored a popular book on out-of-body experiences that made parapsychological research accessible to the public.
>
> J. Gaither Pratt, a psychologist who studied under J. B. Rhine and later was a research associate under the psychiatrist Ian Stevenson at the University of Virginia.
>
> D. Scott Rogo, a writer and musician who until his death in 1990 was probably the most important of the post-Rhinean popularizers. Although he sometimes strayed into the topics that bordered on the spiritualistic, members of the parapsychology establishment grudgingly accepted him because they believed that the field needed a popularizer.[6]
>
> Charles Tart, a professor of psychology at the University of California, Davis. Probably best known as the editor of the volume *Altered States*

of Consciousness, he is also the author of several books on parapsychology written for the general public.[7]

Skepticism

Parapsychologists see themselves as skeptical of the claims of New Agers,
psychics, and other popular advocates of paranormal beliefs; but there
is another, more strident, form of skepticism. The latter is associated with
the book publisher Prometheus Books, the popular magazine *Skeptical
Inquirer* and its readers, and scientists and other writers sympathetic to
the Committee for the Scientific Investigation of Claims of the Paranormal (CSICOP, pronounced "psi cop"). Generally known as "skeptics," the
antiantiscientists tend to lump parapsychology together with the New Age
movement into a category of popular superstition, occultism, and "pseudoscience" for which their social mission is one of debunking and demysti-
fication. Thus, the skepticism associated with CSICOP and its allies — a
coalition of scholars, scientists, writers, journalists, and magicians — provides a strong critical voice that often speaks in the idiom of journalistic
muckraking.[8]

Many of the first critics of mediums and psychics were psychical researchers, but there were also some scientists who rejected not only the
phenomena of mediumship but also the entire project of finding a core
of valid paranormal phenomena among all the outlandish claims. Some
critics of psychical research, such as Joseph Jastrow (1900), were members
of the emerging psychology profession, and others included medical doctors, who viewed mediumship as a form of psychopathology. In addition,
magicians such as Harry Houdini achieved fame by unmasking mediums.
Thus, the skeptics of today can look back to a long and rich tradition that,
like those of New Agers and parapsychologists, dates back at least to the
late nineteenth century.

In 1976 some of the leading skeptics came together under the leadership
of the philosopher Paul Kurtz, then editor of the *Humanist,* the magazine
of the American Humanist Association. Like the Parapsychological Association, the skeptical organization CSICOP included some well-known
scholars, such as the philosophers Sidney Hook and W. V. Quine and the
psychologist B. F. Skinner (Kurtz 1976a).[9] After some initial disagreements
and negotiations, CSICOP began publishing the popular magazine *Skeptical Inquirer,* a quarterly publication which debunks all sorts of claims that
do not meet the skeptics' criteria of valid science.

Kurtz is in several ways the J. B. Rhine of organized skepticism. Both
began from bases in the academy: Rhine was for much of his life a professor at Duke University, and Kurtz is a professor of philosophy (cur-

rently emeritus) at the State University of New York at Buffalo. Rhine, a model scientific entrepreneur, founded the *Journal of Parapsychology* and built up an endowment for the Foundation for Research on the Nature of Man. Likewise, Kurtz led the founding and institutionalization of organized skepticism, from CSICOP and the *Skeptical Inquirer* to the publishing house Prometheus Books. Finally, just as Rhine authored experimental research reports as well as books that explained parapsychology to the general public, so Kurtz is the author of numerous books and articles that range from erudite philosophical discussions to popular expositions of secular humanist philosophy that are accessible to the lay reader.

Skeptics such as Kurtz, then, compete with parapsychologists to occupy the cultural space of a scientific position on paranormal beliefs and popular superstition. Like parapsychologists, skeptics have produced many erudite essays and books on scientific methodology or the details of fraudulent psychic claims. They have also generated complex philosophical studies (e.g., Kurtz 1988, 1989a) and a new subfield of psychology known as the psychology of the psychic (Marks and Kammen 1980, Zusne and Jones 1982). However, like the parapsychologists' experimental studies and philosophical discussions, such studies have little to say about the cultural meaning of the paranormal or the place of skepticism in society, and consequently I do not discuss that category of skeptical writing here. Instead, I focus on skeptical essays that are written for the general public or that describe skeptics' vision of the social importance of skepticism and the cultural meaning of the paranormal. In addition to Paul Kurtz, examples of skeptics whom I will discuss include:

Isaac Asimov, the well-known science fiction writer who was also a science writer and skeptic.

Kendrick Frazier, the editor of the *Skeptical Inquirer* who has also edited two important anthologies of skeptical essays: *Paranormal Borderlands of Science* (1981) and *Science Confronts the Paranormal* (1986).

Martin Gardner, known for his former column in the *Scientific American* on games and puzzles; his column in the *Skeptical Inquirer,* "Notes of a Fringe-Watcher"; and his popular books that debunk paranormal, occult, and New Age beliefs (e.g., 1981b, 1983, 1988).

Ray Hyman, a professor of psychology at the University of Oregon. He has generally written methodological critiques of parapsychology, but his writings occasionally touch on the issue of parapsychology as "pathological science."

James "the Amazing" Randi, a magician who has frequently appeared on television talk shows to debunk psychics and to show how he can replicate their feats through stage magic.

Leonard Zusne, a professor of psychology at the University of Tulsa and coauthor with W. B. Jones of *Anomalistic Psychology*. His psychological portraits of advocates of the paranormal provide interesting materials for a cultural reading of skeptical discourse.

A Note on the Cultural Perspective

Skeptics and others who doubt the validity of the paranormal face an interesting sociological problem. New Age and related beliefs appear to encounter widespread popular interest and growing support in many countries, but these beliefs seem to be doing especially well in a place where they are, on the surface, least expected: the pragmatic, secular, and forward-looking society of the United States, with its relatively literate and well-educated population. Thus, skeptically minded inquirers might ask themselves, "Why is the paranormal so compelling to so many people in a technological, capitalist society that seems to be even more rationalized, materialistic, and disenchanted than it was at the turn of the century, when Max Weber issued his prophetic warning about the specter of the iron cage of rationalization?"[10]

Skeptics sometimes answer this question, what I call the "paradox of the paranormal," by blaming an irresponsible media; but they also think of the growth of paranormal belief as the result of the persistence of a "transcendental temptation" and of magical thinking. To them, the flight from reason is an ostrich-like reaction in the face of an ever-advancing case for scientific knowledge and an ever-receding basis for religious faith.[11] In a world of computers and high technology (according to this view), the paranormal is more palatable than conventional magical rituals and religious faith, yet notwithstanding its veneer of scientificity, paranormal belief represents a new irrationalism that may even pose a danger to society.

Despite the elegant simplicity of the flight-from-reason solution to the paradox of paranormality, it can at best only explain why such beliefs exist and persist, not why specific varieties have emerged rather than others. The solution has all the shortcomings of instrumental and functionalist theories in general: they are good at explaining the existence and persistence of social phenomena, but not their dynamism, their variability, and ultimately their power in society. To answer this second set of questions, we need to ask how the paranormal looks to those who embrace it. That

question constitutes the methodological starting point commonly understood as "cultural" or "anthropological": understanding the world from the
point of view of the people in question, that is, in terms of and *relative*
to their culture.[12]

Upon asking the anthropological question, it will soon become clear
that people who hold paranormal beliefs, such as New Agers, see themselves as skeptics in their own right. They are skeptical not only of the
demands of religious faith but also of the promises made to them by the
corporate world, official science, and the medical establishment. In short,
New Agers are skeptical of orthodoxy, be it religious, scientific, technical,
or economic. From this perspective, the New Age movement may represent not an irrational reaction to rationalization, but an attempt to build
an alternative rationality in a world perceived to consist of irrational and
unjust orthodoxies.

The cultural approach therefore opens up the possibility of seeing New
Age discourse as a contemporary development of — and remaking of — longstanding American values of self-reliance, individualism, egalitarianism,
pragmatism, and even show-me skepticism. In the past, New England Puritans skeptically questioned the authority of the Catholic or Anglican
churches and opted instead for the more empirical and experiential authority of the scriptures, faith, and prayer; and later the transcendentalists questioned many of the dogmas of their Puritan ancestors.[13] In a similar way,
New Agers skeptically question the authority of the scriptures, faith, and
prayer — as well as the authority of official science and mass-market advertisers — and instead they see themselves as opting for what appears to
them to be the more empirical knowledge of experiences such as meditation, channeling, or out-of-body experiences. Likewise, just as the pioneers
of the past lived an ethic of self-reliance and pragmatism, so New Agers
today look for natural healing systems that enable them to avoid becoming entangled in bureaucratic medicine that they see as alienating them
from their own bodies. In short, I see the New Age movement not as a
new irrationalism but instead as a new expression of skepticism within
a framework of religious or spiritual assumptions: a spiritual self-help movement or even a kind of religioscientific consumerism.[14]

The cultural perspective also makes it possible to interpret skepticism
skeptically — or better, socially and culturally. Either in the form of the
antagonistic CSICOP — or in the form of what could be called the kinder,
gentler skepticism of the academic parapsychologists — skeptical discourses
are often constructed as reformist attempts to rescue the country, or even
the world, from the risks of irrationalism.[15] At one extreme, then, members of CSICOP portray New Agers as fools bound to dogmatic supersti-

tions who would lead the country toward an apocalypse of unreason. At the other extreme, New Agers see skeptics as bound to their own superstition of dogmatic materialism that could result in environmental Armageddon. From this perspective, the discourses of CSICOP and the New Age movement can be seen as two variants — or better, as polar opposites — with parapsychology as the mediating discourse. In this "chiasmus" all the actors nonetheless view themselves as "skeptical" in their own way.

Thus, skeptics, parapsychologists, and New Agers are all, in a sense, "skeptics." In the United States, "skepticism" is often a positive trait; it suggests an empirical, pragmatic, independent, self-reliant, and antiauthoritarian approach to the world. The arena of positions, then, is defined not by one absolute form of skepticism, but instead by what might be called the varieties of skeptical experience. A vast dialogue and debate ensues, but the sharp differences of opinion play themselves out over a "doxa" of unstated cultural assumptions and values that the rival orthodoxies and heterodoxies create through their differences (see Bourdieu 1977:168). As the various actors construct their irrational Others and draw boundaries between the credible and incredible, they forge a new paraculture that itself has shared assumptions, histories, and key terms.

In outlining my cultural perspective, I have implicitly been identifying a fourth community in this arena of debate and dialogue: anthropologists, sociologists, historians, culture critics, and various other students from the humanities and social sciences — the human sciences — who are not explicitly aligned with one of the other three communities. Although some human scientists see their role as defending a position that they think is the "right" one, most of us are more interested in understanding the meaning and implications of the debates about who is right or wrong. Nevertheless, we are by no means neutral and impassive observers in these debates, and indeed complicated questions emerge regarding the position of our "fourth voice" in the ideological arena.

I shall return to some of these questions at the end of the study. In the meantime, our "fourth voice" appears most clearly at the end of each of the chapters. In the conclusion sections of the chapters, I relate the discussion of shared metaphors and representations to the values, hierarchies, categories, politics, and myths of the broader culture. Thus, my analysis works at two levels: first, I "deconstruct" boundaries among the three cultures; then I show how this shared "paraculture" is itself part of the broader culture. Some may misunderstand this cultural perspective as a neutral, bird's-eye view that attempts to remain above the fray. At one level, this is true, since I am not concerned with arguing the epistemology, methodology, and so on of claims of the varieties of skeptical and paranormal belief. However, at another level my voice is part of the same arena of dialogue and debate. Implicit in my analysis is the belief that members of the different discursive communities should inspect carefully the political assumptions and implications of their discourse. The result is that at the end of the book I do take a stand on "who's right and who's wrong." However, my criteria for carving my own boundaries within the paraculture are social and cultural ones. Thus, I find points of convergence and agreement with each of the three cultures, just as I find points of divergence and disagreement with each of them.

Having laid out these background issues, I can now turn to the history of the different positions, their details, the predictability of the disputes, and the surprises of the undisputed. The next chapter completes the introductory section by providing a historical account of New Agers, parapsychologists, and skeptics. It is, however, a history that looks toward the present and future, for the chapter ends with a discussion of New Age discourse and the question of postmodernism. In the second part of the book, I provide specific discussions of the three cultures by focusing on three dimensions that reveal continuities of cultural meaning: "Self and Other," "Heroes and Sermons," and "Gender and Hierarchy." The last chapter of the second section, on the paranormal in Hollywood, serves as a check on the analysis presented in the previous chapters: it shows how the cultural meanings inscribed in the texts of skeptics, parapsychologists, and New Agers also appear in Hollywood movies, which play a crucial role in the construction of this emergent paraculture. In the process, I provide the reader with a way to read the wide-ranging popular literature (and movies) on the paranormal in the United States. Rather than get caught up in who's right or who's wrong, I show that a vast dialogue on American culture and society is taking place in an arena that some have dismissed as much ado about nothing.

2

The Historical Context

Spiritualism, pure and undefiled, will by the unfailing conservator of all that is good and true in human beliefs on the subject of the relations of man to time and to eternity, to the universe and to its author.
                                                        —Epes Sargent (1869:400)

Spiritism is the ruck and muck of modern culture, the common enemy of true science and of true religion, and to drain its dismal and miasmatic marshes is the great work of modern culture. . . .
                                                        —G. Stanley Hall (Tanner 1910:xxxii)

To UNDERSTAND contemporary New Agers, parapsychologists, and skeptics in the United States, it is necessary to have a sense of their precursors and historical development. In providing such an account, I have opted to flag how some of the significant discursive boundaries were constructed rather than to narrate a brief "history" of the predecessors of these communities. By focusing on the question of boundaries, I initiate a discussion of the broader theoretical problem that will be important in the chapters that follow: what the sociologist Thomas Gieryn has called "boundary-work," or efforts to distinguish one discursive domain, such as science, from competitors, such as religion (1983a, 1983b, Gieryn and Figert 1990).

Like Gieryn, I do not take the boundary between the scientific and the nonscientific to be a monolithic one, nor do I think science can be defined on purely intellectual grounds by a philosophical argument based on abstract demarcation criteria. Instead, I interpret the boundary culturally as scientists and nonscientists construct it in specific contexts, and I show how in practice the boundary between science and nonscience is recursive, multiple, and changing. Notions of the ascientific, pseudoscientific, or less scientific range from (as the skeptics would see it) the whole gamut of paranormal, spiritual, and occult beliefs to (as the New Agers and their predecessors would see it) a dogmatically materialistic scientific orthodoxy.

17

Furthermore, this chapter will provide a sense of how the boundaries are being constantly redefined as new variations of skeptical and paranormal discourse emerge.

The Precursors of the New Age Movement

Where to begin? The dialogue between skepticism and belief in Western societies can be traced back to ancient philosophers such as Lucretius, and even beyond. Another possible starting point would be the Renaissance magical tradition, as has been explored by the historian Frances Yates (e.g., 1972). However, the present configuration of three more or less distinct discourses is of more recent origin; it depends on the institutionalization of science as a source of authority in society. Hints of the configuration appear in the eighteenth century, such as in the works of Franz Anton Mesmer and Emanuel Swedenborg, but it only becomes clearly articulated in the mid to late nineteenth century with the development of Spiritualism in the United States and Britain, and Spiritism in France.[1]

The Spiritualist/Spiritist movement grew to enormous proportions during the 1850s and 1860s, obtaining an international status with tens of thousands of members. With growth came notoriety, and after the exposure of several physical effects mediums the movement gradually shrank into the status of a small sect, which is its condition today in every country except a few Latin American countries such as Brazil. Spiritualists/Spiritists practiced communication with spirits via mediums, and they believed that mediums' communications were empirical, observable, and therefore "scientific" phenomena. In the United States and Britain, Spiritualists developed more in the direction of religion, whereas in France the educator Allan Kardec authored the more intellectual Spiritist doctrine, which promised to connect scientific research, philosophical principles, and Christian morality. Kardec explicitly described Spiritism as a philosophical movement rather than a religion, and he borrowed from Eastern philosophy the principles of reincarnation and the law of karma, two ideas that further distinguished his doctrine from the beliefs of most Anglophone Spiritualists (see Hess 1991b). Thus, even in the 1850s and 1860s, Spiritists were constructing a boundary between themselves and Spiritualists by defining Spiritualists as less sophisticated, philosophical, and "scientific."

Internal boundaries notwithstanding, Spiritists and Spiritualists alike viewed themselves as putting religious issues on the firm footing of scientific observation. A hybrid of religious and scientific discourses, Spiritualism/Spiritism was to some extent "new." The rupture — or perhaps, tremor —

that they inaugurated in the intellectual landscape was in no small degree a response to the intellectual anxiety that discoveries in geology, biology, and astronomy were generating for the proponents of conventional religious faith. Many of the first American Spiritualists came from Universalist, Swedenborgian, or Unitarian backgrounds (Moore 1977:11, 49–61); they left these already somewhat rationalized religions to embrace Spiritualism, which promised an even more rational basis for the questions of faith and ultimate meaning. Spiritualists were therefore every bit as radical for the Protestant churches of the day as was the Reformation for the Catholic church. Thus, while Spiritualism and Spiritism might not qualify as a second reformation, they nevertheless represented a major transition in the religious domain.

As religious rationalists, Spiritualists were not antiscience. The historian R. Laurence Moore (1977) shows in some detail that they viewed their movement as an extension of science to the spiritual realm, and they saw themselves as providing a scientifically valid and empirically grounded basis for religious experience and faith. One American Spiritualist, Epes Sargent, wrote that no one "who has carefully examined the facts of modern Spiritualism can fail of being struck by the analogy they bear to many of the miraculous incidents recorded in the Bible" (1968:391). Once grounded in the facts of Spiritualism, conventional religion could achieve a new life, as Sargent goes on to explain: "May not some of our professional religious teachers wake up some bright morning to find that their hearers have very generally outgrown a certain style of appeal to their lazy preferences, their self-indulgent hopes, their nervous fears, or their sordid calculations? Should such a change come – and the signs are threatening – we may be sure that Spiritualism, pure and undefiled, will be the unfailing conservator of all that is good and true in human beliefs on the subject of the relations of man to time and to eternity, to the universe and to its author" (400). Sargent's book *Planchette, or the Despair of Science* consists of a defense of Spiritualism as a scientifically grounded belief system, but as this passage shows, he viewed Spiritualism as revitalizing traditional religion. In general, Spiritualists believed that the religious world view could be saved by being placed on the firm foundation of scientific knowledge.

Spiritualism, then, is perhaps the most obvious precursor of the New Age movement, but between the origins of Spiritualism in the nineteenth century and the New Age movement today is a complex history of alternative philosophical and religious groups. Perhaps the most important event was the formation in 1875 in New York of the Theosophical Society, the project of the Russian mystic Madame Blavatsky and the American lawyer Henry Steel Olcott. In many ways, their Theosophical Society was a more proximate precursor of the New Age movement today than Spiritualism, for Theosophists shared with New Agers an interest in ritual magic, astrology, Eastern religion, and reincarnation (Melton 1988:40–41). However, Theosophists and Spiritualists were soon at odds with each other.

Madame Blavatsky accepted much of Spiritualism but like Kardec she gave it a new philosophical basis by adding to it a complex philosophical system derived from Hindu philosophy and various esoteric traditions. Her Theosophical doctrine retained mediumship and spirit communication but shifted the spirit guides from Native Americans and other domestic or Western figures to Eastern sages. As the religious studies scholar and historian Robert Ellwood, Jr., argues, the turn toward Hindu and Tibetan sages made American Spiritualism "look tame and provincial" in contrast with the cosmopolitanism of Theosophy (1979:105). Still, although Madame Blavatsky may have looked cosmopolitan and sophisticated to her followers, she was not well received among Spiritualists. As Moore demonstrates, Spiritualists drew their own boundaries by rejecting Theosophy for its occultism, esoteric philosophy, and lack of scientific attitude (1977:228–35). Some even accused the Theosophical Society's cultlike organization, which centered power around Madame Blavatsky, of the kind of religious dogmatism that had "held mankind in mental bondage" through the years (cited in Moore 1977:228). Thus, while Theosophists rejected Spiritualism as philosophically unsophisticated and uncosmopolitan, Spiritualists rejected Theosophy as unscientific occultism.[2]

Ellwood argues for a genealogy that runs roughly from Theosophy's contact with Eastern religions through the Beatniks into the 1960s counterculture to New Age groups today (1979:136–66; 1987:32–34). To trace out the organizational and doctrinal divisions and schisms among the various esoteric and occult groups in the twentieth-century United States would require an entire volume.[3] Nevertheless, it is worth pausing to discuss in some detail one of the transitional figures between the Theosophy of the late nineteenth and early twentieth centuries and the New Age movement today: Alice A. Bailey, who has been given credit for introducing the phrase "New Age" in the 1920s (Basil 1988:10; Melton 1988:41).

Born in England, Alice Bailey immigrated to the United States in 1907 at age twenty-seven. She joined the Theosophical Society in 1915, only to be dismissed from it a few years later. In 1923 she founded the Arcane School, where students could study the teachings of her own spirit guide, Djwhal Khul, known simply as "the Tibetan" (Melton 1986:21–22). One of Bailey's last books is *Education in the New Age*. Written shortly before her death in 1949, the book is remarkable for the number of themes that foreshadow the New Age discourse of the late twentieth century. For example, although Bailey claims to have received the contents of the book under the inspiration of her spirit guide, the Tibetan states that neither he nor Bailey is "the least interested" in having their books "acclaimed as inspired writings" (1954:xiv). As the Tibetan comments, "If [the writings] present truth in such a way that it follows sequentially upon that already offered in the world teachings . . . then they will have served their purpose" (xiv). As is often the case with channelers today, Bailey is less concerned with documenting, in a way understood by Spiritualists or even psychical researchers, that the text is the product of a spirit guide. Rather, she is more concerned that the text be judged on the basis of its content and the quality of its message.

Another similarity between Bailey's writings and that of New Agers today is her prophecy of a coming Age of Aquarius. She claims that in some sense human evolution has come full circle from the epoch of the religious Atlantean people to the Piscean era that is drawing to a close in the contemporary period (42). In place of the Age of Pisces, the New Age of Aquarius will represent "the noble middle path" that will synthesize the best of the two previous epochs (42). "The conquests of science," she writes, "the conquests of nations, and the conquests of territory are all indicative of the Piscean method, with its idealism, its militancy, and its separativeness in all fields — religious, political, and economic. But the age of synthesis, of inclusiveness and of understanding is upon us, and the new education of the Aquarian Age must begin very gently to penetrate the human aura" (4–5). In describing the transition, Bailey develops a critique of society and knowledge that emphasizes a new holism that predates the work of the New Age writer Marilyn Ferguson. Even Bailey's characterization of the Piscean age as an era of conquest and militancy suggests New Age feminism *avant la lettre.*

The bulk of Bailey's book is devoted to an exposition of the nature of the education needed for the New Age, and she names three new sciences to go with this education: antahkarana, meditation, and service. (The former, antahkarana, involves the study of spiritual energies, the astral bodies, and the wisdom associated with them.) Clearly her understanding of science, which she and the Tibetan spirit guide draw from Asian spiritual teachings, is a long way from that of the Spiritualists, who still maintained a Western notion of science that was rooted in the observation of the phenomena of mediumship (see Moore 1977:230–31). Bailey's focus on meditation, rather than on mediumship, constitutes yet another step that foreshadows the increased interest placed on meditation in New Age groups.

In some ways, the transition to New Age thought involves a rationalization of the heritage of nineteenth-century Spiritualists and Theosophists. The greater emphasis placed on Eastern philosophies and meditation could be interpreted as reflecting increasing psychological sophistication, such that meditation has to some extent displaced both mediumship and the Spiritualists' and Theosophists' dialogue with the spirit world. In a similar way, the rise of UFO cults has transformed the otherworldly discourse of spirits and apparitions into the somewhat more rationalized form of extra-terrestrials and contactees.[4] Even contemporary New Age channelers, who continue the tradition of mediumship by receiving spirits or extraterres-trials, tend to sidestep the question of the authenticity of mediumistic com-munications by sometimes viewing the source of the communication as a higher dimension of their own consciousness, that is, by opening up the possibility of a more psychological interpretation of mediumship. There is some evidence, then, that the transition from late-nineteenth-century Spiritualism to the late-twentieth-century New Age movement reflects a tendency toward a somewhat more psychological and less otherworldly discourse. However, the New Age movement is diverse enough so that "ra-tionalization" can only describe one tendency within it; at the same time other currents enter into New Age discourse, such as the goddess religion, which would be more appropriately characterized as spiritual and other-worldly.

From Spiritualism to Parapsychology

The boundary between Spiritualism and psychical research was at first somewhat fuzzy: the original Society for Psychical Research in Britain in-cluded Spiritualists as well as scholars and scientists among its ranks. How-ever, after a few years many of the Spiritualists resigned and the Society was left in the hands of a group of scholars and scientists headed by the philosopher Henry Sidgwick (Gauld 1968:138). Opinion among the psy-chical researchers was divided on the extent to which their research sup-ported the Spiritualist belief that the human personality could survive death and communicate with the living through apparitions and mediums. Some psychical researchers were quite skeptical, and eventually they exposed as fraudulent several mediums, particularly those who claimed to generate paranormal physical effects. Still, the psychical researchers of the late nine-teenth and early twentieth centuries should not be seen as hostile toward the general ideas behind Spiritualism, nor to religious questions in gen-eral. Rather, like the Spiritualists, they hoped that their research would lead to a less pessimistic answer to religious questions than the materialis-tic temper of the times would have allowed (Gauld 1968:140–43).

An examination of the family backgrounds of the leaders of psychical research provides more evidence for the argument that they were not hostile to religion. The leading British psychical researchers in the Sidgwick group came from religious backgrounds, and they came to question the religious faith of their upbringing without necessarily finding the materialistic alternative satisfactory. Likewise, some of the leading figures of American psychical research—the philosopher James Hervey Hyslop, the psychologists Walter Franklin Prince and Gardner Murphy, as well as Louisa Rhine, J. B. Rhine, and J. Gaither Pratt—came from religious homes or suffered from a religious crisis earlier in life. Furthermore, the most well known American supporter of psychical research, William James, came from a Swedenborgian background; and at Trinity College, which was renamed Duke University a few years before the Rhines arrived, the Methodist university president found in Rhine's work a bridge between "religio et eruditio," to quote the Duke motto. Thus, in several contexts there is a connection between religion and the psychical researchers, although the connection is without a specific religious affiliation. Instead, the early psychical researchers were often attempting to answer the question "Is the universe friendly?"—to use the phrase of the psychical researcher and classicist F. W. H. Myers—rather than to justify any particular religious faith.[5]

Just as Spiritualists thought of themselves as more scientific than the religious groups from which many of them emerged, so psychical researchers saw themselves as more scientific than the Spiritualists. The writings of James Hervey Hyslop provide one example of the boundary-work that took place between psychical researchers and Spiritualists. A professor of logic and ethics at Columbia University, Hyslop resigned his post in 1902 after suffering from tuberculosis. He then worked full-time on psychical research, and a few years later he led the rebirth of the American Society for Psychical Research.[6]

Although Hyslop may not have been typical of American psychical researchers because of his firm belief in spirit communication, he left behind a large quantity of publications that bear on the question of boundary-work and the relationships among psychical research, Spiritualism, and orthodox science. Furthermore, he was outspoken and opinionated, even to the point of being brash and somewhat tactless; and consequently his writings are quite clear about the nature and significance of the boundaries. Examining his work in somewhat more detail therefore provides one example of how a psychical researcher positioned his field of inquiry. It will also reveal several commonalities with the work of J. B. Rhine and some of the parapsychologists of the late twentieth century.

Hyslop believed in spirit communication and, in general terms, in the

Spiritualist project of finding a scientific basis for religion, but he also blamed Spiritualists for the rather poor reception that psychical research was having among the scientific and medical elites. Thus, in criticizing Spiritualism he constituted psychical research as a more scientific alternative. "The Spiritualists themselves," he wrote, "are largely to blame for the slowness of [the general acceptance of their ideas]. They have made it impossible for the intelligent man to touch it without forfeiting the respect of his neighbors. . . . If they had done scientific work in 1850 they would have won their case before science and religion had weakened its appeal" (1918:473).[7] As this passage suggests, Hyslop was equally dissatisfied with conventional religion, which he criticized as follows: "The religious mind has been too intent in the past on combatting science. If it could have clearly seen that scientific method is its best friend, it might have held the materialistic tendencies of this age in check. But it has always had the bad taste and bad politics of antagonizing the method which promised it the best of vindication" (1916:273).

At the same time that Hyslop criticized Spiritualism and conventional religion, he also challenged the materialistic philosophy associated with orthodox science. Scientific knowledge, he argued, had replaced what had once been within the purview of religion, and as a result "religion had to turn to the residual phenomena of life . . . to vindicate its aspirations and interpretation of the cosmos" (1908a:408). The residual phenomena included the areas investigated by psychical research, and in validating these phenomena psychical research implicitly became realigned with Spiritualism and religion in general. Hyslop worried that without some basis in spiritual beliefs, the "materialistic tendencies of the age" could bring about the end of civilization, and consequently he ended up criticizing materialistic science in a way that sounded very much like the Spiritualists:

There are signs enough of social and political upheaval in the dissolution of the older ethical and religious ideals and it will devolve on a new philosophy to aid in the reconstruction of order. The academic world is blind to the needs of the hour and has isolated itself in aristocratic seclusion from contact with the life of those who are the ruling tendencies of the future . . . and if any spiritual ideal be discovered, it must be in the little beacon lights that shine out from the residual and neglected phenomena of mind which promise as wide an extension in psychological knowledge as the new discoveries in the material world have produced in the physical sciences (1908a:409).

Hyslop may remind the reader of President Bush's "thousand points of light," but his rhetoric also foreshadows that of J. B. Rhine, who constructed parapsychology in a similar matrix of science/religion relations and called for the rejuvenation of the present social and moral order. Although this matrix constitutes one point of similarity, Rhine's work also marked yet another schism or boundary in the history of the dialogue between skeptical and paranormal beliefs, again in the direction of orthodox science. He did this by abandoning — or postponing indefinitely — research into the question of postmortem survival and by focusing instead on the narrower problem of the patterns of extrasensory perception and psychokinesis. In addition to moving the primary locus of research from the parlor and field site to the laboratory, he also led the transition of the institutional basis of research from psychical research societies to universities and private research foundations. Thus, parapsychology represented a skeptical version of psychical research, and it can be viewed as yet one more development in the history of skeptical revisions of religion. In other words, parapsychology stood to psychical research as psychical research to Spiritualism, Spiritualism to Universalism and Swedenborgianism, those religions to conventional Protestantism, and even Protestantism to Catholicism.

It is difficult to date exactly the transition toward the narrower and, in some senses, more "scientific" definition of psychical research that J. B. Rhine popularized as "parapsychology." A sharp divide between Spiritualists and psychical researchers had already occurred in 1923, when pro-Spiritualist forces gained control of the American Society for Psychical Research (ASPR), ousted President William McDougall, and demoted Hyslop's chosen successor, the psychologist Walter Franklin Prince, who resigned in 1925. The ASPR lost 108 members in 1923, and the controversy over the claimed physical effects of the medium named "Margery" sealed the division. It was not until the 1941 "palace revolt" that the psychical researchers regained control of the ASPR, and by then Rhine was already established at Duke University. Rhine and the leaders of the "palace revolt" — the editor Laura Dale and the psychologists Gardner Murphy and Gertrude Schmeidler — marked the emergence of an experimentally oriented parapsychology that is still evident today in the Society's publications.

Although J. B. Rhine hoped that the laboratory approach would replace the uncertainties of the case history and observational methods, he encountered increasing hostility from the psychology profession and other scientists who remained skeptical of his claims to have demonstrated ESP in the laboratory. The members of his own department grew restive when William McDougall died in 1938 and Duke's President Few died in 1940. However, Rhine was an extremely successful fund raiser, and by 1947 he obtained support from the administration to set up an independent laboratory separate from the psychology department. Eventually, he garnered the resources to move off campus and start the Foundation for Research on the Nature of Man, an independent organization that was founded in 1962 and continues in existence today.[8]

The historians Seymour Mauskopf and Michael McVaugh argue that Rhine made several strategic errors by founding a separate journal, moving off campus where he lost access to graduate students, and in general working to establish parapsychology as a separate scientific field, which included the formation of the Parapsychological Association (1980:304–5). Parapsychologists would probably argue that to a large extent Rhine was forced into the separatist path by the skepticism of his colleagues in psychology and other sciences. Indeed, just as parapsychologists were attempting to distance themselves from Spiritualists and similar groups, so psychologists were engaged in boundary-work of their own.

Skeptical Counterpoint

Although some psychical researchers believed that some mediums were able to relay messages from spirits, others opted for the more conservative interpretations of psychological "automatism," telepathy, or even fraud. Thus, there were significant divisions of belief among the psychical researchers, with some leaning toward Spiritualism and others toward this-worldly explanations. However, to the "right" of the conservative wing of psychical research was yet another position, the precursor of today's skeptical movement. Nineteenth-century skeptics tended to be members of the medical fraternity, solid materialists who were often as opposed to the emerging psychologies and dynamic psychiatries of the day as they were to Spiritualism. Neurologists and others of similar background such as William Carpenter, George Beard, William Hammond, and Frederic Marvin explained mediumship in terms of pathology and female debility, two images of the paranormal Other that continue to play a role in skeptical representations of psychics and New Agers today. Marvin even spoke of "mediomania," a women's disease that he classified as a subcategory of "uteromania," a mental illness caused by a tipped womb (Moore 1977: 135–37).

One example of an early American skeptic was William Hammond, a professor at Bellevue Hospital Medical College who observed Spiritualist meetings and concluded that some mediums manifested "hysterical phenomena" (1871:51; see also Braude 1989:142–61). As the medical man questioned the rationality of the movement's practitioners, he also rejected the scientific claims of the Spiritualists and pushed them back into the camp of religion. "Spiritualism is a religion," he wrote. "As such it is held tenaciously and honestly by many well-meaning people. To reason with these would be a waste of words, just as much as would be the attempt to persuade a madman out of his delusion. Emotion or interest or accident might change them, but facts never" (1871:84–85). That the ensuing discourse took on the polarities of empowered men versus disempowered (and self-empowering) women has not been lost on historians. For example, Alex Owen shows how husbands resisted and attempted to control their wives' involvements with Spiritualism, which was seen as a threat to the patriarchal order, and at times some of the more radical and independent mediums were even incarcerated in asylums (1989:167; see also Braude 1989, Moore 1977:102–29).

With the founding of professional psychological associations in the United States and Europe (such as the American Psychological Association in 1892), a more sophisticated variant of skepticism emerged, one which included psychical research as its unscientific Other. The year 1900 —when Freud published his *Interpretation of Dreams*—marked what may be the first modern skeptical tract in the United States: Joseph Jastrow's *Fact and Fable in Psychology* (1900). A less polemical and more empirical skeptic than the medical doctor Hammond, Jastrow was a psychologist from the University of Wisconsin, where his colleague Clark Hull and Hull's student Milton Erickson were later to distinguish themselves with a kind of hypnosis research that was disconnected from psychical research. The historian Deborah J. Coon (1988, 1990) argues that Jastrow's book was an example of psychologists' attempts to define their new science by demarcating it from psychical research and the occult. For Jastrow, the new psychology represented the science of the day, whereas its nemesis was the "occult"—Spiritualism, Theosophy, Christian Science, astrology, phrenology, alchemy, etc.—which to the psychologist was "as often the result of bad logic as of defective observation" (ix).

Jastrow characterized the conflict between psychology and the occult by using images that resonate with those of skeptics today. For example, in one passage he used a martial analogy: "The cause of truth and the overthrow of error must sometimes be fought in drawn battle and with the clash of arms" (viii). Likewise, he described the occult in figures of temporal distance: the occult points "back to distant epochs and to foreign civilizations; to ages when the facts of nature were but weakly grasped, when belief was largely dominated by the authority of tradition . . ." (5). Jastrow also viewed the occult as seductive and pathological because it appeals to a certain kind of intellectual temperament, one "that distorts the normal reactions to science and evidence . . . and shades from it through an irregular variety of tints to a vague and often unconscious susceptibility for the unusual and eccentric, combined with an instability of conviction regarding established beliefs that is more often the expression of the weakness of ignorance than of the courage of independence" (3). Those who have this weak temperament are drawn to belief systems such as Spiritualism, which "appeals to a deep-seated craving in human nature, that of assurance of personal immortality and of communion with the departed" (15).

Unlike many skeptics today, Jastrow's pronouncements on psychical research were much more tempered than his depiction of the occult. He dedicated the second chapter of *Fact and Fable* to a discussion of psychical research, and here his tone shifts to what Paul Kurtz (1986) later called neutrality as opposed to debunking. In this chapter Jastrow argues that the proceedings of the psychical research societies "contain valuable material in creditable quantities," and he finds much of interest for psychology in the pages of their journals. Notwithstanding his respect for the psychical researchers, his conclusions are largely negative: "But in my opinion the debit side of the ledger far outbalances the credit side. The influence which Psychical Research has cast in favor of the occult, the enrollment under a common protective authority of the credulous and the superstitious, and the believers in mystery and in the personal significance of things, is but one of the evils which must be laid at its door" (75). Jastrow goes on to blame popular misunderstandings of psychology on the psychical researchers, and he concludes the chapter by stating that the "disassociation" of the term "psychology" from "psychical research" and the pursuit of more psychological investigations are "consummations devoutly to be desired" (77).

Coon has argued that the demarcation problem for the emerging psychology profession was in part one of nomenclature, for the "term 'psychical' was often used interchangeably with our current term 'psychological'" (1990). She adds that Spiritualists sometimes used the term "psychological" to describe their own work, a usage which, I would add, also occurred among nineteenth-century Spiritists in France and Brazil. Likewise, Hyslop used the terms "psychical research" and "psychology" more or less interchangeably. For example, he portrayed psychical research as promising "as wide an extension in psychological knowledge as the new discoveries in the material world have produced in the physical sciences" (1908a:409; see also 1908b).

At the turn of the century, then, the relationship of psychical research to psychology — not to mention the meaning of the very terms — was still ill-defined. William James, who maintained a lifelong interest in psychical research (1960), still wielded a great influence on American psychology (see Coon 1988, 1990). Likewise, hypnotic procedures still retained an important position in psychotherapy, and thus clinicians were more likely to retain an interest in the psychical researchers' studies of trance states. Everything would change with the death of an older generation of psychologists, the advent of behaviorism, and the development of psychotherapeutic procedures, such as free association, that did not utilize conventional hypnosis (see Mauskopf and McVaugh 1980). However, at the time of Jastrow's *Fact and Fable*, the boundaries were much more flexible and undefined, and according to J. B. Rhine (1982 [1967]), they remained so at least until Watsonian psychology had firmly displaced the earlier generation of introspectionists.

An example of boundary-work, Jastrow's book helped to define the new discipline of psychology by developing a psychology of belief and deception as well as of what we would today call altered states of consciousness, both of which remained within the fold of a secular, materialist psychology and replaced the discourse of psychical research. It is therefore possible to view psychologists' rejection or "sacrifice" of psychical research as an intellectual strategy that helped them to construct and legitimate psychology as a scientific discipline. It is difficult to say the extent to which psychologists engaged consciously in this intellectual strategy, just as it is hard to assess the impact of the rejection of psychical research on the legitimation of psychology as a discipline, but certainly the topic warrants further research.

Gieryn (1983a) reminds us that boundary-work should be viewed broadly as a conflict over the authority of science in society, and frequently the struggles involve a contest between groups that represent the authority of science and religion. The conflict between science and religion is more clearly articulated in another early example of psychologists' rejection of psychical research: *Studies in Spiritism*, written by the psychologist Amy Tanner and with an introduction by her teacher, G. Stanley Hall.[9] A long volume that is still contested by parapsychologists today, *Studies in Spiritism* focuses on the American psychical researchers' star medium, Leonora Piper, and concludes by questioning not only spirit communication but also telepathy. For the sociocultural purposes here, it is not necessary to consider Tanner's arguments in any detail; the general point is that the text constructs psychology as the voice of science in contrast to Spiritualism (and, less explicitly, psychical research).

For example, in the introduction to the book, Hall draws the boundary in the spatial and temporal terms that appear again and again in skeptical and even parapsychological discourse today:

Science is indeed a solid island set in the midst of a stormy, foggy, and uncharted sea, and all these phenomena are of the sea and not of the land. If there have been eras of enlightenment it is because these cloud banks of superstition, for which about all forms of modern Spiritism are only collective terms, have lifted for a space or season. Spiritism is the ruck and muck of modern culture, the common enemy of true science and of true religion, and to drain its dismal and miasmatic marshes is the great work of modern culture. . . . But we have great ground to rejoice that science is now advancing into this domain more rapidly than ever before, and that the last few years have seen more progress than the century that pro-ceded. The mysteries of our psychic being are bound ere long to be cleared up. Every one of these ghostly phenomena will be brought under the domain of law. The present recrudescence here of ancient faiths in the supernatural is very interest-ing as a psychic atavism, as the last flashing up of a group of old psychoses soon to be extinct. When genetic psychology has done its work, all these psychic re-searches will take their place among the solemn absurdities in the history of thought, and the instincts that prompted them will be recognized as only psychic rudimen-tary organs that ought to be and will be left to atrophy (1910:xxxii).

The passage deploys many of the images that will reappear in subsequent boundary-work by skeptics, parapsychologists, and New Agers. For ex-ample, the frontier imagery (together with that of the uncharted sea) reso-nates with the faith in progress and the great metaphor of the nineteenth century: evolution. In turn, the Spiritualist Other is relegated to another space (dismal and miasmatic marshes, with their associations to the patho-logical—yellow fever and tropical diseases, as in Panama), as well as to another time (the Other is a "psychic atavism") and even to unreason ("old psychoses"). In the terminology of the nineteenth-century evolutionary an-thropologist Edward Burnett Tylor, Spiritualism is portrayed here as a "sur-vival" from earlier stages of cultural evolution.

However, in the quoted passage there is a curious phrase that one might not expect: Hall portrays Spiritualism as the enemy not only of "true sci-ence" but also of "true religion," a phrase which suggests that he left some room for "true religion." Spiritualism cannot be true religion any more than true science because, to paraphrase the anthropologist Mary Douglas (1966: 35), it is discourse out of place. As Amy Tanner notes in the conclu-sion to her study, "Science is new and faith is ancient" (378), and Spiritualist beliefs belong to the earliest stages of human evolution where "savages" are like "children" (377–79). Instead, however, grown and educated white men are found advocating Spiritualist beliefs. Their advocacy is anoma-lous within the evolutionary framework, and their new synthesis of sci-ence and religion threatens to destabilize the boundaries and hegemony of both orthodox science and religion.

In the place of the Spiritualist's medium and its spirit communicators,

Tanner issues a long eulogy to the brain, "the storehouse of all the experience of the individual and the race" (380). After a tour of nerves and engrams, she ends with a description of true science/religion:

Without irreverence this wonderful creation [i. e., the brain] of the great Spirit of Life may be compared to the New Jerusalem with its many mansions, and its beauties which eye hath not seen nor ear heard nor tongue of man been able to declare. It reveals glimpses of possibilities in development that will place men as far beyond his present state as he now is beyond the simplest protozoan. It opens to the most abnormal and degenerate the door of hope, because, however bad his immediate heredity may be or his circumstances, the very fact that he is here at all reveals that he is the child of God, and an inheritor of the kingdom of Heaven and that—as the revivalists are always telling us—he need only knock at the door and it will be opened to him, or—as some are putting it now—he can draw at any time upon the store of infinite energy that is stored up within man. This conception of man makes all these things literally true. The amount of chemical energy stored up within the brain is beyond calculation. It staggers figures (381).

As Tanner proceeds to explain the origins of modern Spiritualism, her definition of true science and religion becomes clearer. Whereas science has made "wonderful" advances, the Protestant church "settled into a dogmatism quite as narrow as that against which it had protested" (384). She blames the narrow-minded clergy of the time for not guiding the people out of the confusion they felt when faced with the great social, intellectual, and technological upheavals of their time. "What is to be done?" she finally asks, and she concludes on a note that late-twentieth-century skeptical humanists might find satisfactory: "[I]n proposition as man draws near to his fellow-man, and in proportion as he works for and with him, he realizes that the 'other side' can wait till the morrow, while salvation is here and now" (388–89).

As boundary-work, Tanner's final statement clearly dramatizes conflicts over the relative legitimacy of science and religion in early twentieth-century America. Tanner's position, like that of Hall, was not antireligion as much as proreligion, provided that religion did not contest the authority of science. Spiritualism and "dogmatic Protestantism" (the equivalent of fundamentalism and Pentecostalism today) contested the new authority of science, and thus the two psychologists drew the boundary of acceptable religion at liberal Protestantism, and they endorsed what appears to be an early version of secular humanism.

Before concluding this section, I should mention the magician Harry Houdini, and indeed no discussion of the historical antecedents of contemporary American skepticism would be complete without him. Houdini served on the commission that investigated the famous medium Margery in the 1920s, and his decision that she was deliberately committing fraud probably had some influence on the psychical researchers Prince and Mc-Dougall, who eventually decided that the medium showed no evidence for paranormal phenomena (Moore 1977:178). The "Margery affair" is one early example of a member of the magician's fraternity having a voice in the arena of Spiritualists, psychical researchers, and skeptical scientists, a role that magicians of a younger generation, such as James Randi, continue to amplify today.[10] Unlike the psychologists Hall, Tanner, and Jastrow, Houdini did not speak on behalf of materialist philosophies and orthodox science. Rather, as he explained in his 1924 book *A Magician Among Spirits,* he believed in the "hereafter" and had, after the death of his mother, genuinely sought evidence of her survival in his sittings with mediums. Furthermore, as a magician, his interest in Spiritualist phenomena was to show that mediums are, in a sense, magicians in disguise (although he apparently hoped that he might someday find a genuine medium). Houdini believed that unlike true magicians, who admit that their work is legerdemain, mediums use legerdemain but mislead the public by failing to admit it. In a sense, then, they provide unfair competition in the world of psychic entertainment.

The magician's voice is an important one because it adds a third element to the skeptical discourse on the paranormal Other. In addition to interpreting the medium through the prison of psychopathology or a psychology of deception, skeptics may also view the medium as a fraud or charlatan motivated by pecuniary gain. Furthermore, the magician points to another aspect of the ideological arena in which the debate on the paranormal takes place. Already the boundaries among science, medicine, religion, and feminism have entered into the debate; the magician points to yet one more boundary: between religion and entertainment. More on this point momentarily.

The Schismatic Logic in the Contemporary Period

The historical outlines sketched above suggest a pattern in the development of the borderland between science and religion in the United States: each new movement situates itself as a more scientific variant of the previous movement. Members of the previous movement may not always agree, but the general logic of the boundary-work is, "I'm scientific, you're irrational." This pattern occurs in the debates among Spiritualists, Spiritists, Theosophists, and psychical researchers, as well as between psychical researchers and parapsychologists. The pattern also occurs in the transition from a medicalized description of "mediomania" to a more sophisticated (but still materialist) psychology of belief, deception, and trance states that emerged in the writings of Jastrow, Hall, and Tanner. In the case of the Spiritualism/psychical research/parapsychology genealogy, the organizational development moved from the Spiritualist associations patterned on Protestant churches to the psychical research societies to the Parapsychological Association, which is led today by academic researchers with advanced degrees. The process is an example of what the sociologist Roy Wallis has called the "policy of sanitization," that is, "a concerted attempt to distance the theory and practice from its more notorious proponents by means of professional associations," more sophisticated scientific methodology, and other signs of scientificity (1985:598; see also Collins and Pinch 1979). At the same time, the broader process of rationalization through ongoing schisms may be seen as carrying the cultural logic of Protestant sectarianism into a more or less secular domain.

By the 1950s, the configuration of discourses on the paranormal in the United States had begun to achieve its present form. Regarding parapsychology, J. B. Rhine was publishing popular books and the Parapsychological Association was founded. To the side of skepticism, the science writer Martin Gardner was already writing his critiques of pseudoscience. Finally, the beatnik movement was developing the otherworldly tradition of Spiritualism and Theosophy in directions that began to resemble the New Age movement. Nevertheless, any construction of a "present period," one which took its form in the years after World War II, should not overlook the ongoing dynamism of these movements and the ways in which the schismatic cultural logic continues in effect in the more recent past.

For example, consider the interesting split within skepticism that occurred when the sociologist Marcello Truzzi separated the more academic *Zetetic* from the CSICOP fold. The *Zetetic* was the first CSICOP publication, but editor Truzzi resigned when the CSICOP leaders decided to turn the journal into a more popular magazine. The *Zetetic* (today *Zetetic Scholar*) remained in Truzzi's hands as a more academic journal, whereas CSICOP went on to publish the more popular *Skeptical Inquirer* (see Pinch and Collins 1984; Rawlins 1981; Truzzi 1982). The popular discourse of the *Skeptical Inquirer* does not necessarily make the publication less "scientific" than the *Zetetic Scholar*; however, the difference between the academic and popular forms of discourse is one of the ways that some skeptics have distinguished between "science" and "pseudoscience." Thus, by the skeptics' own criteria, the *Zetetic Scholar* might be classified as a "more scientific" publication. However, Truzzi appears to have a more open-minded approach to parapsychology, and to the extent that the advocate/critic division is used as a boundary criterion, a more favorable attitude toward parapsychological and related studies of "scientific anomalies" could be interpreted as a less "scientific" position than that of the *Skeptical Inquirer.*

A second example, this time to the parapsychology side, involves the formation of the Society for Scientific Exploration (SSE), which might be viewed as a further "sanitization" of the Parapsychological Association as well as of various other heterodox sciences. The SSE's membership criteria are — so I have been told — more stringent than those of the Parapsychological Association, and although many members or former members of the Parapsychological Association participate in the SSE, the language used in the journal articles tends to shy away from parapsychological terminology such as *extrasensory perception, psychokinesis, paranormal,* and *psi* (an umbrella term for paranormal phenomena). The SSE also defines its area of inquiry broadly as scientific anomalies rather than paranormal phenomena, and in fact there seems to be a movement to rename the field "anomalistics," a term which reflects the diffusion of one of the key terms of Thomas Kuhn's *The Structure of Scientific Revolutions* across disciplinary boundaries (but not followed by a diffusion of its criticisms). As a discipline, "anomalistics" would include not only some of the better documented reports and quantitative analyses of ufology, cryptozoology, astrology, and parapsychology, but also anomalous findings in astronomy, physics, geology, and other orthodox scientific disciplines as well as sociological and philosophical discussions of issues such as demarcation criteria. Thus, in the SSE areas traditionally classified as "pseudoscience" commingle with anomalous findings within the mantle of orthodox science as well as with social scientific and philosophical discussions of their context and significance.

Together, these changes mark the SSE as a more "scientific" organization — in the sense of being ostensibly more acceptable to orthodox scientists — than the Parapsychological Association. However, at the 1990 meeting of the Parapsychological Association, one parapsychologist informed me that he viewed the SSE as a "less scientific organization," because it allows papers to be given by ufologists and other heterodox scientists whose methods are, from his viewpoint, less scientific than those of parapsychology. He described parapsychology as "an experimental science," in contrast with the qualitative methods of some ufology reports or the correlational methods of quantitative astrology. Other parapsychologists have agreed with this assessment, and my impression is that it represents a widely held view among experimental parapsychologists. Note, however, that their argument that parapsychology is more "scientific" than the SSE is based merely on methodology, whereas, as I have shown, on a number of other criteria the SSE is able to construct itself as more acceptable and therefore more "scientific" to the orthodox scientific community.

Again, the debate over which group is more or less "scientific" depends on the multiple and complex criteria that can be invoked to construct the boundary between science and nonscience. Thus, different demarcation criteria result in a different verdict on which group is the more or less scientific. Furthermore, these contemporary debates show how the schismatic logic discussed for the history of Spiritualists, psychical researchers, and skeptics is not frozen. Rather, the present period continues to evidence similar patterns of schism and dynamism.

There is even evidence that in the late 1980s and early 1990s the New Age "movement" may have started to fragment as some so-called New Agers seek to dissociate themselves from the most scientifically questionable beliefs and practices, such as crystal healing and channeling (Jones 1989b: 14). Certainly by the end of the 1980s some publishers — who must always have a finger on the pulse of popular culture — were dropping the "New Age" label as a marketing device (Jones 1989c), just as some New Age bookstores were diversifying into related areas such as self-help psychology (Jones 1989a). This process apparently should be interpreted less as the "end of the New Age" than as its absorption into the mainstream of American culture. At the same time that New Age bookstores diversify, more conventional bookstores are also incorporating New Age books into their standard stock (Jones 1989a). One New Age publisher described the process as follows: "The New Age publisher's goal for the nineties is to find ways to integrate these ideas within the general culture, and to market the product as the age-old wisdom and good advice that it really is. . . . My hope is that in five years there is no 'New Age' category as such, that all of the material will have been mainstreamed . . . " (Tarcher 1989:32). One example of how this mainstreaming is occurring comes from a publisher who has broken off a "New Science" imprint from a "New Age" series, and in general the New Age label may disappear as spin-offs — apparently in more secular if not scientific directions — come to take the place of a "New Age" line (Jones 1989c). In short, there are some signs that the New Age movement (like the broader historical tradition of spiritual and occult groups) is subject to the same schismatic logic as are skeptics and parapsychologists.

However, I urge caution in applying this framework to the New Age movement, for it is already divided into a welter of groups, positions, and organizations. As a result, the tendency may be just as much toward syncretism and synthesis as it is toward schism and sanitization. Indeed, when I talk to people who are deeply immersed in one or more aspects of the New Age movement, I am most impressed by how open-minded they are toward a wide range of alternative belief systems. It is as if any alternative spiritual path is good because it is spiritual and alternative; in the New Age/ancient Buddhist formula, "There are many paths to the top of the mountain." In this world view, Buddhist meditation, Native American religion, and Judeo-Christian mysticism can coexist alongside crystal healing, neopagan goddess worship, the tao of physics, and new psychotherapies.

Situating the New Age Movement Historically: Popular Postmodernism?

The New Age movement's capacity to absorb a number of discourses and practices, to juxtapose non-Western wisdom of the ages with cutting-edge science, raises the question of yet one more boundary: the New Age and postmodernism. New Agers' wide-ranging, syncretic eclecticism bears some similarities to this other "movement" that is also associated to some extent with the baby-boom generation. Like the New Age movement, postmodernism may be neither very "post" nor much of a "movement." Nevertheless, as a social movement postmodernism achieves a certain degree of coherence through its social roots in a shared generational experience. Although postmodernism originated in the 1960s, it became a force in the academy in the 1980s, a process that is parallel to the transformation of the counterculture and the Movement of the 1960s into the New Age movement of the 1980s and 1990s. The following questions emerge: Are the New Age and postmodernist "movements" in some sense variants of baby-boom culture? Is New Age discourse the popular and spiritual sibling of its more erudite and secular postmodern Other?

Whereas detractors of postmodernism probably will delight in the comparison, advocates will probably not like it. My purpose, however, is not a polemical one, although the existence of polemics on the topic is itself a social fact that strengthens the comparison. To the point, postmodernism has provoked rather heated divisions and reactions in the academic and artistic worlds not unlike the skeptics' critiques of New Agers. For example, the anthropologist Edward Brunner states that in a number of sessions at the 1989 meetings of the American Anthropological Association, anthropologists were divided into two mutually hostile camps, for which the five-syllable "P-word" (as one of my colleagues has called it) served as either banner or banshee. "All the metaphors were on display," Brunner notes, "the phallocentric 'hard' versus 'soft' approaches, masculine versus feminine, fact versus fantasy, real versus imaginary" (1990:28). One person even said to him, "I never want to hear another thing about postmodernism or the search for meaning. I've had it with that nonsense"

(28). Like the debate over the New Age movement, the idiom through which much of the debate over postmodernism is articulated involves claims of lack of scientific status or intellectual rigor, that is, skepticism (which, as I show throughout this book, cuts both ways).

I believe, however, that there are more compelling reasons to think through an admittedly somewhat ornery comparison between the New Age movement and postmodernism.[11] To begin, consider the argument of the literary scholar Fredric Jameson (1984a) that postmodernist discourse is characterized by a peculiar relationship to mass culture, one which inverts the oppositional relationship of modernism. Whereas modernism depended on a "distinction between high and so-called mass culture for its specificity" (64), postmodernism calls this distinction into question and incorporates mass culture.

On those criteria, parapsychology and to some extent skepticism are modernist discourses. Their relationship to popular paranormal and spiritual belief is oppositional, although in different ways: skeptics reject paranormal belief but do so by adopting some of the rhetorical forms and conventions of popular discourse, whereas parapsychologists attempt to filter out what they view as the scientifically valid category of paranormal phenomena from the popular discourse of paranormal belief, much as modernist artists filtered out selected fragments and motifs of popular culture for appropriation into their elite idiom.

Although both skeptics and parapsychologists have written popular texts, the New Age movement is distinguishable as more consistently or more wholly popular, but popular in a way that—like postmodernist art—involves a fluid juxtaposition of erudite and mass culture, particularly of scientific and religious/spiritual discourses. In other words, New Agers incorporate and rework the research of anthropologists, physicists, philosophers, and other scientists and scholars to legitimate a discourse that also sanctions crystal healing, channelers, astral bodies, goddess religion, and other beliefs and practices generally associated with popular culture. Likewise, in New Age writing a variety of time periods—from future-oriented, cutting-edge science to the ancient wisdom of the Mayans, Egyptians, or Hindus—comes together in a syncretic juxtaposition that is similar to the nostalgic aesthetic of postmodern movies known as *la mode rétro* (e.g., "Chinatown" or "Batman"; see Jameson 1984b).

The parallels between New Age discourse and postmodernist art and aesthetics, interesting as they are, should not be overdrawn. One important difference is the "prepostmodern" way in which New Age discourse is mediated to its consumers. In *The Postmodern Scene*, the political theorists Arthur Kroker and David Cook argue that the world of television, with its emphasis on superficialities and entertainment, is a good example of postmodern technology and culture (1986:270–79). On these grounds, the New Age movement is not postmodern (at least, not yet), since its primary mode of mass communication remains books, magazines, or audio cassettes (with some exceptions, such as Shirley MacLaine's television special "Out on a Limb"). On the criterion of relationship to mass media, perhaps a better candidate for postmodern religiosity would be televangelism, where religious discourse becomes part of the culture industry and religious experience merges with entertainment.

A second and even more striking difference from postmodernism (and televangelism) has to do with the economic and organizational structure of the New Age movement. Unlike televangelism with its centralized churches and large corporations, the New Age movement has remained relatively decentralized. Its entrepreneurs tend to work more at the mom-and-pop shop level and under a self-conscious, "small is beautiful" economic ideology that legitimates this economic form of organization (see Satin 1978). For example, the psychic fairs and holistic health "expos" that I have attended in upstate New York and the Berkshires tend to be more like home-and-garden shows or county fairs. As rituals, they are reminiscent of the kind of events that Marcel Mauss linked to a period of "total social phenomena" that antedated *homo oeconomicus* (1967:74–78). They are festivals in which entrepreneurs (often local) display a potpourri of goods and services that are vaguely related to the values of "naturalness," antiestablishment "alternatives," and "appropriate" technologies.

New Age capitalism is therefore still a small-scale, largely entrepreneurial capitalism. It can be distinguished from the large-scale, corporate, and multinational forms sometimes associated with postmodernism.[12] For example, in *New Visions*, the New Age newspaper from the Berkshire region, most of the advertised goods and services — crystals, books, bodywork tables, mountain retreats, natural foods, futons, and a wide variety of therapies, classes, and massage treatments — are offered by small-scale entrepreneurs, that is, the "petty bourgeoisie." The consumer's decision to buy the goods and services — and with them to "buy" the story of their cultural meaning as alternative and natural — is part of what locates the consumer as either belonging or not belonging to the New Age movement. But many consumers have opted in, for there is apparently a healthy market for New Age products, and advertisers across the country continue to buy space in New Age publications, which in the late 1980s and early 1990s were flourishing (Carlson 1990). Part of the appeal of New Age commodities must be that unlike the culture industry, which turns cultural production into commodity production, New Agers view themselves as turning commodity production into cultural production: they produce goods with a heart. Thus, New Age goods and services appear to have little in common with the conditions of postmodern production, and certainly the attempt to market natural and wholesome products is not necessarily new or postmodern.[13]

Nevertheless, there are some parallels between the cultural meaning of New Age goods and services and that of postmodern art. Consider, for example, the Coca-Cola bottle, Campbell's Soup can, or Marilyn Monroe of Andy Warhol, artistic representations that Jameson argues turn "centrally around commodification" (1984b). Warhol takes the commercialized — the reified and commodified visual representation, such as commodity advertising or the fetishized Hollywood star — and turns it into an object that is an artistic representation and therefore a commodity (or representation of a commodity) as well as a critique of commodification. In a similar way, New Age entrepreneurs produce goods and services that are both commodities and, as statements about "naturalness" or "alternativeness," to some extent critiques of the system of commodity production.

New Agers also produce religious discourse in ways that, like their commodity production, bear some similarities to postmodern aesthetics. One might argue that New Age spirituality shares an essentialism with religious discourse that postmodernism eschews. As a result the New Age movement may be seen as one more variant of Americans' seemingly endless capacity for religious experimentation, and therefore New Age discourse bears little similarity to postmodernism. But again notice the difference between New Age discourse and televangelism, this time a difference that makes New Age discourse appear relatively postmodern. Despite the televangelists' adoption of the cultural forms of late-night TV entertainment, amusement-park get-aways, and corporate entrepreneurship, their discourse remains firmly within recognizable religious conventions. Samuel Danforth and Jonathan Edwards could listen to Jerry Falwell or Jimmy Swaggart and find a shared discourse (which is not to say that they would all agree), but the Puritan ministers would listen to Ram Dass or Shirley MacLaine as if they were from another planet or from hell itself. New Age discourse may incorporate elements from the Judeo-Christian religious tradition, but it cannot be characterized as either Judeo-Christian or a formal religion. Just as the social organization of the New Age movement is not built around a central church or even divided into different sects, so New Age discourse might be seen as "pastiching" the multiple discourses of the ideological arena — religion, science, politics, medicine, psychology, feminism, ecology, and so on — not to mention the discourses of other times and other cultures.

To conclude, there are enough similarities between New Age and post-modernist discourse to make interesting the formula that New Age discourse is a popular, otherworldly version of baby-boom culture for which post-modernism is its erudite, this-worldly Other. Such a formula, however, should not lead to the stabilization of the New Age movement (or post-modernism) along a popular/elite dimension. As the situation of New Age publishing in 1990 reveals, emergent divisions within New Age writing and publishing are part of the general historical pattern of sanitization via a more scientific or secular discourse. The internal divisions among the New Age movement thus contribute to a rapidly changing dynamic, which in turn is further complicated by the syncretic and eclectic power of New Age discourse to reincorporate that which splits off from it. While, as social scientists have argued (Chevalier 1986, Wallis 1985), there may be a tendency for some occult or spiritual groups to develop a more scientific or secular discourse because of the authority and prestige of science in contemporary society, there is an opposing syncretic tendency that welcomes a variety of alternative spiritual, medical, and even scientific systems back into the New Age movement.

Those who wish to maintain their distance from the syncretism and synthesis of discourses engage in boundary-work, and a multiple and complex debate occurs among the various positions of those who are for and against, inside and outside, orthodox scientific discourse. In the process, their rhetoric articulates with the surrounding culture. It is the cultural meanings of the boundary disputes to which I now turn.

Part II

The Cultural Construction
of Skeptical and Paranormal Discourse

3

Self and Other

I MAINTAIN a dialogical concept of the "Self"; identity is constituted not by essential characteristics but instead by a set of relationships to the Other, or whatever is *not* the Self. Skeptics, for example, could not really exist — or would certainly be fundamentally different — if they were not situated oppositionally in an ideological arena of parapsychologists, New Agers, fundamentalist Christians, and others who hold what skeptics view to be pseudoscientific beliefs. Likewise, parapsychologists and New Agers construct their identities in similar matrices of "alterity" or "otherness."[1]

In this chapter, I look over the shoulders of New Agers, skeptics, and parapsychologists as they construct their Others. I will show that although each community represents itself as fundamentally different from its Others, they all construct their differences in similar ways. All borrow from a shared set of cultural understandings and categories to distance themselves from their Others and even, as the anthropologist James Boon (1982) has observed, to create a sense of "exaggerated" distance between the Self and the Others. At the same time, as they draw on their cultural heritage to construct the boundaries between Self and Other, they also remake that heritage by conjugating religious, political, and scientific discourses in new combinations.

New Agers

The Other in Marilyn Ferguson's Aquarian Conspiracy

Like many New Age writers, the editor of the *Brain-Mind Bulletin* has a great deal of respect for the achievements of contemporary science. Yet, in the New Age classic the *Aquarian Conspiracy*, Ferguson does construct an Other when she discusses one view of science: the old science of Bacon and Descartes, an outdated approach that implied understanding nature atomistically (1987:156). In place of their mechanical and analytical science, she advocates a "new," holistic, systems-oriented science. Examples include the neuroscientist Karl Pribram's theory that the brain is a hologram (177ff.) and the physicist David Bohm's theory of a holographic universe (180). She also finds inspiration in the chemist Ilya Prigogine's theory of dissipative structures, that is, open systems that she describes as *"flowing wholeness"* (164, emphasis original).

Crucial to Ferguson's vision is her association of the "Other" science with the past, with old ways of thinking. As the anthropologist Johannes Fabian (1983) has argued, the Other is frequently located in a space and time of "there and then," as opposed to the "here and now" of the Self. In its broadest terms, Fabian's formula holds true for Ferguson as well, but the New Age writer adds a new twist to the formula by constructing a future-oriented Self that recuperates the lost wisdom of the distant past. For Ferguson, the future is a time of synthesis between "breakthrough science and insights from the earliest recorded thought" (1987:23). Likewise, she draws on ancient cosmology for the future-oriented title of her book, *The Aquarian Conspiracy*. She states that she was "drawn to the symbolic power of the pervasive dream in our popular culture: that after a dark, violent age, the Piscean, we are entering a millennium of love and light—in the words of the popular song, 'The Age of Aquarius,' the time of 'the mind's true liberation'" (19).

Ferguson's vision of new knowledge provides a template for the new society; she views the opposition between mechanism and holism in science as part of a general cultural transformation that also plays itself out in the domain of social organization. She argues that a mechanical picture of the universe means that people will live mechanically. "On the other hand," she adds, "if we know that we are part of an open universe, and that our minds are a matrix of reality, we will live more creatively and powerfully" (1987:146). Just as in the natural world the theory of dissipative structures shows how the transformation of a part is linked to that of the whole, so in the social world a "dissident minority like the Aquarian Conspiracy" can transform society (166). If the Aquarian conspirators are successful, the new social order will no longer be based on competition, formal institutions, and hierarchies; instead, she argues, it will be anchored in an ethic of cooperation and a social organization of "loose networks" (25).

The new science and new society also entail a new religion, and here Ferguson draws on the theories of the psychologist Herbert Koplowitz, who adds new stages to Piaget's theory of cognitive development. Beyond standard cognitive thought lies systems thinking, which represents simultaneous and inseparable causes, and after this comes a final stage, "Unitary Operational Thought," in which dualisms evaporate and the mind perceives the interdependence of opposites (371). "Unitary thought is holistic," Ferguson adds, as is mystical experience, and she finds many parallels between Eastern mysticism and the new science (372, 379).[2]

In her descriptions of old versus new forms of science, social organization, and religion, Ferguson deploys a series of appropriate spatial similes and metaphors. For example, one of her section titles is "New Mind, New World" (406, a reference to J. B. Rhine's book *New World of the Mind*), and she explicitly compares the "personal paradigm shift" of the new holistic outlook to "a sea-crossing to the New World" (387). Ferguson explains that, like the European immigrants who came to America, voyagers to her New World cannot convince all their friends and relatives "to make the journey" (387). Furthermore, no matter how hard the immigrants try, they cannot maintain the old ways of the Old World; as she phrases it, "New England is not England; Nova Scotia is not Scotland" (387).

Ferguson specifies the space of her new world by linking the new way of thinking to the future-oriented "Pacific Culture," where visionaries "tend to emphasize the future, ecology, high technology, inner development, cultural diversity, coalition, the joining of disciplines, and parallel spiritual truths" (422). Within the United States, she sees California as a "laboratory for transformation" (132). If California is named after a mythical island, as she claims, then it is a myth she embraces, for she reads California as a place of hope and rejuvenation for a decadent country. California "has been an island of myth in the United States, sanctuary of the endangered dream" (132). California is the future: "If America is free, California is freer. If America is open to innovation, innovation is California's middle name. . . . California is a preview of our national paradigm shifts as well as our fads and fashions" (132). California is the home of new governmental experiments, its own group of twentieth-century transcendentalists, and, of course, Esalen and the human potential movement, which, perched on the edge of the Pacific basin, turns to the East for spiritual wisdom (134–38).[3]

Ferguson writes of Flaubert dreaming of China, the Indies, and California, and she quotes Thoreau saying, "There is an orientalism in the most restless pioneer, and the farthest west is but the farthest east" (135). Yet, while the Europeans and New Englanders of the nineteenth century dreamed of California and the mysterious East, the future home to the New Age movement "was already dotted with centers and study groups revolving around Buddhism and 'Hindoo' teachings" (136). The mysterious East beckoned from across the Pacific as a space that is imagined to be as old as California is new and as spiritual as the West is materialistic. In the process, the traditional structures of orientalism (Said 1978) are given a face-lift: it is a New Age orientalism of new psychologies and sciences, of Esalen hot tubs and Taoist physics. The physicist Fritjof Capra (1975) becomes one of Ferguson's prophets (145), and the Western future of a "new" physics is linked to an Eastern past of Hinduism, Taoism, and Buddhism.

Ferguson's Self is therefore constructed in relation to two types of Others: a negative, mechanistic Other that possesses less knowledge than the Self, and a positive, holistic Other that is mediated through exotic imagery.[4] The negative Other is located in the science of Bacon, the existing social order based on competition and formal institutions, and the old ways of Europe (not America) or New England (not California). In contrast, the positive, exotic Other is located in the ancient wisdom of the East that simultaneously serves as a model for the future Self of the Pacific Rim, the new holism, and unitary thinking. As a result, depending on how far we go into the "there and then," we tend to come full circle to an exotic Other that serves as a model for the future-oriented Self.

Crystals Are Good to Think: A Crystal Healer and Her Others

Ferguson's relatively erudite construction of the boundary between Self and Other can be contrasted with popular constructions at the other end of the spectrum of New Age thought. Despite important differences, Ferguson and the more popular New Age writers both construct a double Other, one negative and proximate, and the other positive and distant.

As the mechanistic view of Baconian science played the role of negative Other for Ferguson's new science, so geology occupies a similar position as foil in Katrina Raphaell's art of crystal healing. The famed author of the crystal trilogy begins the first book in the series, *Crystal Enlightenment* (1985), with a survey of the geology of crystals that describes the technicalities of the classes of crystals and the various procedures for mining, cutting, and polishing them (3–7). In short, her description of crystals from the "physical" viewpoint is a straightforward, scientific description.

However, this physical view of crystals is only a point of departure; Raphaell argues that crystals can be approached both "physically" and "esoterically." From an esoteric perspective, crystals contain within them the ancient wisdom of Atlantis, the "legendary civilization of advanced sciences" that had both a technologically and a spiritually advanced understanding of crystals (8). Thus, crystals served "physical and practical purposes," but they could also be used as "telepathic communicator[s]" to the Atlanteans' "universal forefathers" (1985:8).

Raphaell's New Age version of the Atlantis saga is a millenarian tale. She explains how the great lost continent was destroyed "because this sacred knowledge was abused and the awesome power misused for egocentric purposes" (8). The "uncorrupted wise ones" wished to preserve the ancient wisdom from its impending destruction, but they were afraid that if they preserved it in writing, then natural catastrophes would destroy the texts. As a result, they preserved the ancient wisdom in the form of crystals, and the survivors of Atlantis in Egypt, the Americas, and Tibet built pyramids "using crystalline theories and patterning them after the great temples in Atlantis" (8). Crystals and pyramids therefore represent the remnants of an ancient knowledge far superior to that of modern science and technology, but a knowledge which, like modern science and technology, was powerful enough to bring about the destruction of a great civilization.

In addition to connecting the Self to the exotic Other of Atlantis, crystals may also contain the souls of ancient Native Americans, who are said to have believed that after death the soul of those who lived a good life went into a crystal (10). Because of these properties, crystals can help their owners to develop meditation skills, just as they can help to heal (11). Having "power and potential" means that crystals are among the "main contributors to the New Age"; they serve as "a means to transform the human predicament and usher in the Golden Age of Aquarius" (11).[5]

Crystals also represent a harmonious middle ground between the two worlds of the materialistic, scientific Other and the spiritualistic, exotic Other. In this sense, they are mirrors for the New Age Self. For example, Raphaell represents the seven basic groups of crystals as "the seven tribes of the crystal kingdom" (3), and the clear quartz crystal is "the grandfather of the mineral kingdom" (49). Crystal clusters — that is, crystals that are separate on top but linked to a common base — become "many individual crystals who all live together in harmony and peace" (54). Quartz crystals are, like humans, "born out of the womb of the earth," which may make humans and crystals "distant cousins" (49). Quartz crystals are also individuals: they are "unique and unlike any others, each with its own personality, lessons and experiences (as with humans)" (51).

Crystals therefore serve as a natural code in which not only the human body and soul, but also the human social order, may be represented, a kind of thinking that the anthropologist Claude Lévi-Strauss described as totemic (1963). Even from the perspective of orthodox science, crystals share at least one of the properties associated with life — the ability to grow — and therefore they already occupy a mediating position between the physical and living worlds. The New Age crystal healer completes this association by making crystals into complex mediators between the scientific and the spiritual, the physical and the esoteric, thing and being, nature and culture, and body and soul.

Like Ferguson, Raphaell's Self is therefore constucted with reference to a purely physical, materialistic Other (the geology of crystals) and romantic, exotic Others (Atlanteans, Native Americans). Yet, like American society Atlantis is also divided between the wise ones and those who wished to use the power of crystals for "egocentric purposes." The Atlantean Other, then, may serve as a warning to the irrationality of Raphaell's more proximate, skeptical Others: those who doubt her higher spiritual message and who would instead wish to use the power of nuclear energy or other forms of advanced technology for "egocentric purposes."[6]

Native Exotic Others

Atlantis and the wisdom of the East are only two of the many sites that New Agers choose for their exotic Other. The Los Angeles–based writer Lynn Andrews reveals another site for which Raphaell only suggests that crystals mediate: the shamanism of native peoples. In *Crystal Woman: Sisters of the Dreamtime* (1987), Andrews takes her readers on a journey from the Native American shamanism of her earlier books to the Aboriginal shamanism of Australia.[7] She describes herself as belonging to the Sisterhood of the Shields, a circle of women shamans, each of whom represents a shamanic tradition from one of the different cultures of the world (21). To understand shamanism, Andrews writes, "[O]ne has to become a shaman. You cannot write about shamanism like an engineer writes down mathematical theories" (xvi). Once again, negative images of conventional science — here the engineer and mathematics — are opposed to Andrews's exotic Other, the shaman.[8]

Andrews believes that those who wish to become shamans must embark on a spiritual voyage, one which she describes by invoking the images of frontiers and exploration seen in Ferguson's text: shamanism "is the space program of the soul [that] launches you out into the uncharted territory of the stars" (xvi). *Crystal Woman* is therefore a travelogue of both spiritual and geographical discovery. Andrews chronicles how she traveled to Australia, "the oldest continent on earth," where the austere desert is personified as a "she" who appeared to have "rejected the life of man" (4). Here, Andrews — a blonde from California — meets her exotic Other, a spiritual mentor named Ginevee, whose alterity is symbolized in a description of her face: "so dark it became one with the shadows" (4). Whereas the exotic Other of Ferguson and Raphaell is represented by a distant lost civilization, Andrews discovers a living, breathing shaman who lives in the same plane of space and time. Ginevee begins to initiate Andrews into the higher knowledge of the dreamtime, the sacred world of the Aboriginal shamans. As part of that initiation, Ginevee explains to Andrews the importance of crystals, the "sacred beings" from the dreamtime (40). Although they are "made up of physical things," they also transcend the world of matter and science, and instead they are, to quote a phrase that bridges the scientific and the spiritual, "part of the higher arithmetic of the Dreamtime" (172).

Whether the exotic Other is Australian Aborigine or ancient Atlantean, the message of crystals is much the same: they mediate between the other world and this world, between a plane of higher spiritual knowledge and that of the mundane, materialistic world of modern science. Unlike the skeptics, who reject anything to do with spirituality or paranormality, New Agers do not reject modern science as much as complete it by grafting onto it a new plane of existence linked to the wisdom of ancient civilizations. In the process, the New Age writer serves as a mediator who, much like the crystals themselves, bridges the gaps between two worlds.

Biographical Time and the New Ager's Skeptical Other

My last example of New Age discourse on the Self and Other reveals similar patterns, even when focussed on the narrower level of biographical time. In *Out on a Limb*, the actress Shirley MacLaine tells the story of her personal journey from a skeptical, mundane world to higher spiritual awareness associated with an exotic Other. One of the most interesting aspects of MacLaine's biographical tale is that the negative Other is frequently expressed as an internal, skeptical voice.

MacLaine's spiritual awakening begins when she accepts a friend's invitation to visit a New Age bookstore in Los Angeles, an apparently unimportant event that, in retrospect, she sees as a major life decision (1983:46). Her friend David shows her many books, but the ones on reincarnation catch her eye. Despite her lack of interest in "God and religion and the hereafter," reincarnation piques her interest because it involves questions of personal identity. "Who was I?" she asks. "Who was anyone?" (51). Narratives of past lives repeat at the level of individual biography the hermeneutic circle described in other New Age texts: the New Age Self recuperates an exotic Other (a past life) that becomes a model for her future Self. In psychocultural terms, the past lives of reincarnation provide an idiom for people to explore and create new aspects of the Self.[9]

MacLaine's present-time Self, however, is divided into a relatively skeptical side and a more accepting, or even credulous, side. Her port of entry into New Age discourse—the question of personal identity—provides a middle ground between the psychological quest for personal knowledge and the religious quest for spiritual knowledge, that is, between relatively skeptical and relatively spiritual idioms. Despite her awakened interest, MacLaine continues to play the role of the skeptic, particularly when paired off against her friend David. For example, after another conversation with him, she thinks to herself: "Jesus . . . hippy-dippy jargon. He's going to use phrases that are simply not part of my realistic vocabulary" (87).

As MacLaine's narrative progresses, the skeptical voice within begins to make more and more room for the New Age voice, and at times she finds her thoughts beginning to "tumble" from the conflict between the two voices. "On the one hand," she writes, "it sounded plausible in an idealistic sort of way. On the other, it just sounded outrageously impossible and flat flaky" (1983:94). By showing her own doubts about the new ideas she is encountering, she portrays her "conversion" experience as a gradual awakening. She never completely jettisons her skeptical side, but eventually she grants more and more room to her New Age voice.

As MacLaine becomes more immersed in New Age thought, she moves from the exoticism of past lives to that of extraterrestrials and ancient wisdom. She takes off on a vacation/pilgrimage that provides one more variant on the location of the exotic Other in the there and then: the Andes, the home of the ancient Inca civilization. Living in California, the end of the frontier, she must now find a new one, so she leaves America and becomes an explorer of frontiers that are simultaneously spiritual, geographical, and temporal. In the process, she encounters some other explorers: extraterrestrial space colonizers who are believed to have been behind the great advances of the South American civilizations. Her skeptical voice surfaces for a moment: MacLaine finds Erik von Daniken, the writer who has advocated the extraterrestrial colonization theory of ancient civilizations, "a little kooky" (239). Nevertheless, she believes that "he's on the right track," and she even comes to accept the possibility that extraterrestrials founded ancient civilizations such as that of the Incas (239). By tracing the roots of ancient civilizations to extraterrestrial colonization, ancient cultures become colonies and the Earth the New World, thus recreating Ferguson's metaphor of the New World on a global scale.[10]

Still, MacLaine must also encounter the internal negative Other, that is, the skeptical voice within her that simultaneously holds her back from spiritual awakening and protects her from gullibility. When a spirit guide appears through a channeler and tells her how extraterrestrials have been making visitations "since the beginning of time," she becomes doubtful. "Maybe this was all an act," the famed actress wonders. She answers her doubts with another question: "[B]ut what if it wasn't? I didn't want to waste an opportunity to learn something" (202). Thus, she listens to her spirit guide, who tells her that "the only important knowledge is the spiritual knowledge of God" and that "all other knowledge flows from this" (202). He also explains how scientific knowledge derives from this higher spiritual knowledge; in other words, as in the sagas of Atlantis and the Australian dreamtime, spiritual knowledge is greater than the mere materialistic and scientific knowledge of the skeptical Other (202–3).

Shortly after this conversation, the skeptical voice returns, but this time it is external to MacLaine's personal voice; it is heard in the form of friends and acquaintances who now find her "naive and gullible" (205). For example, when she runs into a friend from New York, he asks her cynically, "So you've gone California?" She is not sure what he means, and he explains: "Yeah. Everybody out here is into that stuff. Only California could elect a Governor Moonbeam, right?" (224). Note how the skeptical voice of the New Yorker associates California not, as Marilyn Ferguson would have it, with the Pacific rim future of new ideas, but instead with the flaky and faddish.

When MacLaine is with her skeptical friend, she advocates New Age beliefs; however, when she is with her New Age friends, her skeptical voice tends to reappear. For example, at one point she challenges her friend David in terms similar to those of the cynical New Yorker she encountered earlier: "[W]hat proof is there that all this stuff is true? I mean really." (233). When she relays her friends' skeptical questions to her spirit guide, he acknowledges that skepticism is healthy, but not when it "becomes so profound and demoralizing that it restricts the potential of learning glorious truths" (206). MacLaine's spirit guide advocates leaving the skeptics alone and not trying to convert them. Eventually, he says, "[T]here will come a time when they too will want to know and they will be drawn to dimensions which are more true" (207). He therefore situates skepticism as an earlier position, one which MacLaine herself once held and her friends who have not yet opened themselves to New Age consciousness still hold. Yet, she never completely jettisons her own internal skeptical voice; it remains a part of her, although supplementary to her New Age voice. The two voices have always been a part of her, but as her personal narrative develops, their relationship is inverted.

MacLaine's tale of personal discovery reveals one more layer of complexity to the processes of boundary-work. In her case, the boundaries between the skeptical and the spiritual, the scientific and the paranormal, are internalized as two voices of the same Self. Furthermore, the boundaries also shift fluidly across changes in personal relationships and life history. Thus, even a complex notion of multiple boundaries, such as I have articulated in the previous chapter, is now rendered even more complicated: we all live out complex and shifting boundaries in our individual lives as we move across different roles and stages of development.

MacLaine's story is also interesting because it confirms some of the patterns found in other exemplars of New Age discourse, such as the construction of exotic and negative Others that are located in different degrees of spatiotemporal proximity. MacLaine may take us to the Andes and talk of extraterrestrials, but in her quest for the exotic Other she could have substituted without much difficulty a voyage to Aboriginal Australia or the mysterious East. Likewise, just as in the societal narratives of Ferguson, Raphaell, and Andrews, where the future Self and society synthesize both recent scientific knowledge and ancient wisdom, so MacLaine's developed New Age Self synthesizes a skeptical, scientific voice of an earlier phase of her life with a believing, spiritual voice of past lives and ancient knowledge. Furthermore, like other New Agers, MacLaine's spirit guide constructs the negative Other as an earlier version of the Self, one which lacks the Self's knowledge but has the potential to obtain it, since he states that eventually skeptics, too, will be won over to their truth.

Parapsychologists

Mediating Religion and Science

Do parapsychologists also define the Self in opposition to a proximate, negative Other and a more exotic, positive Other? The answer, both yes and no, is consistent with what I see as the mediating position of the parapsychologists between the two extremes of the New Agers and skeptics. I begin to answer this question by looking more closely at J. B. Rhine's book *New World of the Mind.*

It may not be entirely accurate to label J. B. Rhine a dualist — according to Louisa Rhine he only called himself a "relative dualist" (1983:265–66) — but whatever qualifications one wishes to attach to the term, Rhine's vision of parapsychology and its object, paranormal phenomena, rested on mind/matter dualism (see Edge 1985). The point is important, for it distinguishes Rhinean parapsychology from both the materialism of most of the skeptics and the spiritualism of many New Agers. Indeed, Rhine's entire vision of parapsychology rested on its role as a mediator between its two antagonistic, negative Others: science and religion, or matter and mind.

Rhine articulated his "relative dualism" on many levels, but perhaps the most obvious was the name he chose for his new science. In place of "psychical research," he popularized the term "parapsychology," a word which had already been coined but was not very frequently used. Literally, the word "parapsychology" means "beyond" or "alongside psychology," but Rhine often used the term to mean "beside" or "alongside physics." For example, in *The New World of the Mind*, he introduces parapsychology as "science's first new world beyond physics" and its subject matter as that which not only "cannot be explained in terms of physical processes" but also "takes one well out of the world with which physics deals" (1953:8). Unlike physics, which he describes as a "space-time system," the Cartesian parapsychologist expects psychic phenomena to be as "independent of time as they are of space" (17). Rhine therefore recognizes mind and body as separate orders of existence, and he even subdivides paranormal (or psi) phenomena into two major categories that are like the sensory and motor aspects of mind/body relations: extrasensory perception, "a form of experience," and psychokinesis, or "physical effects" (89, 107).

Rhine is quite explicit about the broader philosophical implications of his dualistic science. He argues that in the past psychic phenomena have been explained as supernatural, and that the explanatory hypotheses he entertains have until then only been considered reasonable "in the field of religion" (46). Unlike New Agers, he seems to have little romantic nostalgia for the mystical knowledge of ancient civilizations. Instead, he aims to bring the "findings" of religion and the supernatural to science, and conversely the "methods" of science to religion and the supernatural (46). Parapsychology therefore does not fit "either kind of prevailing orthodoxy," and its challenge to the twin dogmas of "physicalism" and "supernaturalism" is so great that Rhine labels its import "revolutionary" (47).

Not unlike crystals and mediums for New Agers, paranormal phenomena for Rhine mediate between the physical and spiritual realms. On the one hand, he insists that psi phenomena are "not unlawful, unnatural, supernatural, or anything of the sort" (84); parapsychology is a science, the science of the soul, and therefore it, too, has laws. On the other hand, he believes that although official religion has not paid much attention to parapsychology (221), there is a close relationship between the two fields: "[P]arapsychology is to religion what biology or physics is to engineering" (220). Rhine considers himself a scientific pioneer and explorer, but he reminds the reader, "The founders of the religious systems were themselves explorers, pioneers, revolutionists!" (219).

New World of Metaphors

The explorer analogy is crucial to the whole organization of *New World of the Mind*, and examining the analogy in detail reveals important similarities with New Age and skeptical texts.[11] Paranormal phenomena themselves, rather than the wisdom of ancient civilizations, constitute Rhine's exotic Other. He returns to the analogy of discovery of the new world throughout the book, but nowhere is it more clearly formulated than in the opening paragraphs:

> This book is about a new world that science has discovered, a region within what we call the mind, a world that has throughout the past been shrouded in dark mystery and superstition.
>
> Many new worlds have been discovered by man—worlds that lie outside himself. He has been less successful within. His new worlds of the past range from deep within his own planet—and even inside the atom—to far beyond the visible spectrum and beyond the visible stars. But the great discovering human mind has never yet thoroughly explored its own puzzling complex nature.
>
> It now looks very much as though here and there a few pioneer explorers have broken through to a truly new world within man, a world of distinctively mental reality (1953:ix).

Rhine's introduction should remind the reader of Ferguson's metaphors of exploring new frontiers, not to mention those of Andrews and MacLaine. Even if the nature of the exotic Other has shifted to a figurative frontier, the Self remains a future-oriented explorer.

Rhine goes on to argue that, like Columbus, explorers usually do not know if they have discovered a new world or only an illusion (ix). Nevertheless, although parapsychology has only glimpsed "a few small islands" of the new hemisphere (x), Rhine confidently deploys the metaphor of the new world as an organizing device for the entire book. The first section of the book, for example, is titled "Explorations in the New World"; the first chapter, "A Chart of the Areas Discovered"; and the concluding section, "The Prospect for Further Exploration."

Because Rhine views himself as a mediator between science and religion, he is hesitant to construct orthodox science as an entirely negative Other. Indeed, when he discusses the relations between parapsychology and the "other worlds" of natural science, his new world shrinks and gradually dissolves. "The science of psi is not an island," he writes. "New though it may be to the explorer, it has connections with the mainland; it is really only one section of a vastly larger order that has many and varied parts" (147). Furthermore, to emphasize the connections between parapsychology and the sciences of the "mainland," Rhine tends to drop the explorer analogy altogether. In its place, the former botanist describes physics, biology, and psychology as the three "branches" of natural science that are closest to parapsychology, which itself is later described as "a small branch of biology" (190). The natural sciences also become "the roots" of parapsychology, whereas the implications that parapsychology has for society, religion, and politics are likened to its "fruits" (147).

Finally, the analogy of a tree with roots, branches, and fruits shifts to that of a mine, an image that appears in a more developed form in Louisa Rhine's writings. J. B. Rhine argues that parapsychologists and other scientists can "work back from their several points of departure to any such deeper lying, undifferentiated root reality as there may be" (165). The "root" reality is both that of a tree and a mine, for as Rhine continues, it will "most likely be the physicists whose picks the parapsychologist will strike first if the digging progresses and the tunnels converge as it would seem they should do" (165).

Why does J. B. Rhine shift his analogy in this way? The new world analogy is a powerful one because it resonates dramatically with a cultural heritage of frontiers, discovery, and exploration, and it conveys the excitement and adventure that Rhine senses in his encounter with psychic phenomena. However, although he wants to emphasize the novelty and importance of his voyage of scientific discovery, Rhine simultaneously wants to stress that parapsychology is connected to the orthodox sciences.

Louisa Rhine and the Mechanistic Other

In *ESP in Life and Lab* (1967), Louisa Rhine develops and amplifies some of the metaphors of the earlier book by her husband. Unlike J. B. Rhine, she is less reluctant to view orthodox science as a negative Other. As she puts it, sciences such as physics and chemistry give the impression that "human beings" are "just machines" or even "nothing but a glorified supercomputer" (1967:1).[12] In their place, she argues that parapsychology points to a nonreductionist view of the mind and human nature. The discovery of a mind freed of its material constraints would "tell us something very important about man's nature. It would mean that deep within his personality, at the center of all the regular processes that run according to the laws of chemistry and physics, is another *order* of operation, one which, whatever its ultimate secret may prove to be, means that the mechanistic model of human beings is incomplete" (1967:4; emphasis original).

Notice that the place of a mind freed from its ordinary limitations is given a location: it is "deep" within "man's" personality, and psychic abilities come from "deeply unconscious levels" (35). In other words, the depth of the exotic psychic Other is opposed to the superficiality of the negative, mechanistic Other. Images of depth are, in Louisa Rhine's writings, part of a family of recurring terms or "terministic screens" (Burke 1966:44ff.) that include depictions of paranormal phenomena as "secret," "obscure," "elusive," and a "mystery." For example, Rhine invokes the picture puzzles of the children's magazine *Highlights* to describe paranormal phenomena as "like the hidden figure in a childhood puzzle, which once spied among the obscuring foliage stands out, never to be missed again" (1967:259). The image of the childhood puzzle—which, incidentally, also appears in Marilyn Ferguson's *The Aquarian Conspiracy* (1987:30)—suggests a hidden secret to be unveiled. Indeed, Louisa Rhine's last book, an autobiography and biography of her husband, is titled *Something Hidden,* and the epigraph reveals the source of this phrase as Rudyard Kipling's poem "The Explorer," where he describes "something hidden . . . behind the Ranges" (Rhine 1983:xv).

Louisa Rhine also employs images of the deep, the elusive, and the hidden to help distinguish between spontaneous case research, the gathering of case reports for which she became known, and experimental parapsychology, the domain of her husband. Here, the Self/Other distinction as parapsychology/materialistic science is recreated internally as the distinction between spontaneous case research and experimental parapsychology.

The difference between real-life and laboratory situations is something like that in mining: sometimes a real vein is struck, but at other times the miner must be content to screen out fine particles of ore from the sand of the riverbed. If he is in the latter situation, he is glad to get even a small residue. He knows he well might have failed even to find that much.

The situation in the laboratory, then, is one of sifting out the particles of ore and being thankful that it is possible to find a residue. In this case the residue may be considerably dulled by impurities, so that the bright, true color of the ore (the conviction) seems absent (1967:68).

Louisa Rhine's almost alchemical images take us deep into a mine, a metaphor for the psychological depth of spontaneous case research, which is contrasted with the superficiality of experimental research. In either case, however, the object of discovery—paranormal phenomena that are imagined as gold—is the same, but her own brand of parapsychological research is viewed as more profound. While J. B. Rhine takes us across oceans to penetrate new continents, Louisa Rhine helps us to explore the depths of the unconscious and subterranean mine shafts.[13]

Louisa Rhine and the Occult Other

Just as Louisa Rhine is more explicit than her husband about the negative Other of mechanistic and materialistic science, she is also more explicit about the negative Other to the side of religion and the supernatural. In a subsequent book, *Psi, What Is It?* (1975), Louisa Rhine adds to this complex web of Self/Other relations a negative Other that is in some ways similar to that of the skeptics' negative, paranormal Other. Writing in the wake of the 1960s, when the term "New Age" and its reconfiguration of occult and metaphysical traditions had not yet gained currency, Rhine still referred to this nexus as "the occult fringe."

Consider, for example, a brief passage that reveals many similarities with the discourse of the skeptics: "Just as in medicine, for instance, proper research has given us 'modern miracles' in place of old-fashioned charms to drive out evil spirits, in parapsychology by controlled experiments much has already been learned to show the dividing line between truth and shadowy old occult beliefs. Those untested beliefs still hang like a cloud, a fringe, around the field. This poses a danger for it, namely, that these loose, sensational, and often well-advertised approaches to psychic mysteries could well eclipse the slow, careful, and factual method of experimental parapsychology" (1975:15). In this passage, Rhine likens parapsychology to modern medicine, whereas she compares the occult fringe to "old-fashioned charms." The latter is somehow also very modern, for she describes the occult fringe as "sensational" and "well-advertised," terms which associate the occult Other with commercial materialism. Whatever the occult is—ancient superstition or modern hype—it is described in images of darkness and ill definition, of shadow, cloud, or eclipse.

In another passage, Louisa Rhine weaves together images of commercial sensationalism and pathology with other negative elements that will also turn out to be characteristic of skeptical discourse: "The acceptance of quick, sensational, publicized claims about psychical matters is evidence of a general need to know the answer to 'What am I' and to know it now. Like a cancer victim, the general public wants a cure and quickly without waiting for the slow, painstaking way of science. But the same impatience leads to quack cancer cures in medicine and to the occult fringe of parapsychology" (21). Rhine therefore links occult belief to the imagery of disease, and in a later chapter, "The Occult in School," she describes occult belief as spreading "like a virus in a population with no immunity" (196). She then shifts metaphors and returns to the image of media hype, stating that "with the help of the media, this one has been spreading like a flame in the wind" (196).

Although Louisa Rhine writes like a skeptic in these passages, there are some important differences. For example, she repeatedly returns to the question of "Who am I?" in a way that indicates that she accepts the question as a legitimate one that parapsychology asks alongside Spiritualists, New Agers, or even the occult "fringe." Furthermore, although Rhine symbolizes "the fringe" as the Other much as the skeptics do, for her it is not quite as negative. For Rhine, the occult Other represents an exaggeration of tendencies already found within the Self, an unsuccessful attempt to answer questions of deeper meaning that nevertheless remain important. She envisions the relationship between parapsychology and the fringe more as a friendly dialogue than as a debunking session. "The careful person," she writes, "must therefore beware of unproven claims, even while he keeps an open-minded attitude toward new ideas which may seem impossible, but are as yet untested. With this attitude the fringe beliefs will not smother the good research as it slowly separates the true from the false. And some of those fringe beliefs may have in them elements of truth that will be needed before the entire secret is revealed" (21–22). Like New Agers, Rhine thinks of the paranormal in terms of a "secret" to be revealed rather than unmasked. Since she recognizes an underlying similarity between parapsychology and its occult "fringe," she creates a relationship that could be described as nonantagonistic, even friendly. Thus, her image of "fringe" does not imply the sense of a lunatic fringe or the fringes of the earth implied in the title of Martin Gardner's column for the *Skeptical Inquirer:* "Notes of a Fringe-Watcher."

It may be helpful at this point to recapitulate the complex nature of the boundaries that the two Rhines have drawn. J. B. Rhine constitutes parapsychology as a mediating discourse between two negative Others, science and religion. In a similar way, Louisa Rhine places parapsychology between the two negative extremes of mechanistic science and the occult fringe, but Louisa Rhine also suggests that this division is repeated within parapsychology in the form of the opposition between experimental and spontaneous case research. For both, paranormal phenomena themselves constitute a positive, exotic Other, and like the New Agers, the Rhines recognize some connections with the beliefs of past civilizations. However, unlike the New Agers, as modernists and rationalists the Rhines see their task less as recuperating ancient wisdom and more as separating superstition from true paranormal phenomena.

Dualism and Contemporary Parapsychology

Both J. B. and Louisa Rhine died in the early 1980s, and although for many years in the United States the names "Rhine" and "parapsychology" were almost synonymous, they always shared the field with other parapsychologists. Indeed, parapsychologists comprise a diverse community, and among their ranks today are many who are embarrassed by the Rhines' popular texts and clumsy dualism. The Rhinean imagination therefore should be treated as a baseline for understanding American parapsychology in the last decades of the twentieth century.

In some cases, the basic parameters of Rhinean dualism remain unchanged. The philosopher Hoyt Edge has argued that the Rhinean tradition of Cartesian dualism "has guided the thinking of parapsychologists for a number of years," and indeed there are dualists among parapsychologists today (1990:133). Nevertheless, Edge is among the parapsychologists who believe that the Rhinean view is outdated because in fundamental ways science is no longer materialistic, atomistic, reductionistic, or mechanistic. Instead, he argues that contemporary science is characterized by a "new mentalism"—an increased recognition of cognitive and mental processes as characterizing a level of reality in themselves—and a "minimal naturalism," in which higher levels of the natural world (including mental processes) are emergent and self-sufficient but also ultimately dependent on spatiotemporal entities (1990:140–48). In other words, the scientific understanding of matter is less "material," but at the same time the understanding of the mind is less "mental" (149). The engineer and psychologist Dean Radin (1989) articulated a similar position in a presidential address before the Parapsychological Association. Radin also argued that science studies a world composed of a hierarchy of levels running from the physical to the biological, psychological, social, and cosmological. In this holistic world of interdependent levels, causation runs both from the bottom up and from the top down.

The position of Edge and Radin is more like that of Marilyn Ferguson than that of J. B. or Louisa Rhine. Like Ferguson, their negative Other is someone who has an outdated, nonholistic view of science. Still, Edge and Radin represent only one tendency within contemporary parapsychology, a "conservative" perspective that attempts to locate parapsychology in frameworks that are consistent with contemporary physics and the contemporary scientific world view. Notwithstanding titles such as that of Radin's presidential address, "The Tao of Psi," these parapsychologists tend to avoid discussing the implications of their science for religion. At the other end of the spectrum, there is a strong current of parapsychological thinking that continues the Rhinean tradition of situating parapsychology in some way as a mediator between science and religion.

For those few parapsychologists who engage in spontaneous case research, there is still the conflict between "survival" interpretations of paranormal phenomena and "super-psi" interpretations. For example, poltergeists may be interpreted as the expression of some kind of otherworldly intervention (literally "noisy ghosts") or, as is more widely accepted in contemporary parapsychology, as the expression of "recurrent spontaneous psychokinesis" generated by the living. Likewise, cases of children who claim to remember past lives may be interpreted as the product of reincarnation or as the result of imagination, clairvoyance, or some other psychological or parapsychological process that does not necessarily support the postmortem survival hypothesis. Thus, spontaneous case research remains one area where parapsychology may still be situated as a bridge to religious discourse.[14] Likewise, it is among the spontaneous case researchers that one is more likely to find a defense of a dualist perspective similar to that of the Rhines (e.g., Stevenson, 1981).

There are also some examples of parapsychologists who argue that their science may have direct implications for religious or spiritual questions. For example, in the introduction to the popular book *Psi: Scientific Studies in the Psychic Realm*, the psychologist Charles Tart considers parapsychology in the context of the question of "the conflict between science and religion" (7).[15] His approach is considerably more measured than that of Rhine. "Yes and no," he writes. "On the *yes* side, I am more certain than ever of the reality of psi events that point toward a much wider, more meaningful picture of the universe and our place in it than orthodox science has provided. I do not believe in the teachings of any spiritual tradition, but I am inclined to be open-minded about the ideas in them and respect the impulse behind spiritual seeking. On the *no* side, my work as a psychologist has made me frustratingly and disappointingly aware of the degree to which we fool ourselves to satisfy our often neurotic desires" (Tart 1977:7).

In the conclusion to the book, Tart outlines a "radical view of consciousness" and grapples with the dualism question. He begins by describing mind/body relations in terms of a software/hardware metaphor (214–15), that is, a metaphor that is consistent with the Edge/Radin view of emergent levels of reality. However, Tart invokes a different analogy to explain out-of-body experiences in the context of mind/body relations. He asks the reader to imagine a man connected to a car in such a way that he is able to satisfy his bodily functions while continuing to drive, such that he becomes a "gestalt of vehicle-plus-driver" (217). If the man is thrown from the car, he may be unable to move, since he tries to press down with his foot, but there is no accelerator to move. Eventually, however, he may learn to adapt to his new carless state. The experience may be frightening, or it may be joyful, just as may be the case of a person having an out-of-body experience (217–18).

Tart's automobile analogy brings him close to Rhinean dualism, but he cautions the reader not to take the analogy too literally. Instead, the psychologist remains ambivalent about the idea "that we definitely have some fully developed soul inside us that just happens to be temporarily driving the physical body" (218). Unlike J. B. Rhine, this post-Rhinean psychologist allows readers to draw their own conclusions. Nevertheless, the matrix of cultural categories that characterizes the Rhinean imagination still provides the framework in which the post-Rhinean psychologist constructs his discussion of the broader implications of parapsychology: dualism versus spiritual or materialistic monism; the paranormal versus mind or body; and parapsychology versus religion or science.

Thus, while I recognize differences among parapsychologists, as a group they nevertheless construct themselves in a different matrix of Self/Other relations than New Agers. For parapsychologists, the positive exotic Other is the world of paranormal phenomena itself and not the romantic wisdom of lost civilizations. Likewise, whereas New Agers see themselves as the spiritual Self that encompasses the materialistic Other, parapsychologists tend to see themselves as mediators who bridge the gap between contemporary, negative Others: science and religion, dogmatic materialism and occultist credulity, body and mind.

Skeptics

The Paranormal Other

Skeptics also constitute themselves through a strong sense of a negative Other. Although they distinguish between "New Agers" and parapsychologists, they tend to be more interested in showing how both belong to one grab-bag category of pseudoscientific irrationalism: their paranormal Other. For example, the philosopher Paul Kurtz recognizes the specifics of the New Age movement as a "religious or quasireligious movement," but he also emphasizes that New Agers "embrace . . . a wide range of psychic phenomena: precognition, psychokinesis, astral projection, levitation, clairvoyance, and so on" (Kurtz 1989b:365–66). Frequently, the central rubric for the skeptic's irrational Other is the word "paranormal." For example, the title of one of the volumes edited by the science writer and *Skeptical Inquirer* editor Kendrick Frazier, *Science Confronts the Paranormal* (1986), sharply frames the central conceptual opposition of skeptical thought: the scientific Self and the paranormal Other. However, when we go beyond this crucial difference that constitutes skepticism as a discourse, we encounter many similarities with parapsychologists and New Agers.

For the skeptics, the paranormal is a highly negative cultural domain that is similar to the New Agers' materialistic Other and Louisa Rhine's occult fringe. Consider, for example, the list that Frazier uses to characterize the paranormal in the opening essay of *Science Confronts the Paranormal:* "exaggeration, deceit, fraud, misperception, self-delusion, and other prominent foibles of the human race" (1986:ix). Other skeptics have added to this list by depicting belief in the paranormal as a kind of disease. The psychologist Ray Hyman sees parapsychology as a "pathological science," a "sickness" that requires a "remedy" (1982:163), and in an implicit comparison to homosexuality, he "strongly urge[s] the scientific community to bring the pathologies out of the closet and to openly work towards developing a more appropriate and rational response" (1982:163). The pathology metaphor appears throughout the writings of skeptics, and it is sometimes applied to New Age channelers, who have been labelled "persons of hysterical personality, displaying classical dissociative features" (Reed 1989:390). Likewise, another skeptic describes the New Age movement as "a symptom of a much graver illness that infects the late-twentieth-century soul" (O'Hara 1989:373).[16]

Commercial greed is another negative characteristic that skeptics attribute to their paranormal Other. Citing the *Reader's Digest* and the Time-Life book series on the paranormal, Frazier notes crisply: "The paranormal sells" (1986:x). Skeptics frequently charge that the public is victimized by an irresponsible press and media who print what will sell and therefore spread paranormal beliefs throughout society. For example, the science writer Martin Gardner laments that the American press has not reported exposures of fraud with the same enthusiasm as favorable evidence for the paranormal, and he complains how one television official defended pseudoscientific programming by exclaiming, "I'll produce anything that gets high ratings!" (1981b:57, xv). The result of such irresponsibility is that the average citizen is not informed enough so that popular "pseudoscientific" books become "unprofitable" (57). Gardner further comments: "And as long as they are profitable, you can be sure they will be written and printed" (57). Skeptics Frazier and Gardner therefore associate a certain kind of materialism, a profit-oriented commercial materialism, with advocates of the paranormal. The skeptic, in contrast, is someone who undertakes the scrutiny of paranormal claims at the potential loss of professional gain, scientific advancement, or prestigious publication (Frazier 1986:ix).[17]

Why is there so much demand for news on the New Age and paranormal? Frazier provides two reasons: "the intrinsic appeal of the subject" and "the understandable need for comforting beliefs" (1986:x). Here the skeptic, who has set his discourse apart from the world of material gain, now distinguishes skepticism from religion. Frazier notes that it is understandable that some people would resist strongly scientific challenges to their belief systems, such as skeptical readings of the Genesis story, since scientific accounts could cause their "belief structure" to "crumble," but he thinks religion must give way to science (xi). Sustained belief in the paranormal, notwithstanding its lack of support from science, can only be explained because paranormal beliefs "operate at the level of deep-seated psychological needs" (xi). In a similar way, the skeptical philosopher Paul Kurtz refers to paranormal beliefs as the "transcendental temptation" (e.g., Kurtz

1985–86). Likewise, according to Martin Gardner, supporters of the paranormal are "true believers" (1981b:323), a term that not only compares them with religious zealots but also implies a level of gullibility that violates the culture of pragmatic street smarts and common sense.[18]

In short, the skeptical Self (identified with science and secular reason) is untainted by material interests and irrational needs, whereas the paranormal Other is tainted by commercial materialism, religious belief, and emotional needs. In this social drama between the skeptical Self and the paranormal Other, the skeptic is cast in the role of the underdog. Skeptics who oppose the paranormal do so against great odds: both against the media, which overwhelmingly favors the paranormal, and against widespread popular support of supernatural belief, evidenced by a list of statistics that Frazier cites from a Gallup Poll. These two axes of the skeptical construction of the paranormal — commercial materialism and religious credulity — come together in a single phrase penned by the philosopher Paul Kurtz: "On the current world-scene, belief in the paranormal is fed and reinforced by a vast media industry that profits from it; and it has been transformed into a folk religion, perhaps the dominant one today" (1986:5).

However, the skeptical construction of the paranormal becomes caught up in a paradox. If scientists who debunk the paranormal cannot expect prestige or financial gain (a questionable claim, given the popular forums that debunking often obtains and the trade paperback editions in which such texts are published), whereas advocates of the paranormal can, then science and the skeptical project are set apart from the social and the economic. This "setting apart" is what Émile Durkheim found to be crucial to the idea of the sacred (1965). In locating skepticism on a plane above this-worldly values such as social prestige and material success, skeptics portray themselves as motivated by the loftier values of mind and reason rather than material interest and emotional needs. The paranormal, in contrast, is permeated by the economic and the social; it is the profane. Thus, skepticism implicitly constructs itself and science as sacred because they are untainted by this-worldly, material interests. Consequently, the confrontation between science and religion becomes obscured by a second contrast: the sacred and the profane. From this perspective, skepticism takes on some aspects of a sacred discourse, the discourse of a pure science in opposition to the profane discourse of the paranormal, which is also linked to religious sentiment.

Here, then, is another point of contact with New Agers and parapsychologists, who also see themselves as motivated by purer motives. Each community sees its own position as the "rational" one, and it reads the other as motivated by materialistic philosophy or material gain. The Other is always "profane" in the sense of being linked to this-worldly concerns and values, whereas the Self is above the fray.

The Ridiculous Other

The skeptics' paranormal Other is a complex construction: it is disorderly, pathological, and commercial, not to mention motivated by deep psychological needs and the emotional pull of the religious world view. In addition, the skeptics' paranormal Other is also funny. One might not ordinarily associate the sense of humor with science and scientists, particularly in a context where skeptics associate the scientific with the rational and the nonscientific with the emotional. However, the sociologists G. Nigel Gilbert and Michael Mulkay have demonstrated that humor is, in fact, commonplace if not fairly widespread among scientists and part of their scientific practice (1984:172–87). The sociologists' work focuses on an ironic form of humor in which scientists generally poke fun at themselves, each other, or their enterprise. In contrast, an analysis of skeptics' humor will reveal another form, one which is directed toward a stereotyped nonscientific Other and which might be better characterized as ridicule. If New Agers, parapsychologists, and other advocates of the paranormal were merely greedy or religious, they might still be taken seriously; thus, ridicule further discredits the paranormal Other.

Take, for example, Martin Gardner's review of *Powers of Mind*, by Adam Smith (1975), an author who is perhaps best known for his popular book on the stock market.[19] According to Gardner, Smith's "machine-gun style is exactly right for the short attention span of his readers" (Gardner 1981b: 302), and Smith's guidebook to what would be called today the New Age movement turns out to be a parody of the spiritual quest: a "short-cut tour of what he calls the 'consciousness circuit'" (301), where "anecdotal wonders chase one another like one-liners in a Henny Youngman routine" (302). Gardner lumps parapsychologists with New Agers, and the former fare no better than Norman Cousins and the consciousness circuit. For example, Gardner describes the parapsychologists' Ganzfeld protocol, an altered state of consciousness experiment which they claim has achieved some degree of replication, as "the sliced-ping-pong-balls-over-the-eyes bit" (302).

Descriptions of the paranormal as comic slip into comic descriptions of the comic. Gardner notes, for example, that Smith gives "a big play" to the New Age guru Baba Ram Dass, Timothy Leary's "sidekick," despite the sobriquets bestowed on the guru by his father, "Rum Dum," and his older brother, "Rammed Ass" (1981b:302). Gardner also clowns around in his discussion of Smith's chapter on the human potential organization known as "est," or Erhard Seminars Training. For example, he makes a pun on the out-of-body experience (or "OBE," but which Gardner abbreviates as "OOB" to make the joke): he notes that Erhard founded est after working for Mind Dynamics, "a California outfit now OOB (out of business)" (303).[20] The skeptical comic calls Smith's chapter on est the book's "saddEST chapter . . . about the latEST and hottEST of the new strawberry short cuts [sic]," and he goes on to indulge in further horseplay and wordplay (303).

Est may be funny, but it is also a business, and the paranormal Other once again becomes inscribed in images of commercial materialism. For example, Gardner claims that est takes money from "thousands of poor souls" (304) only to submit them to a humiliating weekend during which they are locked in a room and not allowed to go to the bathroom. The est instructors argue that their clients learn to see themselves as a tube in which food and liquids enter through one end and leave through the other, but Gardner says these practices turn the human being into a "mechanical asshole" (304). People speak about est training in terms of "getting it," but according to the skeptic the person who is getting it is Erhard, who is "getting rich" (304). "They are," Gardner adds, "naturally, advanced seminars. They cost more" (305). Thus, the skeptic's negative Other is once again constructed with the imagery of the material: material gain and the body, the rational mind's material Other that is degraded by emphasizing its most basic material functions. To the point, Gardner ends the essay by transforming one sign of the spiritual associated with the New Age, the Hindu mantra, from the spiritual into the material. He urges his readers to chant over and over again *owah tanah siam*, and he adds, "Come to think of it, Erhard might even approve" (306).

Space, Time, and the Paranormal Other

Like parapsychologists and New Agers, skeptics also use spatial and temporal metaphors to situate their Other in the "there and then." For example, in the introduction to *Paranormal Borderlands of Science*, Kendrick Frazier describes "the borderlands of science" as a very negative place: "the land of pseudoscience, fringe-science, and the paranormal" (1981:vii).[21] In his words: "If the frontiers of science are a newly discovered ocean for exploration, the borderlands of science are a murky, backwatery swamp right here on land. If science is an advancing, forward progression of the frontiers of knowledge, the pseudosciences are a much-trodden farmed-out field at the rear flanks. If science is the cutting edge of discovery, pseudoscience is a dull blade left behind amid the sawdust and debris" (viii). Frazier does not develop the analogy, but for many American readers, a series of metonyms may come to mind: the "newly discovered ocean" brings to mind the New World, Columbus, and the pilgrims; just as the images of "a much-trodden farmed-out field" and "a dull blade left behind" resonate with the rocky, desolate soils of lands always to the east/past: Europe, New England, or perhaps even the midwestern dustbowl of the Great Depression. Thus, whereas the skeptical editor situates the scientific Self as an "advancing, forward progression," he locates the paranormal Other in multiple pasts of there and then.[22]

In the book *Flim-Flam! Psychics, ESP, Unicorns, and Other Delusions*, the magician James "the Amazing" Randi also situates the paranormal Other in the there and then. Randi describes the credulity with which the courts of seventeenth-century France received a dowser who apparently helped locate a criminal. He then notes, "The use of 'psychic powers' in a court of law is not confined to medieval France" (Randi 1982:5), and he goes on to describe the legal practices of the city of Watkins Glen, New York, where he claims that a psychic helped a prosecuting attorney to select prospective jurors by measuring their auras. He concludes this example with the comment: "The Dark Ages have not quite ended in Watkins Glen" (5).

In the essay "Magical Thinking and Parapsychology," the psychologist Leonard Zusne develops another aspect of the connection between the paranormal Other and the past. After discussing Piaget's ideas on childhood thinking and applying them to what he believes to be the magical thinking of parapsychologists, Zusne draws on the anthropologist Lucien Lévy-Bruhl's discussion of primitive mentality in order to connect parapsychology and magical thinking to past times both phylogenetic and ontogenetic: "The connection between the 'primitive' mind and the mind of the child is that in both cases we are dealing with individuals whose conceptual development has not yet reached the stage of the educated adult in an industrial society. For this reason, both may show magical thinking under similar conditions, and the magical thinking of an adult who ought to know better is occasionally described as 'primitive' or 'childlike'" (1985:694). Anthropologists (myself included) would question the ethnocentrism implicit in Zusne's recapitulationist thinking; but, skeptical questions aside, the passage does bring together in an explicit way two strands of the temporal distance that skeptics sometimes use to describe the paranormal Other: childhood and the primitive or medieval past.[23]

By employing the analogy of primitive thinking, or by comparing beliefs in the paranormal to medieval superstitions, Randi and Zusne locate their paranormal Other in such distant times and places that it might also be considered "exotic." Like Louisa Rhine on the occult fringe, they equate the negative, proximate Other with the negative, exotic Other of ancient superstitions. But do skeptics also have a positive, exotic Other like that of the parapsychologists and New Agers? Consider again Frazier's introduction to *Paranormal Borderlands of Science*, which begins on a lyrical note: "What an age of discovery this is!" (1981:vii). Frazier goes on to eulogize the marvelous discoveries of the space age, from the soil chemistry of Mars to astronomical wonders more than eleven thousand light-years away (vii). In a trajectory reminiscent of the opening paragraphs of *New World of the Mind*, the skeptical writer then switches from discoveries of outer space to those that take us down to the bottoms of oceans and into the inner recesses of the brain. He concludes the opening paragraph on a note reminiscent of the epigraph from the "Star Trek" series, "Space – the final frontier," or Reagan's "Star Wars" rhetoric: "These are the frontiers of science," he writes (vii). This passage is probably as close as the skeptics come to a positive, exotic Other: the frontiers of science situated in exotic spaces such as outer space or the bottoms of oceans.[24]

Conclusions

Cultural analysis leads to a paradox: skeptics, parapsychologists, and New Agers see themselves as very different from each other, but they go about constructing their differences in similar ways. The solution? They are all drawing on – and at the same time helping to recreate – their cultural heritage as Americans at the end of the millennium. How exactly are they reproducing and remaking American culture in their constructions of Self and Other?[25]

To begin, consider the metaphors of space and time. Certainly many cultures locate the Other in the "there and then," but these three communities do so in American ways. For example, the "there and then" of the negative Other tends to be figured as the Old World (or New England), whereas the "here and now" of the Self is situated in terms of a forward-looking explorer of new frontiers where a positive, exotic Other may be located (e.g., Ferguson's California and Pacific Rim, J. B. Rhine's New World, and Frazier's outer space).[26] Thus, while the geographical location of the frontier may vary, the writers all tend to imagine themselves as pioneers blazing the trail toward new forms of knowledge.

Similarities, of course, commingle with differences. For example, the skeptics' exotic Other is located in the future of scientific frontiers and space exploration, not in the distant past of ancient civilizations. Thus, the skeptics' view of time and the Other is linear rather than cyclical. Unlike the parapsychologists, skeptics see nothing to recuperate in old superstitions, and unlike New Agers, they find unromantic the spiritual knowledge of ancient civilizations.[27] Nevertheless, parapsychologists and New Agers locate the discourse of their skeptical Other — modern science as materialist ideology — prior to that of the Self. In other words, even if parapsychologists and New Agers have a cyclical approach to time and the exotic Other, they still construct the coming world of their new knowledge as an event in a linear trajectory of historical evolution with the negative Other located behind them. In this sense, members of all three cultures share the forward-looking, optimistic spirit associated with Americans' self-representation of their culture and society.

Another similarity among the writers involves the list of attributes they assign to the negative Other: greedy, materialistic, egocentric, and sometimes disorderly and pathological. The negative imagery of the skeptics is most developed, but Louisa Rhine also writes of an "occult fringe" in very similar terms. Likewise, Katrina Raphaell warns of the perils posed by those who threaten the future of the world due to their greed and materialistic interests. Furthermore, all three sides see the Self as somehow above the fray, as not motivated by greed and material gain, and therefore as somehow more rational than the Other.

At the same time there are examples from each of the three cultures that portray the irrationality of the Other through the frame of religious dogmatism. As we have seen, skeptics view their paranormal Other as hostages to age-old occult superstitions or victims of a transcendental temptation. Likewise, J. B. Rhine compared science and religion by using terms such as "dogma" and "orthodoxy" (1953:47). More recently, in an article titled "Irrational Rationalists," parapsychology sympathizers charged that the skeptics associated with the *The Humanist*'s "crusade against parapsychology" had used a number of illogical rhetorical techniques as well as "apocalyptic rhetoric."[28] Even among the New Agers one writer describes the skeptics as the "New Inquisition," and more generally we have seen how New Agers believe that the reductionistic materialism of orthodox science represents a dogmatic and outmoded approach to science.[29]

Thus, members of the three cultures construct the negative Other as both materialistic and religious. A paradox rather than a contradiction, the underlying similarity is a sense that the Other is dogmatic. All three communities share a belief that theirs is the open-minded, rational system that is grounded in some notion of "factuality": in the sense of observable evidence (the skeptics), experimental and case-study evidence (the parapsychologists), or experiential evidence (the New Agers). In other words, all three communities agree that theirs is the discourse of reason, whereas that of the Other is irrational and dogmatic.

The commonality should not be surprising, for a constant theme of the

American religious tradition is the struggle against the religious dogmatism of established churches, from the Puritans and slave religions to the transcendentalists and on to the welter of religious sects today. Furthermore, the Protestant tradition has also left a legacy of discomfort with the merely material. As Max Weber (1958) pointed out nearly a hundred years ago, the Calvinistic Puritans valued material success only as a sign of success on a higher plane. Thus, when the three cultures construct their Other as dogmatic and materialistic, they are drawing on the repertoire of the dominant cultural heritage.

Even when skeptics, parapsychologists, and New Agers do not share values and representations, they rely on a shared set of cultural categories such as disinterested/commercial, spiritual/material, holistic/mechanistic, mind/body, rational/irrational, scientific/religious, future-oriented/past-oriented, and frontier/backwater. These terms do not appear in every version of the construction of Self and Other, and some discourses or texts may privilege one side over the other. Furthermore, the elements do not always line up, so that, for example, rationality may be linked to materialism in one case and spirituality in another. Still, these "elements" — or, to invoke in a playful way the crystalline metaphor of classical Lévi-Straussian structuralism, the atoms or molecules of the diacritics of borderland science — are shared among the three faces of the paraculture.

At the same time, there is a historical dimension to the ways in which they all are constructing Self and Other. Skeptics, parapsychologists, and New Agers may draw on the cultural categories that are available to them, but they do so in ways that put into question conventional categories such as the boundary between religion and science. The Other is no longer constructed in purely religious terms — evil, Satanic, Godless, wicked, and so on — or in purely scientific terms — weak evidence, bad arguments, and so on. Instead, religious and scientific categories are brought together in ways that construct a new discursive arena that is neither scientific nor religious, neither psychological nor political: it is "paracultural." Furthermore, as I shall show, the syncretic quality of the boundary disputes spills over into a number of other arenas of discourse and practice, such as individualist ethics, homiletics, gender, and the body.

4

Heroes and Sermons

FOR parapsychologists, skeptics, and New Agers, the distinction between Self and Other is more than a mere descriptive assertion of difference. They frequently imply that the Other is not merely different, but morally wrong. The Self, in contrast, becomes a heroic crusader who can redeem the corrupt world of the Other and restore a sense of right community. As a prophet or crusader, the Self becomes an "individual" who is defined in terms of values and ideals rather than relations and group memberships. Contestations over "is" shade into polemics of "ought," and texts that are meant to convey special knowledge also double as sermons.

New Agers

Individualism and the Aquarian Revolution

For Marilyn Ferguson, the dawning of the Aquarian Age represents a new stage in human history that will require a shift in thought of revolutionary proportions. She describes the transformation in terms borrowed from the historian Thomas Kuhn (1962): the Aquarian Age represents a "paradigm shift about how paradigm shifts happen, a revolution in understanding how revolutions begin" (37). She warns us that many are blind to the signs of this new revolution, but she claims that it is located "not in the distant future" but in the "imminent future" and even the "dynamic present" (38).

The Aquarian conspirators, "a leaderless but powerful network that is working to bring about radical change in the United States," form the vanguard of Ferguson's envisioned revolution (1987:23). "Without political doctrine" and "without a manifesto," they are leaders of a revolution with a difference (23). Hers is an individualized, personalized revolution in which people's lives, as opposed to their political system, "become revolutions" (24). "You will look in vain," she warns the reader, "for affiliations in traditional forms: political parties, ideological groups, clubs, or fraternal organizations" (25).

Ferguson's imagery switches back and forth between revolution in a psychopolitical sense and in the Kuhnian sense of a paradigm shift, and this motion allows her to translate the idioms of social and scientific transformation. She compares the old paradigm of politics and power to the mechanistic and atomistic view of the universe reflected in Newtonian mechanics (212). In their place, her new paradigm of holistic social transformation is, as she describes it, "the counterpart in politics of modern physics" (212).

Ferguson's vision of political transformation is therefore a far cry from a Marxist-style revolution, and indeed she turns to the spirit of 1776 as a better model. Like her Aquarian conspiracy, the American Revolution was primarily an affair of hearts and minds: "*The revolution was in the minds of the people.* This radical change in the principles, opinions, sentiments, and affections of the people was the real American Revolution. Long before the first shot is fired, the revolution begins. Long after truce is declared, it continues to overturn lives" (121). The revolution continues in the nineteenth-century transcendentalist movement, which she describes as "a logical extension of the American Revolution," with spiritual liberation the counterpart to constitutional freedoms (122).

An inner-directed, personal revolution nonetheless has implications for society. Ferguson believes that "the second American Revolution" must also involve a "critique of injustices" that leads to better environmental management and greater social justice (125). The revolution from within will lead to an outward change in all aspects of American and even international culture: "politics, society, international and interracial relations, cultural values, and technology and science" (125).

By weaving a tapestry of scientific, psychological, political, and social revolution, Ferguson reins in her rhetoric of political change and keeps it within the boundaries of a constitutional, Lockean framework. Just as paradigm shifts within science remain within the boundaries of accepted notions of scientific methods, so reformist social and political movements remain within the accepted notions of constitutional government. Radical rhetoric notwithstanding, the political vision of *The Aquarian Conspiracy* remains a reformist one that lies in the mainstream of Anglo-Saxon political thought. Ferguson even defines government in the familiar terms of social contract theory as "a community of people" who decide on a set of rules not unlike the "established scientific paradigm" of normal science

(196). Likewise, she writes of a utopian "government by the self" in which "social harmony springs ultimately from the character of individuals" (192).

In short, Ferguson's Aquarian conspirators are heroes who are out to change minds more than social institutions. She sees her job as one of moral uplifting, of writing homilies, rather than of organizing for political activism and profound institutional change. For Ferguson, the conflict between individual and community, which runs like an Ariadne's thread through American political culture, is resolved by making social change the effect of individual, personal change. As a result, society is relegated to an epiphenomenal existence, and the fundamental reality becomes the individual. With the appropriate changes at an individual level, a new community spirit will emerge, and the old conflict between individual liberty and social order will be transcended, marking the inauguration of the New Age utopia.

Ferguson accentuates the positive; she does not bog down her followers with a prophecy of gloom and doom. She does, however, locate the future in opposition to a negative present characterized by "tragic wars, alienation, and the bruising of the planet" (43). Invoking the poet Wallace Stevens, she claims that her Aquarian conspiracy is "the Yes on which the future of the world depends" (43). Just as her heroes are cheerful, smiling do-gooders, her sermon is a sunny, Californian message of optimism.

Short-Circuiting the Armageddon Script

I wish to consider here a second kind of New Age sermon and heroism, but in a more popular text: *The Mayan Factor: The Path Beyond Technology* (1987), by José Argüelles, art historian and architect of Harmonic Convergence, a celebration held in 1987. Harmonic Convergence marked, according to Argüelles, the beginning of the new era when Quetzalcoatl and other ancient heroes were to return from the farthest reaches of the galaxy. "Amidst spectacle, celebration, and urgency," Argüelles promised, "the old mental house will dissolve, activating the return of long-dormant archetypal memories and impressions" (1987:170).

In *The Mayan Factor*, Argüelles develops a complicated numerology that links the ancient Mayan calendar to the Chinese wisdom of the *I Ching*, but his discussion of galactic harmonies and genetic codes also connects these systems of ancient wisdom to today's world of scientific discourse. His calendrical numerology looks backward to ancient civilizations as well as forward to the year 2012, when, so he predicts, a New Age will begin (1987:150). The new, "post-technological" phase of history is a future utopia characterized by a return to the wisdom of the ancient Maya, Argüelles's exotic Other. In the future utopia, we "shall find ourselves as planetary

Maya" who possess a nonpolluting technology that is "brilliantly simple" and sophisticated, and based on the "matching of solar and psychic frequencies" (173). The new world will consist of harmonious "bioregional groups" that will have more leisure time and thus "collectively come to know as one" (173).

Argüelles presents his utopian vision of "the coming solar age" — where the sun is now a source of mystical as well as physical energy — only as a possibility, as a model for a future and not necessarily a model of the future. The ancient Mayan calendar provides a warning of a coming apocalypse that he believes will be the direct result of "the untenable position of proclaiming the superiority of suburban automobile and television existence" (149). Argüelles argues that after 1945 "environmentally impactful events" have set up a "dissonant vibratory wave" that could affect the planet's spin in a way similar to an "uncontrolled nuclear reaction" (146). He warns that if the process is not stopped, the Earth's spin could get out of control and ultimately the planet could shatter and become another asteroid belt (146). Writing in the mid-1980s, Argüelles encouraged people to join in the celebration of Harmonic Convergence — the great "evocation" of August 16–17, 1987 — to help ensure that "the Armageddon script is short-circuited" (148). Argüelles's message is clear: if we mend our ways, there is still time to avert the coming apocalypse, an apocalypse of technological unreason — or, to use the political theorist Langdon Winner's phrase, of "technics out of control" (1977).

Like Raphaell on Atlantis, Argüelles warns of a civilization that destroys itself because the people became corrupted by the egotistical use of their technical advances and consequently forgot their spirituality. He shows the danger of the improper adoption of materialistic values and the abuse of technology that could lead to a catastrophic downfall not unlike nuclear Armageddon. The mass ritual of Harmonic Convergence offered a way out of our technological predicament and our materialistic backsliding. Unlike Ferguson, the revolutionary who speaks in a secular language, Argüelles adopts a form of heroism more like that of a biblical prophet. Yet, both Ferguson and Argüelles wish to save the world by leading it toward a New Age, and both fashion themselves as heroic individuals: prophets who, because of their mission, are set apart from society.

After the Revolution: Further Comments on
Individualism, Heroism, and Community

Ferguson and Argüelles both imagine a future, utopian society, but they are vague about its details and, like most prophets, they focus on winning converts to their plan of action. However, through channeled descriptions of life in the next world, New Age writers do have a way of imagining in more detail their utopian "Other society." The topic leads to the sizeable literature of mediums or "trance channelers," from which I have selected one example: Ruth Montgomery's *A World Beyond* (1971).

In the late 1960s Montgomery had sittings with Arthur Ford, a leading Spiritualist medium who died in 1971 (Melton, Clark, and Kelly 1990:290). In *A World Beyond* Montgomery records through automatic writing the communications she claims to have received from his spirit, apparently beginning the very day he died.[1] Ford is perhaps best known for his claim to have communicated with the spirit of Houdini after the magician's death in 1926, and to have successfully received Houdini's secret code, a claim that was subsequently contested. After much hubbub and press coverage, the medium passed into a period of relative eclipse that included bouts of alcoholism. He emerged in the 1960s as a medium for the Bishop James Pike, and subsequently Ford's famed abilities were once again exposed (see Gardner 1981b:251–61; Spraggett with Rauscher 1973). Although Ford led a somewhat checkered life in this world, he seems to have fared better in the next world, which he describes in detail through the mediumistic channel of Ruth Montgomery. As an otherworldly ethnography or travelogue, *A World Beyond* is a rich source for the cultural meaning of the one aspect of New Age thought: other worlds, a site for the exotic Other next to which all other sites pale in comparison.[2]

That there is culture in heaven should be no surprise to most readers (see McDannell and Lang 1988), and I have even found the proposition acceptable to Spiritists in Brazil, who recognize that spirits take with them their this-worldly cultural baggage and that the depictions of heaven by their North American siblings are somewhat different from those channeled through the hands of Brazilian mediums. In previous studies, I showed how the channeled texts of Brazilian mediums could be read as descriptions of the social conflicts of life in this world: on earth as it is in heaven (1991a, 1991b). Here, I will focus more on the instructive, homiletic side of otherworldly ethnographies and on the question of paracultural heroism.

Consider, for example, Ford's parables of two spirits, the narrow-minded, dogmatic schoolteacher and the greedy, selfish man. (The two figures should not come as a surprise; we are in the familiar landscape of the dogmatic, religious Other and the materialistic, greedy Other, now marked clearly for gender.) During terrestrial life, the spinster schoolteacher was the "soul of generosity," but she was also "narrow-minded," unoriginal, and dogmatic (1971:16–17). As a result, in the afterlife, she expects to find "harps and angels floating amid palaces and sylvan glens," and she is at first disappointed when she discovers the realities of the afterlife (16–17). "But this will pass as she develops, provided that she works at it," the spirit Ford points out (16–17).

At the other extreme, Ford describes the "stiff-necked, educated, and polished man" who "never gave thought to anyone but himself" (39). When he dies, his afterworld consists of "other greedy souls, who because they are in a like situation, welcome him gleefully to the hell that they have created for themselves" (39). Shocked, he tries to break away from the "fiendish group," but he cannot escape, and no one can rescue him. Forced to suffer this torment for some time, he eventually achieves "full repentance" and is able to free himself from the hell of his own making. "For a long time thereafter he searches his own soul to review his past mistakes" (40).

The situation of the educated but greedy spirit in this modern purgatory corresponds to, just as it inverts, that of the generous but dogmatic spinster. The female spirit has compassion but lacks knowledge, just as the male spirit has knowledge but lacks compassion. Both find their way when they develop the missing side of their personalities, and consequently they become whole like the spirit Arthur Ford, who, as the wise spirit guide, has both knowledge and compassion.

The spirit Ford has his own teachers, and indeed the dominant activity of life in the other world seems to be communion in the temple of wisdom. The spirit describes the temple of wisdom as "not a place, of course, but a state of mind" (55). The "wise old masters" who teach in the temple of wisdom are spirits "who have lived on various planes, but because of their goodness return for a time each day to the plane" of their pupils (57). Is the temple of wisdom a school? Not quite. In the temple of wisdom, souls who "are in the proper state of advancement" gather for religious communion, although there is "no single sermon or service" (51). Instead, "[E]ach draws from it according to his needs, and the cup needs never to be replenished, for the wisdom is bottomless and pours forth in the amount for which the soul thirsts at the moment" (51). The individual's growth and development therefore take place with others of like mind, who gather "in good fellowship" to share their learning experiences (51).

The temple of wisdom, then, is both a school (knowledge, science) and a church (compassion, religion), but it is also a model of an ideal society. It is a place where the problem of society is resolved, and there is no competition among individuals for scarce goods, no reality of offering plates in the house of God. The system works according to a rule that echoes with Marx's communist utopia, with the souls gathering and learning "each according to his own needs" (51). As in Ferguson's, Argüelles's, and Raphaell's visions of the New Age, in this spiritual utopia the individual is so deeply transformed by inner spiritual and moral knowledge that the conflict between individual and society is transcended. It is no longer necessary to construct a revolutionary or a prophet—that is, a loner hero who must go outside of society in order to redeem it—because the conflict between the individual and society no longer exists. In the spirit world of Arthur Ford and Ruth Montgomery, the relationship between transformed individual and society is carried to its logical conclusion: there is no longer any need for a government and political leaders. In their place, we find yet a third New Age hero to add to the pantheon of revolutionaries and prophets. Arthur Ford may have led a questionable life on earth, but in death he becomes the spirit guide, guru, wise master.

Parapsychologists

J. B. Rhine, Cold Warrior

Let me return to a detail mentioned in the previous chapter: J. B. Rhine described his new science of the mind as "revolutionary" (1953:47). Rhine therefore shared with Ferguson a metaphor as well as a vision of how his ideas would contribute to a better society. However, the parallels should not be overdrawn: Rhine thought of himself as a scientific rather than a social revolutionary, and as far as society was concerned, he was quite conservative. He enlisted parapsychology as crucial in a reactionary battle against philosophical materialism at home and dialectical materialism abroad. As a hero, Rhine was a scientific revolutionary who was also an arch cold warrior, and he used parapsychology as a platform for urging the American people to mend their ways. In doing so, his discourse often shaded into prophetic and homiletic rhetoric.

In the chapter of *New World of the Mind* titled "Bearing on the Conduct of Life," Rhine argues that American society needs "a more effective moral code, an adequate ethical philosophy" (259). Despite all of its "progress and strength," the country lacks "moral fiber." "The conduct of human beings in the present era," he declares flatly, "is not good" (260). From Rhine's perspective, the reason for the moral failures of his day was that religion had lost its hold on the modern imagination, but at the same time science could not replace religion because science was limited by materialistic and mechanistic values. "Moral values," he argues, "are not relevant to a physical world" (263).

Rhine claims that parapsychology is the key that "unlocks the gate of a materialistic philosophy of man" (262) and that "the discovery of a nonphysical element in [the] personality . . . makes all the difference in the world to ethical values" (263).[3] It is only a short step from the science of the psychic to the social ethics of voluntarism: because parapsychology points to the existence of a nonphysical mind, a "soul," free will becomes a logical and scientific possibility. In turn, the idea of free will helps legitimate the political value of freedom. "The entire institutional system of the 'free world,'" he writes, "is manifestly built around the assumption that human beings are voluntary individuals" (264–65). As voluntary individuals, they take "for granted not only a freedom for the rightness of a given way of living, but the freedom to choose or reject it" (264–65).

All of this is a "different matter in the camp of communism" (264), where the materialist philosophy that threatens the West has taken over entirely. As a cold warrior, Rhine sees in communism "a threat to the whole ethical life of mankind" that "supplants the entire value system by which the West has civilized itself" (267). He likens communism to "the Frankenstein story," in which "the philosophy of Western science . . . [is] taking a wild destructive turn in the new setting the Communists have given it, a setting in which its materialistic logic is accepted literally and applied to everything" (267).

The Frankensteinian story of materialism-out-of-control serves as a warning for the free world.[4] Because Western science is also materialistic, the evil is, to some extent, already festering within the West. "Is it not significant that Western scholars have not been attacking communism on the level of its root ideas?" Rhine asks (269). He goes on: "In the present world struggle of ideologies the West cannot afford to let its people remain half physicalistic and half idealistic (that is, spiritualistic) in their philosophy" (269).

Parapsychology to the rescue: this science of the mind can help free Western science from its materialistic bias and in turn save the West from communism. As the "science of the spiritual aspect of nature" (227), parapsychology can successfully encounter that "chief enemy of religion . . . the philosophy of materialism" (226). Rhine grafts his philosophical critique of materialism onto a social mission that will rescue the American way of life by shoring up American religiosity against the threat of materialist philosophies both at home and abroad. Parapsychology gives religion a new life, and "religion can yet save the world . . . if it can save itself from becoming completely a relic of the past" (235).

Rhine therefore links parapsychology to a sweeping social vision by bringing his thoroughly dualistic science — one based on dichotomies such as physical/nonphysical, science/religion, body/mind, PK/ESP— together with the equally sharp dichotomies of the surrounding cold war culture: freedom, voluntarism, individualism, and the American Way of Life versus materialism, communism, totalitarianism, and the Red Menace. Rhine's root metaphor, the new world, now comes to mean not only the new world of science but also that of America, with its pioneer spirit and dedication to the freedom of new frontiers. In the process, parapsychology begins to have the qualities of a millenarian religion. As a hero, J. B. Rhine is more than a cold warrior and scientific revolutionary; he is also a prophet who issues a warning about the impending end of the world in terms comparable to those of Argüelles.[5]

More Revolutionaries

Most parapsychologists today would regard Rhine's sermonizing on the cold war as a quaint expresson of the times, but they are probably less willing to recognize how they share with Rhine a belief that their field of inquiry has a profound meaning that bears on the way human beings view themselves and ultimately their world. Thus, the metaphor of revolutions and revolutionaries has continued to play an important role in parapsychologists' construction of their place in science and society.

Before discussing examples from the 1970s and 1980s, Rhine's former student and colleague J. Gaither Pratt deserves to be mentioned. Perhaps best remembered for the hotly debated Pratt-Pearce and Pratt-Woodruff experiments, which became paradigmatic for the early ESP card-guessing tests, Pratt was a farm boy from Winston-Salem, North Carolina, and hardly a revolutionary in the conventional sense of the term.[6] Indeed, his colleague at the University of Virginia, the psychiatrist Ian Stevenson, describes Pratt as a calm man whose few "vices" included being a merciless croquet player (1980:287). Yet, in his book *Parapsychology: An Insider's View of ESP* (1964), Pratt uses the analogy of revolutions and "revolutionists," terms which he quickly distinguishes from their radical and violent connotations:

In 1936 I became a professional revolutionist. This book is about the revolution I joined.
   Before you start looking for the beard or calling the FBI, consider the meaning of the words. Webster says, "Revolution: A total or radical change; as a revolution in thought." And a bit farther on: "Revolutionist: One engaged in a revolution."
   One tends to think of a revolution as an act of violence and bloodshed, a power struggle that results in the overthrow of the government when it is successful and in the execution of the revolutionists when it fails. But the truth is that the political upheavals that hit the headlines are only passing symptoms of larger changes spanning decades or even centuries of history (1964:1).

Pratt then claims, like Ferguson, that "the really important thing about a revolution is a basic advance in ideas," and he argues that one such case is "the revolution of human thought," the "benign revolution" that the new science of parapsychology will bring about (2). In this revolution of ideas,

Rhinean dualism is still the fundamental principle — "as physics is the science which deals with matter, so parapsychology is the science of the mind" (3).

Images of revolution and revolutionaries appear in a series of other statements by parapsychologists in the 1970s and 1980s. One example can be found in an invited address before the Parapsychological Association in 1983, where the engineering professor Robert Jahn invokes the metaphor of American revolutionary soldiers and other underdog heros to describe his fellow psi researchers: "There are many detractors and, let's be honest, we are somewhat of a rag-tag army. But rag-tag armies have prevailed in the past. Think of Valley Forge; of the Russian resistance of Napoleon and much later of the Nazi armies; or of that marvelous description in Shakespeare's *Henry the Fifth* of the agonies of the young king on the eve of a critical battle with the French on the plain of Agincourt" (1983:21). Jahn ends his address with an image of victory of Shakespeare's English soldiers when faced with overwhelming forces on the fields of Agincourt (1983:22–23). Jahn's analogy suggests that the revolutionary image, especially in the American cultural context, may be less about radicalism than about the appeal of the image of the virtuous and ultimately victorious underdog.

Other parapsychologists have used the revolution/revolutionary metaphor more explicitly, particularly when it is connected with the Kuhnian theory of paradigm revolutions. By the mid-1970s, Kuhnian analyses had become the rage in parapsychology as in other disciplines, and talk of paradigms and paradigm shifts abounded at an international parapsychology conference held in Copenhagen (Shapin and Coly 1977). To give one example of Kuhn's influence, the physicists Russell Targ and Harold Puthoff begin the first chapter of their popular book *Mind Reach: Scientists Look at Psychic Ability* (1977) with the provocative title: "When the Normal Becomes the Paranormal: Where Will You Be Standing When the Paradigm Shifts?" Even Pratt, in one of his last published articles before his death in 1979, adopted the Kuhnian framework, fretted over the "paradigm crisis within parapsychology," and claimed, once again, that the success of parapsychology would have "a revolutionary effect upon all of science" (1979:26–27).[7]

By the 1980s, uncritical use of Kuhn's ideas, plus criticisms in the philosophy and social studies of science, led parapsychologists and others to reassess the rhetoric of paradigm revolutions as a way of describing the relations between parapsychology and orthodox science (see Blackmore 1983; Hövelman 1984). One of the first examples is a paper by the anthropologist Michael Winkelman, who questioned facile applications of Kuhnian frameworks to parapsychology and argued that parapsychology "cannot be conceived of as a paradigm within normal science as long as it has a different metaphysic" (1980a:4; see also 1980b).

Despite critical comments about the applicability of the framework of paradigm revolutions, Winkelman argues against rejecting the metaphor of revolution for parapsychology. Instead, he suggests that a new parapsychology could result in an "ideological revolution" (1980a). Apparently that would be even greater than Kuhn's paradigm shift or a revolutionary science: "The differences between parapsychology and mainstream science suggest a strong resemblance to the Copernican Revolution, which was an ideological revolution within science. An ideological revolution involves a basic change in the assumptions as to the nature of science, humankind and the universe; it involves a whole new set of observations and evidence, an entirely new world containing a new view of the human being and our capacities for knowing new observational language, new means of observation, new frames of reference, and new conceptions of frame of reference" (1980a:4–5). The rhetoric in the passage, even down to the phrase "new world," appears to be winking at J. B. Rhine, but Winkelman parts with the Rhinean framework when he questions the apparent contradiction between Rhine's antimaterialist metaphysics and his experimental, mechanistic methodology. Instead, Winkelman appears to be supporting something even greater than the Rhinean revolution, which he sees as flawed because it "implicitly contained the main influences and assumptions of the materialist/mechanist tradition in the models, analogies, and experimental methodology it borrowed from the dominant scientific tradition" (1980a:3).[8]

In an invited dinner address before the Parapsychological Association, the social scientist Willis Harman also invoked the revolution metaphor when he speculated on the "social transformation" that research in parapsychology and the psychology of consciousness were helping to support. He left to future historians the task of determining the extent to which the last years of the twentieth century will be seen as a "revolutionary era" (1976:236), but he argued that the current dilemmas of our industrial society will not be resolved without a "fundamental transformation" of values, institutions, and "the very roots of our culture" (236). Harman proceeded to articulate parapsychology with New Age values and the possibility of a broader social transformation of ethics, institutions, education, health care, and science. Regarding the latter, Harman noted that "science would be clearly understood to be a moral inquiry," and it would "promote wholeness — in much the same way that present-day nutritional science deals with what foods are wholesome for man" (240). Harman's post-1960s revolu-

tionary science is therefore substantially different in ideological orientation from the revolutionary parapsychology of J. B. Rhine; the metaphors
shift from foot soldiers of the cold war to health-food consumerists. Still,
in either case parapsychology is part of a "benign revolution," to return
to Pratt's phrase.

Because Harman's lecture was an invited address, it does not necessarily
express the perspective of the parapsychological community, which in
general tends to distance itself from anything having to do with transpersonal psychologies or the New Age movement. Still, in the chapter on the
"Sociocultural Aspects of Psi" in the textbook *Foundations of Parapsychology* (Edge et al. 1986), several leading parapsychologists discuss Harman's
ideas and also refer to Ferguson's *Aquarian Conspiracy*. Their evaluation
is fairly favorable: "Such a society promises much: a societal organization
in which there will be less competition and more cooperation, and the feel-
ings of the unity of society being greater than the assertions of the individual; less of a work ethic and more of a merging of work and play
and learning; a greater tolerance of difference and experimentation; a greater
respect for the potentials of consciousness; and institutions which support
these goals" (Edge et al. 1986:377). The term "revolution" does not come
up, but the changes described represent a utopian social development, or,
as they say, "a fundamental change in culture" (377). The fundamental
change involves a reorientation of individual/community polarities: cooperation over competition, community spirit over individual assertions, play
over work, and diversity over intolerance. Here, then, is a case where a
similarity between New Age and parapsychological discourse shades into
convergence, with parapsychologists turning to Marilyn Ferguson for a vision of how their scientific revolution can be linked to a new social order.

Parapsychology, Apocalypse, and Rebirth

In addition to invoking the metaphor of revolutions and portraying
themselves as scientific revolutionaries, contemporary parapsychologists
also occasionally give sermonizing prophecies of doom that can be compared to J. B. Rhine's warnings about the communist menace or Argüelles's
discussion of environmental Armageddon. One example is an invited address that the parapsychologist and biologist Robert McConnell gave at
the 1982 convention of the Parapsychological Association and the centen-
nial meeting of the British Society for Psychical Research. Titled "Parapsychology, the Wild Card in a Stacked Deck: A Look at the Near Future
of Mankind" (1983b:117–45), McConnell's address provides a wide-ranging
catalog of current trends in the global ecology, economy, and society: the
depletion of fossil fuels, food and water shortages, acid rain, the green-

house effect, deforestation, rapid population growth, Third World bank-
ruptcy, lower educational standards, increased crime, "moral decay," and
starvation. McConnell's ominous list appears to be fairly complete, and
his only mistake — at least what appears to be a mistake as I write in 1990–
91 — is his prediction of the emergence of "a new military philosophy" that
sees war as "[p]sychological rather than physical conflict" (1983b:138).

More than a prophet of doom, however, McConnell also points the way
to future-oriented action when he concludes his sad reflection on the present state of things with a flicker of hope: parapsychology, "the wild card
in the deck." As a wild card, parapsychology may be harnessed for military purposes, but McConnell argues that "the philosophical implications
of psi . . . offer the only hope I know — and slim it is — for a continuation
of the human experiment" (1983b:140). Like Rhine, McConnell believes
that parapsychology might provide the basis for a "code of ethics to which
all could subscribe" in a world where "old-time religion is dead" (1983b:
140–41). While McConnell is unsure of what discoveries will be made in
parapsychology, he says with certainty that "as a species, Homo sapiens
is doomed unless we experience a moral rebirth within the next decades"
(1983b:140). McConnell's glum vision is therefore very similar to that of
Rhine, but he also transforms the Armageddon by giving it a more contemporary ecological and North-South dimension in place of the East-West
polarities.

McConnell is part of an older generation of parapsychologists, and it
is therefore worth considering a few other examples of similar visions of
apocalypse and rebirth as described by a younger generation of parapsychologists.[9] In some cases, the role of parapsychologist as prophet is only
suggested in very faint terms. The psychologist Charles Tart, for example,
argues that "the bright, shiny scientism" that he learned early in life is not
enough to provide the answer for the new value system for which he sees
himself and others searching (1977:5). He warns of a "fanatic religious re-
vival" as a possible future that could even entail rejecting free scientific
inquiry (5). Instead, he prefers to have more scientific research in "the
neglected aspect of the human mind and human spirituality" in order to
integrate "the scientific and the spiritual" (5). Thus, in limited terms he envisions parapsychology's role as helping to bring about a better future
world and to stave off a potentially negative one.

A better example of the parapsychologist as prophet of doom appears
in *Leaving the Body: A Complete Guide to Astral Projection*, by the parapsychologist and writer D. Scott Rogo. In the final pages of the book, Rogo
claims that the out-of-body experience can be used to experience "the cosmos at first hand," resulting in a type of knowledge that goes beyond "the

cold art of scientific measurements and statistics" (1983:182). Like Rhine, Rogo locates parapsychology as a mediator between science and religion that can restore the spiritual dimension to an overly material world. In his words,

Even with all its limitations, science is a marvelous art. From its advances have come the great citadels of industry, technology, and worldly knowledge. But these noble citadels have become polluted by the dungeons of horror. Nuclear arms, modern materialism, and the rejection of spiritual values serve to remind us of science's double-edged legacy. Voyaging inward and outward — through zen, meditation, yoga, and out-of-body travel — may not lead to any great scientific advancement on our part. But these practices may lead to a cultural revolution — a return to the primal spirituality with which humankind is endowed and which the materialism and hedonism of modern society has sought to smother (1983:183).

Rogo's description of the present state of the world is not uniformly apocalyptic, since he contrasts "noble citadels" to the "dungeons of horror." He thus portrays the present state of the world in terms of opposing tendencies marked as "upper" and "lower," "good" and "evil." Calvinist imagery then shifts to romantic imagery when Rogo sets our sights on the future "cultural revolution" that returns us to "primal spirituality."

Another example of a vision of apocalypse and rebirth is articulated in the last chapter of *Out-of-Body Experiences: A Handbook* (1981), by the psychologist Janet Lee Mitchell, who is known for having worked at the American Society for Psychical Research with the psychic Ingo Swann on the out-of-body experience (OBE) experiments that she describes in the first chapter of the book.[10] In the last chapter, "Social and Ethical Considerations," she describes the philosophical and social implications of the out-of-body experience. The problem with the current situation, she argues, is the contradiction between the spiritual and the material. Noting that the United States was founded by a minority "who held nontraditional and spiritual ideas" (like New Agers and parapsychologists?), she argues that this rational and technological society has reached the point at which "complex, ecstatic experiences have been devalued as naive, uneducated, or delusional" (1981:125–26). She adds that America's churches are not "satisfying the basic spiritual needs of the people," and this condition is linked to the specter of vast world problems such as "poverty, resource shortages, overpopulation, famine, and environmental degradation" (126).

In the face of such overwhelming problems, the OBE might seem trivial, but Mitchell argues, "Most social ills derive from the fact that we identify ourselves as separate bodies" (1981:127). Among the ills are bigotry, elitism, sexism, and racism (notice the shift in the catalog of ills from that of J. B. Rhine). Mitchell claims that today's problems are rooted in the deeper cultural presupposition that the body is merely a machine, or, as she states later in echoes of Louisa Rhine, "a marvelous and priceless piece of equipment" (129). The OBE is a liberating experience equivalent to, in her metaphor, getting out of the car and walking on a nice day. The nature of this liberating experience is spiritual, to such an extent that "a large majority" of people who experience the OBE report "no fear of death" (128; cf. Tart 1977:217–18).

Just as spiritual liberation requires separation from the machine-like body, so social liberation requires separation from materialistic values. Mitchell argues that a shift from "material and monetary gain" could lead to "a societal ethic . . . that would affirm our sense of unity and abundant life" (1981:134). The emergence of such an ethic, however, is stymied by "a self-image" based on "physical limitations and bodily definitions," and in order to achieve the new social ethic this self-image must first be transcended. Thus, in ways very similar to the Rhines, Mitchell defends a dualistic perspective on mind/body relations that she believes can help society to achieve a solution to its pressing social problems.[11]

The humanistic psychologist Stanley Krippner provides one last suggestion of a similar vision of parapsychology's importance for society. Although he comes from a somewhat older generation than Tart, Rogo, and Mitchell, he was part of the consciousness scene during the 1960s counterculture, and he even met with Timothy Leary at Millbrook, as he explains in his book *Song of the Siren: A Parapsychological Odyssey* (note the explorer metaphor in the title). Furthermore, in the essay "Parapsychology and Postmodern Science," Krippner provides perhaps the first discussion of the relationship between parapsychology and the intellectual/artistic movement characteristic of the baby-boom generation.

Krippner's rhetoric is, in general, more restrained than that of the other parapsychologists considered here, and indeed he discusses the topic with the distance of a reporter who is merely representing the views of a segment of the parapsychological community. Nevertheless, he shares with his parapsychology colleagues a sense of anxiety about the present and a hopeful vision of the future that is linked, however tentatively, to parapsychology. For example, Krippner argues that the scientific and modern world view can be mechanistic, scientistic (challenging religion), materialistic, reductionistic, anthropocentric, Eurocentric, patriarchal, and militaristic (1990:133–34). In contrast, parapsychology provides a hint of a more holistic and "postmodern" world view. Although Krippner is a long way from the prophetic soteriology of J. B. Rhine, he still finds a role for parapsychology in the construction of a new era: "If the postmodern age is to represent a substantive advance over the modern age, the world's antagonistic superpowers and sects will need to be reconciled; the earth's ecology will need to be restored; the dispossessed peoples of the globe will need to be empowered; the planet's dwindling food and energy resources will need to be augmented and carefully allocated; effective treatments for old and new diseases will need to be discovered. Psi research data, whatever their ultimate explanation, suggest forms of information and influence flow that are unitive in nature" (138). He concludes by suggesting that the unitive and connective aspects of the paranormal may help, even in a modest way, provide the background to some of the great problems facing the world today.[12]

Clearly, parapsychologists such as Krippner have come a long way from the conservative social vision of J. B. Rhine. Theirs is a politically progressive, environmentally oriented vision that is arguably closer to the laments of Argüelles and other New Age writers than to that of J. B. Rhine. Still, parapsychologists today share with Rhine a more erudite discourse than the New Agers, and they invoke dualistic oppositions that resonate with those of J. B. Rhine. Thus, there are commonalities to both sides. Indeed, all the visions share the common structure of an apocalyptic present and an ominous future that a certain kind of science or knowledge, as well as heroism, can help avert. To differing degrees, New Agers and parapsychologists play the role of prophets of gloom who threaten the end of civilization if the people do not wake from their slumbers and heed their call to change their ways. As scientific revolutionaries, parapsychologists, like Aquarian conspirators, also battle heroically the entrenched forces of science in order to help bring about a new knowledge and society.

Skeptics

Skeptical Sermons

Do skeptics also situate themselves in a social world of heroes and sermons, ominous presents and hopeful futures, or are they skeptical of such rhetorical figures? I will argue that they do, and their analogies are one more aspect of the paraculture that they are forging with New Agers and parapsychologists. Consider, for example, skeptics on the threats posed to society.

Martin Gardner finds much that is ridiculous and humorous in New Age, paranormal, and pseudoscientific beliefs, but he also worries about the serious and dark side of his paranormal Other. For example, in the introduction to *Science: Good, Bad, and Bogus,* Gardner subdivides his Other into cranks, crackpots, and charlatans. For the most part, Gardner does not take them seriously, and in general he does not believe that the books now available on "worthless science, promoted into bestsellers by cynical publishers," pose much of a threat to society (xiii–xiv). However, he believes that in areas such as medicine and anthropology pseudoscientific beliefs constitute a clear threat to society (xiv). Pseudoscientific diet books and medical cures, for example, have resulted in the senseless deaths of some people. Likewise, "The idiocies of Hitler were strengthened in the minds of the German people by crackpot theories of anthropology" (xiv). In cases where cranks, crackpots, and charlatans pose a danger to society, Gardner reserves his right to express "moral indignation," even as he still defends his Others' right to free speech (xiv).

Whereas Gardner does not extrapolate by arguing that society itself is in grave danger, other skeptics are more willing to don the cloak of the prophet of doom. The religious studies scholar Carl Raschke, for example, argues that should the New Age movement "continue to 'catch on' with sundry professionals and pace-setters among the baby boomers, [it] will surely 'transform' the American economy and social order in much the same way as AIDS transforms the body's immune system" (1988:332). He continues with a dire prophecy: "The impact on economic productivity and America's capacity to compete in the global arena will doubtlessly be affected" (332).[13]

The writer Isaac Asimov issued a similar prophecy of doom. In reply to a journalist who had seen no harm in uncritically reporting claims about a perpetual motion machine, Asimov warned that such reports could mislead the public into thinking that there is no energy crisis, and as a result the public might avoid making "hard decisions" or taking "strenuous action" (Asimov 1982:xiv). The science fiction writer concludes, "That might just add the necessary amount of heedlessness that will keep humanity from solving this life-and-death problem and will therefore send civilization crashing" (xiv). Against this backdrop of the end of civilization, Asimov points to science as the source of human salvation: "Never in history has humanity faced a crisis so deep, so intense, so pervasive, and so multifaceted. . . . If we are to pull through, we must thread our way carefully through the rapids that lie ahead. . . . If we are careless and over-hasty, we may destroy ourselves through the misuse of science. If we are forethoughtful and knowledgeable, we may find salvation through the wise use of science" (xiv).

Not all skeptics believe they should issue such prophecies of doom. The philosopher Paul Kurtz, for example, questions those skeptics who "have assumed that a new Apocalypse of Unreason is about to descend upon us," and he warns that "such doomsday forecasts are probably overly speculative" (1981:xiii). Still, Kurtz's comment shows that skeptics do occasionally issue warnings about an "apocalypse of unreason," and his choice of metaphor suggests that he also recognizes the connection between these prophecies and their biblical prototypes.

Skeptical Heroes

As heroes, then, skeptics occasionally play the role of prophets of doom who harangue their paranormal Others and the general public. They do not, however, share with New Agers such as Ferguson and many parapsychologists the self-image of revolutionary. To the contrary, skeptics view themselves as defenders of the established order. What kinds of heroes are these? Consider some examples.

Asimov suggests two types of heroism in his characterization of the magician James "the Amazing" Randi. He begins by noting that his skeptical colleague has been called the "hit man" of CSICOP, a label that Randi himself apparently does not deny (Asimov 1982:xv; of course, the term is not meant to be taken literally). Asimov also compares the magician to a medieval knight (and part American boxing champion): "Randi has, at one time or another, assailed every wall and buttress of the vast Castle of Pseudoscience and has never pulled his punches" (Asimov 1982:xv). Indeed, Randi himself seems to like the martial metaphors, and in his introduction to the same book, *Flim-Flam!* he develops a similar image: "We critics of supernaturalism are accustomed to having words put into our mouths by the opposition and by the media, and it is about time that we struck back. In this book I will hit as hard as I can, as often as I can, and sometimes quite bluntly and even rudely. Good manners will be sacrificed to honesty, and the Marquis of Queensbury [sic] be damned" (Randi 1982:3).

The images of mafioso hit men and rogue boxers imply that the work of skeptics is somehow shady or outside established social norms, but the name of the skeptics' organization, CSICOP ("psi cop") also suggests that they see themselves less as outlaws than as the police of the republic of science. Thus, a second set of heroic images links the skeptical heroes to the role of the good citizen. As Kendrick Frazier makes clear, "[I]f an informed and rational citizenry is indeed important to a democracy (as I believe it is), then scientists have an obligation to help the public understand the difference between sense and nonsense, good science and bad science, scientific speculation and outright fantasy" (1986:xii). The metaphors now shift to military ones — and the prose to short, declarative phrases — as Frazier conjures up images of the battle to save science and the republic: "It is not enough to state positions. One must be armed with the facts. And one must be prepared for attacks from unexpected direc-tions. Sometimes these attacks are carried out with surprising cleverness and effectiveness" (1986:xii). The game now shifts from one of cops and robbers, boxers, or hit men to serious warfare, one in which the fate of democracy itself may be at stake.

Martial metaphors also appear in Gardner's *Science: Good, Bad, and Bogus*, which he dedicates to other skeptics, whom he likens to "fellow warriors in the never ending battle against dishonest and deluded science" (dedication page). The phrase "never-ending battle" suggests a comparison with Superman's struggle for truth, justice, and the American way. Super-man serves on the side of justice and the police to uphold the law of the land, just as skeptics serve as police for the law of science. Sacrificing per-sonal gain and emotional needs, and fighting against the tremendous forces of media interest and popular credulity, skeptics fight an uphill battle for the salvation of science and the republic. In the process, skeptical discourse lines up science with the civil religion (Bellah 1975), and it pits both against religious faith and superstition.

By depicting themselves as fighting an uphill battle, skeptics portray themselves not just as heroic figures but as heroes in a specifically Ameri-can sense. Like Superman/Clark Kent, Batman/Bruce Wayne, and other American superheroes, skeptics are double: they are part of the social and scientific order that they seek to uphold, but they also work somewhat outside of it, because it is corrupt even at the highest levels. Another mar-tial image that better conveys the double nature of the skeptics' role is one used by two sociologists: skeptics are "scientific vigilantes"; that is, they act in the name of society even as they may transgress some of its rules (Collins and Pinch 1982:42). Just as superheroes may overstep the bound-aries of the law in order to preserve the rule of law, so skeptics may over-step the boundaries of scientific methods in order to preserve the rule of science.

Another heroic image that reveals the complexities of skeptical heroism is their self-representation as supporters of the underdog consumer with respect to commercial interests. At the 1988 CSICOP conference, the skep-tic Jay Rosen argued that the New Age movement is tainted with "con-sumer culture" and plagued by the "culture of narcissism," and thus CSICOP should become a corresponding "consumer movement" (Shore 1989:233). As a further expression of this perspective, CSICOP members formed a Legal and Consumer Affairs Subcommittee, the goal of which is to help victims of psychic and New Age fraud. By representing itself as a con-sumer movement, CSICOP counters otherworldly spirituality with this-worldly consumer protectionism. However, the conflict between spirituality and consumerism, between the idioms of religious experience and caveat emptor, should not obscure the deeper similarities, for the New Age movement is itself constructed in opposition to official religion, science, business, and medicine. As such it represents a consumerist movement in its own right, as is most evident in New Age alternative medicine and natural products.

Thus, both skeptics and New Agers can be seen, in their different ways, to invoke an ethos of consumerism and a heroism of consumer protectors (like the heroic "Nader's Raiders"). Clearly, their targets are different: skeptics aim at the New Age and "pseudoscience" in general, and New Agers aim at big business and official science and medicine. In turning to the fierce independence of the consumer ethos, both skeptics and New Agers articulate the American value of independent thinking and self-reliance, the latter a value that the anthropologist Francis Hsu (1972) finds distinctive of the American form of individualism.

Conclusions

Consumer watchdogs, psi cops, hit men, revolutionaries, spirit guides, prophets of doom — how are these diverse heroic figures related? Once again, consider the "doxa" that is left undisputed through all the conflicting orthodoxies and heterodoxies. As I suggested in the previous paragraph, an obvious place to begin is the question of individualism and American culture.

The anthropologist Louis Dumont (1980) associates individualism and egalitarianism with modern Western societies, and frequently social scientists point to the United States as the country where such values have received their greatest elaboration. The self-reliance of the pioneer, the fierce independence of the revolutionary patriots, and the self-righteous moral indignation of the Puritan divines are closely connected heroes in a national mythology that calls upon its citizens to question authority and class privilege. Arguably, the three figures are all variants on the Puritan divine, who either stayed in England and became a revolutionary or moved to the shores of Massachusetts to become a pioneer and to build the New Jerusalem. The Puritan, the pioneer, and the revolutionary therefore all locate themselves outside of society, either to renew a corrupt social order that has been backsliding or to build an alternative society of their own that will resurrect lost values.[14]

Thus, one commonality is the hero as self-righteous underdog. Parapsychologists and New Agers explicitly see themselves as marginal and heterodox defenders of a true knowledge that the various orthodoxies of science, religion, and the government deny. Skeptics may not be revolutionaries, but they still see themselves as players in a social drama that pits them against the representatives of powerful social interests. Like David before Goliath, they also face enormous odds in their drama of the battle against the tide of popular opinion and profiteering opinion-makers. Thus, the topdog switches from the social and scientific orthodoxies of the day (for the New Agers and parapsychologists) to a powerful media establishment that supports the paranormal for pecuniary motivations (for the skeptics).

As underdogs, these heroes are located "beyond" or "alongside" society: they are paraheroes. In their struggle for the lofty goal of a better knowledge and society, they sometimes violate the very rules of the knowledge and society they seek to preserve. Thus, parapsychologists and New Agers propose a new form of knowledge that violates the assumptions (and sometimes the methods) of existing science, and skeptics at times engage in rhetorical strategies, such as debunking and ridicule, that also violate the ideals of scientific decorum. Therefore, members of all three communities are caught in a paradox: in order to redeem society, they must leave it and in some sense become marginal figures—hit men, dirty boxers, revolutionaries, disembodied spirit guides.

By making a journey outside of society, the heroes undergo a trajectory that begins to look like a rite of passage: the ordinary citizen is transformed into a hero by passing through a "liminal" or marginal social position toward reinstatement into a better and reformed society. The sociologist Robert Bellah and his colleagues find a similar trajectory in two other types of American hero, the cowboy and the detective, both of whom to some extent must leave society in order to redeem both it and themselves (Bellah et al. 1985:145–46). In the process, the hero doubles, becomes a kind of outlaw, and reveals a rottenness at the core of society. Bellah and colleagues explain that in detective stories at first the crime appears to be an isolated incident, but the detective's investigation soon shows that the crime is "linked to the powerful and privileged of the community. Society, particularly 'high society,' is corrupt to the core. . . . The hard-boiled detective, who may long for love and success, for a place in society, is finally driven to stand alone, resisting the blandishments of society, to pursue a lonely crusade for justice" (Bellah et al. 1985:145–46).

The passage "outside" of society is therefore restricted; the hero in fact remains in society but must make a passage outside of the corrupt high society of the topdogs. The economic and social power that all three communities believe shores up their Others can be seen as a signifier of the corrupt and powerful forces that they challenge as underdog crusaders.

The heroic loner, set apart from the everyday concerns of success and material gain, suggests an individualistic form of heroism that constructs itself as, to use the term of Bellah and colleagues, "heroic selflessness" (Bellah et al. 1985:145–46). Thus, the classic American conflict between the individual and the community is resolved by a hyperindividualism that becomes social through dedication to the cause of remaking a corrupt society in the individual's image.

The role of the underdog hero is similar to that of the biblical prophet; both stand somewhat outside society and urge it back to its original principles. Like our classic Hollywood westerns and detective movies, the story of the parahero is a morality tale of good guys and bad guys. The Self is the elect, the voice of self-righteous knowledge wrapped in its smug self-conviction that the Other is wrong. The Other, in turn, is motivated not by a quest for knowledge (which seems to be the unique privilege of the Self) but instead by impure interests: greed, materialistic gain, dogmatism, zealotry. The terms of the Self/Other distinction therefore participate in and reproduce what Bellah has discussed as Americans' self-representation as the chosen people (1975). In the story of the pilgrims, the (increasingly contested) foundation myth portrays Americans as the chosen people who, like the ancient Israelites, left their oppressors in Europe/Egypt to come to the promised land. Americans continually tell variants of the foundation myth in their tales of virtuous underdogs, from the success of the pilgrims in New England to the Horatio Alger stories of the nineteenth century to the civil rights, antiwar, and other activists in the current period.

One other aspect of the doxa of the emerging paraculture, then, is a shared representation of the Self as prophet, which in turn is reflected in the sermonizing quality of the writings of all three communities. All three issue laments about the state of the world, about the perils imposed by the way of the Other. Conversely, they point to an optimistic future represented by the way of the Self and an antagonistically constructed notion of scientific truth. Langdon Winner (1989:51) traces the future-orientedness of the ideology of American science to the Puritan jeremiad, which the literature scholar Sacvan Bercovitch argues served to spur the community toward an optimistic future time in which "fact and ideal *would be made* to correspond" (1978:61).[15] Unlike the European form of the jeremiad, which ends with a pessimistic lament, the American jeremiad opposes a lament of doom to an affirmation of the world with an optimistic future (1978:7). The anxiety in the writings of skeptics, parapsychologists, and New Agers is a peculiarly American anxiety that has to do with backsliding, with losing the status as the world's chosen people. As J. B. Rhine stated in a phrase of blunt eloquence that still rings true thirty years later: "The conduct of human beings in the present era is not good" (1953:260). But the lament of the American jeremiad is a preface to the call to build a better future, to an optimistic hope that the dream can still be fulfilled.

Even the "pagan" sagas of Atlantis and Harmonic Convergence become recognizable as expressions of the American preoccupation that it has broken its sacred spiritual covenant and begun to serve mammon in the place of God. At one point, Argüelles makes the religious metaphor explicit, when he asks, "Is there a Mayan Second Coming, a Mayan Return?" (1987:166). Later he comments that to some people Harmonic Convergence would appear as "another Pentecost and second coming of Christ" (170). Likewise, when the skeptic Kurtz laments that his own colleagues have adopted the rhetoric of an "apocalypse of unreason," he applies a religious image that confirms my argument that these rhetoric structures are part of the American religious tradition. Like the Protestants of the seventeenth century, who attempted to weed out magic from their churches by smashing stained-glass windows and icons, the skeptics of the twentieth century issue blanket condemnations of popular superstition and call for purity in the church of science.[16]

My discussion of doxa, then, leads to doxologies, to the religious and moral systems that these writers put into play in their stories of difference. The three communities are not by any means typical representatives of what we might call "mainstream" American religiosity. Skeptics are often atheists; New Agers are more likely to be drawn to non-Western philosophies than to the standard Judeo-Christian theologies; and parapsychologists, to the extent that they discuss the religious implications of their work, have sometimes described their project as finding "religion at the point-o-five level of significance." Yet, the visions of heroism and the urge to issue jeremiads reveal how much they all have in common.

Thus, the prophets and heroes of paranormal culture are both drawing upon and rewriting their cultural history. They are speaking in conventions that may be recognizable as the American jeremiad, but they are also transforming the genre by translating it into new idioms. To borrow a metaphor from the historian/culture critic Donna Haraway (1991), these new hybrids of science and religion, politics and prophecy, are "cyborg" discourses and practices. Puritan divines and hardshell preachers are no longer part of this scene; in their place are mediums, gurus, revolutionaries, and psi cops, who occupy much the same cultural space of issuing laments and prophecies. Likewise, we may find hints and references to George Washington–style revolutionary soldiers, but the patriots are also transformed into scientific revolutionaries or Aquarian conspirators, just as crime-fighting cops become consumer watchdogs or scientific vigilantes who police the boundaries of acceptable knowledge. Thus, while New Agers, parapsychologists, and skeptics follow the well-worn grooves of their cultural legacy, they simultaneously cut their own figures and forge a new "paraculture."

5

Gender and Hierarchy

LIKE systems of political and religious morality, notions of gender frequently serve as a contested arena where questions of is and ought merge in highly charged language. I use the word "gender" to refer to cultural understandings of what is masculine and feminine, including those having to do with perceived differences between the sexes as male and female. In Western societies (if not all societies), gender is frequently constituted as a hierarchy that privileges men and masculine attributes and in turn relegates women and the feminine to a secondary role. My concept of "gender," then, is a complicated one related to the question of hierarchy and power.

One may or may not wish to take gender as the prototype of all forms of social hierarchy, but certainly the relationship between gender and hierarchy is a close one. The anthropologist Louis Dumont (1980), for example, recognizes implicitly the close relationship when he chooses the story of Adam's rib to explain his concept of hierarchy. Dumont describes hierarchy as a relationship in which two terms are in opposition at one level, but at another level one of the terms is used to define the whole. For example, in Western cultures Adam and Eve are in opposition, but in the biblical story Eve is also derived from Adam. In the conventional, patriarchal usage of English, the words "man" and "woman" stand in opposition at one level, but at another level the word "man" is given priority by being used to stand for the whole species. The relationship between the first and second term is one of "encompassment," or, to switch disciplinary vocabularies, one of "supplementarity" (Derrida 1974).

Gendered hierarchies play an important role in the social construction of the boundaries among skeptics, parapsychologists, and New Agers. In addition, they play a role in the construction of internal boundaries, what I call "internal Others." The use of gendered language and metaphor, as well as the parallel construction of internal Others, therefore constitutes one more way in which skeptics, parapsychologists, and New Agers build a common culture through their disputes and differences.

New Agers

Feminisms and New Age Thought

As has become clear from my discussions of New Age writers, Ferguson's voice is a relatively erudite one in the vast Babel of New Age voices.[1] Her vision of science is in some ways arguably even less heterodox than that of parapsychologists, because she tends to stick to new developments within the orthodox sciences rather than to find empirical evidence for controversial phenomena such as extrasensory perception. Likewise, in *The Aquarian Conspiracy* Ferguson does not advocate channeling, crystal healing, goddess religion, or any of a number of more controversial New Age practices, and she seems to see the "so-called New Age movement" as just one aspect of a broader social and spiritual transformation that she advocates (1987:423).[2] Terms such as "revolution," "paradigm shift," "new consciousness," and "transformation," rather than "New Age," are more characteristic of *The Aquarian Conspiracy*.

One important area that Ferguson shares with the more popular New Agers, and that distinguishes them both from the skeptics, is her open endorsement of feminism. The link between feminist perspectives and alternative religion in the United States is a deep one that dates back at least to nineteenth-century Spiritualism. As the historians Ann Braude (1989), R. Laurence Moore (1977), and Alex Owen (1989) have amply demonstrated, women's suffrage and independence were interwoven into the otherworldly discourse of women mediums. The connection between women's perspectives and religion continues today in the New Age movement.

Ferguson is hopeful that women will lead the way in her Aquarian transformation. Indeed, she writes, "Women represent the greatest single force for political renewal in a civilization thoroughly out of balance" (1987: 226), and she believes that women will not only redefine political issues, but they will redefine leadership and even "thinking itself" (227). Ferguson's feminist vision, however, is reformist rather than separatist. She believes that women and men will work together to create a new social order, one in which the "yin perspective" of women "will push out the boundaries of the old yang paradigm" (226). Likewise, she compares the societal sharing of powers between men and women to the beneficial mixing of masculine and feminine characteristics on a personal level (226).

However, there are many feminisms, just as there are many New Ages, and Ferguson's vision is therefore only one among many. Before making any statements about feminism, women's perspectives, and New Age discourse, it is therefore important to consider some of the alternatives in this already alternative world.

Goddess Religion

At the popular end of the New Age spectrum, one is more likely to find separatists or other radical feminists who might view with suspicion Ferguson's accommodationism. For example, the shamanic world of the writer Lynn Andrews is based on a sisterhood, and at one point Andrews finds herself "looking at the face of the goddess" (1987:68). Her shamans are all women, and in *Crystal Women: Sisters of the Dreamtime* (1987) Andrews's mentor Ginevee describes how her people became patrilineal long ago; that is, she suggests that they had a distant past of matriliny if not matriarchy (60). As a writer, Andrews is a feminist version of Carlos Castaneda: a goddess way of knowledge.[3]

A perhaps even more developed example of feminism and New Age thought is found among the neopagans, that is, those who believe in ancient pagan gods.[4] Feminist neopagans frequently support ecofeminism, a movement that has been dated to 1980, when about four hundred women gathered at the University of Massachusetts at Amherst for a three-day conference titled "Women and Life on Earth: Ecofeminism in the Eighties" (Albanese 1990:176). One example of an ecofeminist neopagan perspective is Diane Stein's *The Women's Spirituality Book* (1986), a text that is interesting from the cultural perspective because it develops an explicit critique of the skeptical, patriarchal Other. Perhaps best known for her book *The Kwan Yin Book of Changes* (1985), the "first women's I Ching," Stein also wrote *Stroking the Python: Women's Psychic Lives* (1988), and she has been active in a number of movements, including Vietnam antiwar, lesbian, women's rights, disability rights, antinuclear, and women's spirituality (1988).

The Women's Spirituality Book opens with a description of the Michigan Womyn's Music Festival, a "workshop on ritual" in which "sixty or seventy women of all ages, sizes, colors, styles meet in a circle in a fern-green wilderness field" (1986:xiii). Some are dressed, others appear "skyclad," that is, in their natural state in this natural setting. Together they perform a ritual in which they first tie skeins of purple yarn to each other's wrists. They then break the yarn and thus symbolize their liberation from the yoke of patriarchy, and finally they retie the yarn as a "symbol of retying women's bonding" (xiv–xv).

In performing this ritual of female bonding, the women each call out the name of one of the bonds of isolation that they are breaking—unemployment, distrust, nuclear power, separation from their bodies, not caring, patriarchy, loneliness, racism, poverty, fear — and then they name the new bonds that they affirm: sisterhood, caring, love, goddess, friendship, community, equality, and peace (1986:xiv–xv). Like Lockean individuals, these women come together in a glen to rewrite the social contract in their own terms, to sign their new Magna Carta with purple yarn, and therefore to establish a new community of "womyn" (the "y" takes the "men" out of "women"). They form their new community under the sign of the goddess, of covenant turned coven. Like the other world of the medium Ruth Montgomery or the post-Aquarian world of Marilyn Ferguson, in this new community the women resolve the individual/community dilemma: they emphasize "individual creativity" as well as "pooling skills and sharing trust" (3).

Goddess religion draws its inspiration from an exotic Other that "has much to do with re-newed and re-membered forms of witchcraft, the Old Religion or wicca, and nothing at all to do with Satanism or the repressions of Judeo-Christian and Islamic patriarchy" (3–4). Like Atlantis and other sites for the New Age exotic Other, goddess religion dates back to the time before the great world religions, before "God or gods," to the time of "the goddess, the great mother" (4). Stein claims that the "evidence of anthropologists and archaeologists indicates that pre-God (goddess) civilizations were both matriarchal and peaceful, and structured far differently from today's world" (4).[5] These ancient matriarchies portray the birth of the world as an act of goddesses, just as women are responsible for "the beginnings of agriculture, tools, and the survival skills collectively known as civilization" (5). Here, women are situated as the transition point between nature and culture, not in the synchronic sense of cultural orders but in the diachronic sense of the passage of humanity from nature to culture.

As in the original transformation from nature to culture, women will now play a historic role in the current reawakening of spirituality: "The goddess is here and now, and no longer sleeping or lost in patriarchy's winter trance" (17). As for the French Revolution, a new symbolic landscape and calendar accompanies the historic transformation. In the new calendar, the sea and the moon become sacred zones (26) and the change of the seasons is ascribed to a feminist version of the myth of Persephone and Demeter (41). The calendar is broken down into sabbats, which correspond to solstices, equinoxes, and ancient pagan ceremonies such as "Hallow's Eve" (100).

Patriarchy is the negative Other in this symbolic world, and nuclear reactors serve as the great sign of the evils of the patriarchal world: they epitomize centralized technology, a lack of concern for the environment, and bureaucratic and patriarchal hiearchy. The women whom Stein describes are activists at Diablo Canyon, Greenham Common, and the Seneca Women's Peace Camp, and their activism is based on the conviction that "women's spirituality is a growing re-cognition of the goddess as planet, as the earth herself, and of women as part of the earth and her divine being" (1). To these women, nuclear leakage "violates natural law," the law of the earth and the planets, and "the inner stresses of technological patriarchy" (2–3).

Likewise, "crystals, messages, colors, and herbs, [and] learning the tarot and I Ching" are signifiers of a gentler technology that is closer to the Mother Earth. Healing (feminine) is opposed to medicine (masculine), which "was and is a business" and "began and remains in competitive exclusiveness" (151). Medicine, like nuclear energy, represents "knowledge hoarded and hidden, dispensed only to those who can pay for it and held as power over women, children and the poor, and all minorities" (151). Healing, in contrast, represents an ancient, democratic knowledge that the medical profession drove underground and that the "womyn's" spirituality movement is reviving (152).[6] This "caring and nurturing medicine," for which the "basic models are those of mother and child and of women who are sisters" (152), contrasts with patriarchal medicine: "The doctor doesn't know the patient's name and is judgmental of her life, and raw science and interminable forms do little [in the way] of comforting. The doctor writes a prescription for chemicals to mask the woman's symptoms or cuts some body part out, if the woman can afford to pay for it, and the experience is physically and emotionally traumatic" (152).

Whether in the form of biomedicine or of nuclear power plants, modern science and technology represent the patriarchal order that "womyn's" spirituality opposes. This conceptualization of the world would probably not satisfy Marilyn Ferguson. Although Ferguson also welcomes a new form of holistic spirituality, she seems to be more at home with the "tao of physics" types than the feminist neopagans. Likewise, although Ferguson shares with Stein a critique of patriarchy, the Aquarian conspirator is much more optimistic about what modern science can offer. At one level the same, at another the opposite, these two New Age feminists are internal Others.

Parapsychologists

Life and Lab: The Two Cultures of Parapsychology[7]

A similar divide occurs within parapsychology between the exponents of quantitative, experimental, laboratory-based studies and the supporters of case histories and field methods known as "spontaneous case research." Although some parapsychologists do both kinds of research, there is a tendency for them to fall into one or the other camp.

In the work of the famous husband-wife team, J. B. Rhine was the experimentalist and Louisa Rhine was the spontaneous case researcher. In Louisa Rhine's terms — borrowed from the title of her book *ESP in Life and Lab* — her husband studied ESP in the lab, whereas she studied it in real-life situations. The husband/wife division of labor immediately raises the complicated issue of the role of gender and social hierarchy in the internal divisions of parapsychology. Certainly I would not want to make too much out of a single example. There is no general pattern that correlates spontaneous case researchers with women and experimentalists with men (the majority of both types of researchers is male). Yet, even if there were such a pattern, it could be a red herring. What I wish to examine is more the gendering of the research than the sex of the researchers. Thus, my question is: to what extent is the opposition between spontaneous case research and experimental research a gendered hierarchy?

Let me begin by considering the extent to which the relationship between the two methods was hierarchical. Certainly, Louisa Rhine's analogy of mining for gold positioned spontaneous research literally "under" experimental research, but it is also not clear from the analogy that she saw the relationship as a hierarchy (1967:68). Likewise, in an essay written near the end of her life, Rhine appears to describe spontaneous case research as a clearly supplementary activity. At the beginning, she states, her goal was "to explore the possible suggestive value of case material in order to provide an adjunct to the planning of experiments" (1977:68). However, she adds that the purpose was "extended," and eventually her project grew "into an extensive study of psi as a human ability as it seems to be indicated in spontaneous experiences" (68–69). Here, she seems to be suggesting that spontaneous case research became its own project, one which might even be broader than the experimental project. Did Rhine, then, accept a hierarchical relationship of experimental parapsychology over spontaneous case research, or was she attempting to reverse the terms of this hierarchy?

Perhaps the answer is neither; in other words, Louisa Rhine may have been attempting to articulate a delicate complementarity in place of a hierarchy. Such seems to be the position in *ESP in Life and Lab*, where she argues that the "life side gives a much wider range of perspective than it has yet been possible to obtain in the laboratory. It can thus suggest or indicate what the truth may be in an area still unexplored experimentally. In addition, it can help in the understanding and interpretation of some of the experimental results and give them deeper meaning" (1967:7). The ambiguity is evident. On the one hand, Rhine introduces the life side as having a "wider range of perspective." On the other hand, she states that the value of spontaneous case research is to suggest areas for exploration in the lab or to help understand the experimental results. Later, she adds that "while the life side gives perspective, the experimental side gives reliability," and together the two "can give a clearer, more meaningful concept than either side alone can give" (7).

For this alchemical wedding between life and lab, it is difficult to tell whether Louisa Rhine is confirming the hierarchy, putting it into question, or perhaps arguing for equality. In any case, her writing clearly points to an internal division within parapsychological discourse, one which J. B. Rhine and his experimentalist colleagues understood as a hierarchy that favored the laboratory method as the more scientific alternative. Thus, the Rhines reinscribe the boundary between the relatively more and less scientific within the confines of their own community, and once again we see how boundary-work is a multiple and recursive process.

Louisa Rhine and the Gender of the Paranormal

The question of gender is more evident when we turn from Louisa Rhine's construction of parapsychology to her construction of paranormal phenomena. A psychoanalytic reading would suggest the obvious, that her description of the paranormal as the hidden, deep, and elusive may be read as vaginal metaphors, just as her husband's project of conquering new continents might be seen as a masculine fantasy of penetration. Likewise, when Louisa Rhine pairs off the mechanistic and superficial view of the mind with the elusive and disorderly paranormal, she is arguably working with gendered oppositions that some psychologists, such as Freud, have used in descriptions of the female psyche (see, e.g., Kofman 1985). The question then emerges: what connection is there between Rhine's vision of the paranormal and Western notions of the feminine?

In *ESP in Life and Lab*, Louisa Rhine does discuss gender in the context of three case studies of psychic experiences. The first involves a mother and her daughter, the second a woman who was trying to locate a trunk that contained her dresses, and the third a woman who dreamed that her husband's brother had died, which was later confirmed by her sister-in-law. All three cases involve women, and in another of her books, *Hidden Channels of the Mind*, Rhine makes the linkage even more explicit: "Women have the reputation for being the more 'intuitive' sex. Are women, then, more psychic than men, or in modern terms, do they use ESP more than men do?" (1961:121). She concludes that at least women report their psychic experiences more frequently than men.

The connection between women and paranormal experiences also appears in Rhine's discussions of her correspondence with people from all over the world, who wrote to her about their psychic experiences. In *Psi, What Is It?* (1975), many of the letters she cites are from young women and girls. For example, the chapter titled "The Fringe" begins with a letter from a student named Angela, who writes for advice on her experiences with the Ouija board. "No, no, no, Angela," Rhine responds, "the answer to all your questions is no. But it is well you asked about this gadget. It is a real fooler. How could you ever tell if it was really a spirit? The idea is just a guess, a fantasy, though it is one that has often been made" (1975: 17). Although at one level her answer appears to be similar to one that a skeptic would give, there is a difference in tone. Rhine's voice here is like that of a mother chiding her daughter for mistaken notions.

The same voice is heard again in the chapter "The Occult in School," which begins with a letter from an eleven-year-old, Nancy Green, who wants to know if ESP can be used to hurt someone. "No, Nancy," Rhine reassures her, "ESP could not possibly be used to hurt anyone physically or mentally" (1975:197). The dialogue continues through three more letters from Nancy, each of which is accompanied by a response from Louisa, then it shifts to letters from a Mary Sue A. and Daisy W. Rhine's responses are written, like a Dear Abby or Ann Landers column, partly to the letter writer and partly to the unidentified reader. Like the columnist, she chides, scolds, lectures, explains, and gives advice to her pen pals, but she never adopts the self-righteous tone of the skeptic-patriarch.

In *Psi, What Is It?*, the characters drawn to the occult fringe are generally innocent children and, perhaps not coincidentally, generally schoolgirls. The voice of the occult Other is therefore mediated through that of the child, whereas parapsychology is encoded as adult. But remember that the parapsychologist is also female, as are her pen pals in general, and therefore the exchange between parapsychology and the occult takes the form of a nurturing dialogue, as between a mother and her daughter.

In contrast, the skeptics' paranormal Other tends to be less the curious schoolgirl than the money-grubbing charlatan or the incompetent experimenter, and the skeptics' genre of writing is less like an exchange between mother and daughter than a college debate, political broadside, or Puritan jeremiad. While it is true that some of the skeptics' essays (just as some of the parapsychologists' replies to skeptics) adopt the epistolary form, the dialogue between skeptics and parapsychologists generally takes the form of an exchange of polemics and accusations, and the exchange is arranged carefully to give one side the last word (e.g., Gardner 1981b). The Other is, from the perspective of each side, left in shreds (or, as a direct mail solicitation from CSICOP put it, "tatters"), rather than admired as fringes.

Because parapsychology is associated with the paranormal, skeptics may gender it feminine in opposition to orthodox science. However, as a science that studies the paranormal and attempts to find laws for it, parapsychologists gender it masculine with respect to its elusive, hidden, and deep object of study. The curious gender ambiguity of parapsychology is reflected in the dialogue with the occult Other, which can be characterized as a dialogue between mother and daughter. This relationship encodes the equality of female/female relations (both are interested in the paranormal) and the hierarchy of the relations between older and younger generations (one is more scientific than the other).

Life and Lab in Contemporary Parapsychology

The implicit hierarchy between experimental and spontaneous case research that was evident in the work of J. B. and Louisa Rhine continues today in contemporary parapsychology. The existence of this hierarchy is easily demonstrated; perhaps less obvious is how the relationship between the two methods is also gendered.

I know from informal statements from many experimental parapsychologists that they continue to value spontaneous case research as a source of hypotheses for testing in the laboratory. Parapsychologists may think of both methods as scientific, but they view experimental research as the more scientific of the two. Likewise, experimentalists may pay attention to the insights of spontaneous case research, but they pay more attention once these insights have been converted into variables that can be quantified in the lab. Even the very word "spontaneous" suggests the perceived weakness of this kind of research: spontaneous cases are nonrepeatable and uncontrolled.

Furthermore, in the inner circles of the international Parapsychological Association, the experimentalists are the dominant group. One indication of the hierarchy is the number of papers presented at the conventions of the Parapsychological Association. On this point, the historian Carlos Alvarado (1987:346) conducted a survey of publications in *Research in Parapsychology* between 1981 and 1985, and he found that of 196 research reports, 25 were spontaneous case studies (surveys and single case studies), whereas 171 were experiments (including semi-experimental protocols). Spontaneous case research continues to exist within contemporary American parapsychology, but it is clearly less important.[8]

To experimentalists, spontaneous case research is a literary venture for which the basic materials are, to borrow the word used by one British pro-experimentalist, Robert Thouless, "stories" (1972:10–11). As Thouless goes on to explain, the first psychical researchers were generally classicists or philosophers, and "few had had any training in scientific research" (15). Furthermore, he argues that even those spontaneous case researchers who have "scientific" training — the term "scientific" here apparently excludes the human sciences — must always grapple with the "weakness of the evidence," and their studies easily lend themselves to skeptical questions (10). For Thouless, the place of spontaneous case research is "to indicate possible conclusions that are to be tested afterwards by experiment" (17).

A similar position is found in a subsequent essay by the German philosopher Gerd Hövelman and the American psychologist Stanley Krippner. Writing with some recommendations for the future of parapsychology, they urge parapsychologists "not [to] rely too heavily on so-called evidence from spontaneous cases or from data obtained in quasi-experimental settings" (1986:2). Hövelman and Krippner go on to establish the hierarchical relationship between experimentalism and case studies in no uncertain terms: "Parapsychologists must realize, therefore, that the only value that reports of such occurrences have is that they stimulate inventions of novel designs for rigid testing and that they can be used to derive testable predictions" (3).[9]

Thus, while many parapsychologists recognize a place for spontaneous case research, there are also some experimentalists who would probably like to refine the canon of parapsychology texts and methodologies, to free it from spontaneous case research, which often becomes fodder for the skeptics' cannons. In the main American textbook of parapsychology (Edge et al. 1986), spontaneous case research receives only one chapter, and some experimentalists would probably reduce this visibility even further. For example, in the address before the Parapsychological Association, "On the Representation of Psi Research to the Community of Established Science," the engineering professor Robert Jahn recommended that parapsychologists concentrate on "clean, conservative experiments," and his discussion did not even include consideration of the role of spontaneous case research (1983:11). Although experimentalists rarely take the additional step of labeling spontaneous case research "pseudoscience," they clearly mark it as less scientific than the experimental alternative.

In addition to expressing a preference for experimental parapsychology as the more scientific option, parapsychologists sometimes explain the difference between the two methods in temporal terms: the division results from an evolutionary development in the history of their discipline from its less scientific past of psychical research to its scientific present of experimental parapsychology, a progression which the title of Thouless's book expresses as moving "from anecdote to experiment" (1972). In this scheme, laboratory and experimental studies represent not only the more "scientific," but also the later, development. With a few exceptions – such as the psychiatrist Ian Stevenson (1987a), the editor Rhea White (1985), and the philosopher Stephen Braude (1986) – most contemporary psi researchers believe that the evidentiality of experiments is more "scientific" or "reliable" than that of spontaneous case studies or observations of mediumistic performances, and they view their preference as an expression of the historical progress of the methodology of the field.

If the relationship between the two parapsychologies is a hierarchical one, is it also gendered? Spontaneous case researchers study reports of psychic experiences that generally occur outside the laboratory, often at home. As a social space, the laboratory is outside the home, much like the workplace, which in traditional American culture is marked masculine. In addition, the laboratory is filled with equipment, as in a factory, garage, or workshop – that is, spaces that are all marked masculine in the culture.

Furthermore, the main feature of the laboratory – its equipment (with its material solidity and its domesticating function of measurement) – opposes that of paranormal phenomena, the immaterial and unquantified human faculties of ESP and psychokinesis. Once experimental parapsychologists coax psi into the lab, researchers can, as Francis Bacon said of nature, "conquer and subdue her" (cited in Keller 1985:36). They see themselves as able to "manipulate" variables and therefore to have the power to predict psi, control it, and give it laws that must be obeyed. The lab is where parapsychologists construct names for paranormal phenomena: sheep-goat effect, variance effect, salience effect, decline effect, etc. Like Adam naming the animals, when experimentalists give names to the paranormal, they can see themselves as making it orderly and law-abiding. Therefore, parapsychologists may think of the laboratory as a place where they *domesticate* the paranormal. For example, McConnell writes, "Despite great effort by a few investigators, it was fifty years before psi phenomena were partially domesticated for laboratory experimentation by J. B. Rhine at Duke University" (McConnell 1983b:71).

As a setting, the lab is therefore foreign to the paranormal; the paranormal comes into the lab from the disordered outside world, from the home and the emotional contexts of love and death. The place of the paranormal is in the home, since the paranormal is an affair primarily of the heart, of family ties, and frequently of mothers and daughters and women and children. When the paranormal is removed from its home in the domestic space and placed in the lab, parapsychologists say that psi is taken out of its "naturalistic" setting. In the process, parapsychology is marked as the cultural and the paranormal as the natural, while the laboratory becomes a space where they transmute nature (or supernature) into culture. However, when the paranormal comes into the laboratory, it finds itself constrained, as—to use Louisa Rhine's simile in her book *ESP in Life and Lab*—"a barefoot boy in boots" who feels "cramped and stylized" (1967:225). To make sure they do not cramp their paranormal phenomena, some parapsychologists have attempted to make the laboratory as comfortable and "homelike" as possible; disguise notwithstanding, the laboratory remains a space of order and control, of measurement and naming.

It should not be surprising that one prominent critic of laboratory research in contemporary parapsychology is a woman and a feminist. The editor Rhea White argued in her presidential address before the Parapsychological Association that experimental parapsychologists, like their skeptical critics, are "repressive about psi" (1985:178). They do not want to study paranormal phenomena unless they "can control the conditions" (178). She suggests instead that parapsychologists should begin with people's psychic experiences and try "to understand *their* language and what their *experiences mean to them*" (179; emphasis original). Rather than attempt to dominate and control psi in the laboratory, she urges parapsychologists to "let our data lead us" (179). As she puts it, "We hardly ever 'sit down like a child' before the data nature has given us" (179), and in a later article she argues even more explicitly that the experimental method of parapsychology has been a failure (1990).

Although in her presidential address White is not explicit about the connection with gender, her critique of the methodology of control and domestication is implicitly connected with feminist concerns. An alternative approach that focuses on listening to the subjects, interpreting the meaning of their experiences, and letting the data lead them to their conclusions are discursive strategies that other feminist scholars have connected with feminist or feminine approaches to methods of inquiry (see Harding 1986, Keller 1985). Furthermore, in a subsequent article, White connects her project with feminist and postmodern approaches to science (1991). What was in Louisa Rhine's writing an often implicit connection among gender, parapsychology, and the paranormal is now being transformed into a feminist critique of the project of experimental parapsychology. The gender polarities of experimental and spontaneous case research remain the same, but the meanings have shifted toward an explicit recognition of feminist critiques of science. Once again, then, the inheritors of the Rhinean legacy show both continuities and changes.

Skeptics

Skeptical Yin and Yang: Skeptics' Internal Others

In the previous chapter, I flagged the double quality of skeptical discourse by showing how there was a tension between "outlaw" heroes (hit men, dirty boxers) and more socially acceptable heroes (psi cops, citizens of the republic of science). To some extent, this tension also points to a division within skeptical discourse between the demystifying popularizer and the more erudite scientific or philosophical critic. These divisions also constitute a hierarchy, with the erudite critic seen as having the more sophisticated role.

In the essay "Debunking, Neutrality, and Skepticism in Science," which is the first chapter of Frazier's edited volume *Science Confronts the Paranormal*, Paul Kurtz outlines the skeptics' complicated, double strategy of what he terms "debunking" and "neutrality." Kurtz bases part of his discussion on an inherent paradox of skepticism. In philosophy, he notes, extreme skepticism can lead to solipsism, and likewise in science it can lead to "methodological anarchism" (1986:10). Kurtz argues that this form of universal skepticism can lead to an extreme "neutralism," for whom the exemplar appears to be the philosopher Paul Feyerabend, and the resulting discourse is "negative, self-defeating, and contradictory" (10). Because universal skepticism implies that one must doubt even one's own skepticism, he maintains that "the most meaningful form of skepticism is a selective one. . . . We cannot at the same time doubt all of our presuppositions, though we may in other contexts examine each in turn" (10). Kurtz therefore recognizes that skeptical discourse must be founded on some unexamined beliefs; otherwise, it cannot function at all. His argument suggests that at the heart of skeptical discourse is a kernel of irrationality, not unlike the field of irrationality skeptics see in the discourse of the paranormal. To borrow a gendered metaphor that is more common at the New Age side of the spectrum, there is a seed of yin within the skeptic's world of yang.[10]

Likewise, Kurtz also recognizes that the discourse of the paranormal may itself retain a small kernel of scientifically valid notions: "[I]f a paranormal claim is seriously proposed and if some effort is made to support it by responsible research methods, then it does warrant serious examination. I am not talking about antiscientific, religious, subjective, or emotive approaches to the paranormal, which abound, but efforts by serious inquirers to present hypotheses or conclusions based upon objective research" (8–9). Kurtz then specifies what might be called the yang in the sea of paranormal yin: parapsychology and "some aspects of recent UFO and astrological research" — and he argues that neutrality is the proper approach for these more scientific aspects of the paranormal (9). The term "neutrality" may be a misnomer, since as the chair of CSICOP Kurtz is not at all "neutral," and his term should probably be interpreted to mean that he advocates a more "measured" or "erudite" dismissal of claims of the paranormal — that is, one supported by arguments — rather than outright dismissal.

Kurtz goes on to caution against applying the "neutral" approach to "fortune telling, horoscopes, tarot cards, palmistry, fortune cookies, and other popular fields" (9). Regarding those practices, the humanist philosopher argues that a more suitable strategy is "debunking." He quotes Martin Gardner quoting H. L. Mencken that "one horse-laugh is worth a thousand syllogisms," and he adds, "Sometimes the best way to refute a claim is to show how foolish it is" (7). Kurtz defines the word "debunking" by recourse to a list from *Roget's Thesaurus*, but Martin Gardner gives perhaps a better etymology and apology for the word that he describes as a pejorative term used "when defenders of pseudoscience want to put down critics" (1988: 65). In the nineteenth century, a U.S. Congressman became known for his speeches for Buncombe County, North Carolina. The word then was shortened to "bunkum" and "bunk," and it came to mean "political claptrap." Gardner concludes: "In today's dictionaries bunk is defined as nonsense, and debunking as the exposing of sham or falsehood. Who could object to that? Nevertheless, it may be that debunk is becoming a term of reproach, like the old word muckraker, now replaced by the more dignified 'investigative reporter'" (65).

Gardner's comment reveals a sense that debunking may be a somewhat tainted activity. In straying from the straight-and-narrow path of "serious" science, it slips off into other discourses that are marshaled to serve the interests of science. Likewise, Kurtz warns that debunking "should not be abused" and that it must be rooted in "the facts" (1986:7). He goes on to state, "One horse-laugh in its appropriate setting may be worth a dozen scholarly papers, though never at the price of the latter" (8). Nevertheless, he believes the horse-laugh is a useful strategy, particularly where public credulity is concerned. Not only does the large number of paranormal claims make strict neutrality and careful investigations impossible for all cases, but debunking may also be a more effective tool for disabusing the public of its superstitions.

Kurtz therefore articulates a division within skepticism between what I would characterize as a scientific means of dealing with what the skeptics view as pseudoscience and a relatively less scientific — or even "pseudoscientific" — means. Skepticism, which serves to articulate and clarify the boundary between science and nonscience, therefore reinscribes this bound-ary — in the relative terms described here — within its own discourse. The division within skepticism becomes the internal reflection of the external reality: skeptics see the discourse of the paranormal as itself split into more or less credible claims, and the external reality is reproduced in their double strategy of neutrality and debunking.

The division between neutrality and debunking may also correspond to the social positions of the different skeptics or their intended readers, and as a result the dimension of social hierarchy may come into play. Note that Kurtz is a university professor, as are Ray Hyman and Stephen Toulmin, who also contributed essays to Frazier's volume and adopted a stance that could be characterized as "neutrality" in Kurtz's terms. In contrast, debunking tends to appear among writers and magicians, such as Kendrick Frazier, Martin Gardner, and James Randi. To venture a hypothesis, the discursive divisions among skeptics may also correspond in some rough way to internal divisions marked by education, occupation, or even class. However, there are cases of professors who write popular texts and journalists who write erudite ones, so a second dimension crosscuts the first: the perceived audience. Skeptics writing for the general public will adopt a more popular style, just as when they perceive their reader to be an experimental parapsychologist, their style will tend to be more erudite. The question of the relations between social hierarchy and discursive styles is therefore very complicated, but a defensible gloss is that neutrality is a relatively more erudite discourse, whereas debunking is more popular.

Is this hierarchy also gendered in some sense? In the New Age movement, the feminine and female are more clearly marked in the popular discourse of goddess religion, just as in parapsychology the "less scientific" method of spontaneous case research is also marked as feminine and female. If this pattern held up for skeptics, we would expect that debunking would be marked as feminine. However, the opposite is more the case. Debunking is a very masculine, even macho, art: it represents to skeptics a form of intercourse in which they can roll up their sleeves and have a good fight as hit men, psi cops, boxers, or knights who assault (violate) the castle of pseudoscience. Could it be that in some sense both science and the paranormal are feminine to skeptics? It is almost as if they see science as the defenseless virgin and the paranormal Other as the threatening whore.

Female, Male, Supernature, Science

Whether skeptics are debunking or merely attacking on an intellectual plane, the tone of their writing in general reflects a confrontational, even aggressive, approach to the paranormal Other. Thus, notwithstanding the existence of an internal Other, on the whole skepticism is a very masculine discourse. It is also a predominantly male movement: although there are women skeptics, the leaders and the vast majority are men. The partial list of over fifty CSICOP fellows, published in the winter 1991 issue of the *Skeptical Inquirer,* includes only four members who are, from their names, obviously women (Susan Blackmore, Dorothy Nelkin, Eugenie Scott, and Carol Tavris).[11] Furthermore, in a report about a CSICOP meeting, a journalist writing for *New Science* noted: "During a quizzing of the executive board, a questioner pointed out that, if the annual meeting were any guide, skeptics in the U.S. were slightly geriatric and were predominantly white and male. The audience and board agreed" (Anderson 1987:51).[12]

In contrast, many of the leading figures of the New Age movement are women, including most of the authors whom I have discussed: Lynn Andrews, Marilyn Ferguson, Shirley MacLaine, Ruth Montgomery, Katrina Raphaell, and Diane Stein.[13] True, there are many men in the New Age movement, and men number among its prominent figures (such as José Argüelles, Ram Dass, and David Spangler); however, women play a much more prominent role in the New Age movement than they do in organized skepticism. The image of yin and yang, discussed above to describe the opposition between the discourses of skeptical and paranormal belief, is relevant once again, this time as a gendered opposition.

Unlike both skepticism and the New Age movement, parapsychology has been dominated by men, but it also has included women among its leading figures, ranging from Eleanor Sidgwick and Louisa Rhine in the past to Margaret Anderson, Eileen and Lisette Coly, Anita Gregory, Renée Haynes, Betty Humphrey, Diana Robinson, Marilyn Schlitz, Gertrude Schmeidler, Debra Weiner, Rhea White, Nancy Zingrone, and others in more recent years (see Alvarado 1990; Zingrone 1988). The number of women participants is neither as outstanding as in the New Age movement nor as negligible as among the skeptics, so again parapsychology can be situated between these other two communities.

The pattern of sex does not mean, however, that I can automatically characterize the "gender" of skeptical discourse as masculine. Nevertheless, given the pattern in the breakdown of sexes between skeptics and New Agers, with parapsychology located somewhere in between, it makes sense to investigate skepticism as gendered discourse.

Consider, for example, some skeptics' representations of women. The reader familiar with early psychical research may remember the famous adage of Frank Podmore, the skeptical psychical researcher (in those days the boundaries were more fluid) who argued that poltergeists were little more than the work of "naughty little girls" (1898–9:135). In an investigation of the 1984 Columbus poltergeist case, which centered around a fourteen-year-old girl living in a home with her foster parents, James Randi adopted more or less the same point of view. In his article on the case, Randi tells us little about the girl herself, and instead he focuses on how she probably faked the phenomena of flying objects, such as the much sensationalized attack of the "killer" telephones. Randi presents an unfavorable view of the press, the parapsychologist who investigated the case (the psychologist William Roll), and the parents, all of whom emerge as gullible perhaps to the point of fault. As for the girl and her life, we learn only that she was hyperactive and emotionally disturbed, so much so that she had been taken out of school to be privately tutored, and that she wanted to trace her true parents against the wishes of her foster parents (Randi 1986:145). Randi concludes by suggesting that the girl faked the poltergeist phenomena because she wanted to use the media exposure to trace her true parents, against the wishes of her foster parents. In his words, she was "was a girl looking for attention. And she got it."[14]

The portrayal of the female paranormal Other as manipulative and her victims as gullible reappears in another of Randi's articles: "The Will to Believe," published in his book *Flim-Flam! Psychics, Unicorns, ESP, and Other Delusions* (1982). In an exposé of a "doctor of magneto-therapy" named Sue Wallace, Randi describes how he listened to one of her clients, also a woman, "rave on" about a diagnostic session with Ms. Wallace (1982: 205). He then recaps the session from his own viewpoint based on his notes, and he proceeds to describe a conversation between Ms. Wallace and one of her woman clients, in which Ms. Wallace apparently tried to find a way out of a bad diagnosis by insisting to her client that the doctors were wrong (206). Randi then brought Ms. Wallace back to his New York office, where he states that he tested her with a double-blind experiment. He notes that during the period when she was waiting while he was testing others, she was "out in the hall charming some of the young men from my office" (209). In short, the women in this article appear as gullible or manipulative, or both.

Similar representations emerge in an attempt by skeptical psychologists to put together a profile of the typical occult believer. Leonard Zusne argues that a review of the literature suggests that the occult believer is "female, unintelligent, misinformed, poorly educated, authoritarian, and emotionally unstable."[15] The list of negative traits associated with the female is cause for suspicion, and it is highly reminiscent of masculinist discourse that runs throughout the history of Western science. One might argue that although the list associates the female with a series of negative attributes, it does not necessarily imply that Zusne and his colleague Jones are sexist; instead, one could further argue that they are providing an accurate description of the personality traits and demographic characteristics of a "typical" paranormal believer, and the sexism lies in the general culture, not in their portrayal.

In general, skeptics could argue that when Randi and his colleagues point the finger at charlatans, cranks, and quacks (as Martin Gardner would call them), it is not their fault that women number prominently among the ranks of undesirables. Still, it is worth probing the implicit cultural meanings in these constructions of the debunked female Other. Even if we agree that the client is gullible and the healer manipulative, we might go on to ask what permits the gullibility and manipulation to work. Stupidity and immorality are possible answers, but they also direct attention away from other potential interpretations, such as the gender politics inherent in a conversation between two women who employ the idiom of the paranormal to contest the authority of a still largely male medical profession.

Likewise, turning to poltergeists, in my own, more anthropologically oriented investigations of some Brazilian cases (all of which involved women), I diverge from both skeptical and parapsychological approaches by bracketing the issue of evidence for the paranormal and by probing instead questions of gender, psychocultural meaning, and domestic politics. I suggest that there are more cases in which poltergeist children, particularly young women, are victims of domestic violence or abuse (1990). Even where domestic violence or abuse is not evident, the perceived poltergeist attack may still alter domestic power relations or serve to empower the apparent victim of the poltergeist. Therefore, an alternative might be to move beyond an accusation that a fourteen-year-old girl may be troubled or manipulative, and instead to ask in what ways she has been a victim and how her desire for attention, if indeed that is her motivation, reflects a cry for help in a situation that evidently is not meeting her needs. In short, in the cases of poltergeist victims, as in those of women healers and clients, the question of paranormal powers may be closely linked to domestic or sexual power and politics. Those are readings that the idiom of skepticism, at least in its current formulation, precludes.

Skeptical discourse also occasionally reveals gender-laden images that reflect an even more overtly masculinist viewpoint. To return to the early skeptical study by the psychologist Joseph Jastrow, the occult is associated with a particular kind of temperament marked for gender: "The man or woman who flies to the things not dreamt of in our philosophy quite com-

monly does not understand the things which our philosophy very credit-
ably explains. The two types of mind are different, and, as Professor
James expresses it, 'the scientific-academic mind and the feminine-mystical
mind shy from each other's facts just as they fly from each other's temper
and spirit'" (1900:42–43). Note that Jastrow adds an "or woman" during
a period when gender-free writing was not part of the intellectual agenda;
obviously he sees some connection between the female and paranormal
belief. Furthermore, his citation of William James, with whom Jastrow dis-
agreed on many issues, suggests that this perception is shared with the
leading American supporter of psychical research of his time. Jastrow then
develops the meaning of the dichotomy when he equates scientific rationality with adulthood and the maturity of the race. "For many this development remains stunted or arrested," he comments, "and they continue as
children of a larger growth" (43). Women, children, and other races all
suffer in this formulation of occult belief.

   An example from skeptics today is Kendrick Frazier's discussion of the
differences between science and pseudoscience, where he defines the scientific attitude as a search to understand nature that must always face new
revisions. In science, he states, "There is a strong, no-holds-barred, let-
the-facts-fall-where-they-may attitude," whereas "[p]seudoscience clings
emotionally to comforting ideas long after they've been shown to be most
likely wrong" (1981:ix). Here images that in Western cultures are traditionally associated with masculinity—strength, fighting, dispassion—
contrast with images associated with femininity—clinging (as a child to
a mother's apron), emotionality, and comforting. Isaac Asimov writes, "Inspect every piece of pseudoscience and you will find a security blanket,
a thumb to suck, a skirt to hold" (1985–86:212). To skeptics, the whole
field of the paranormal represents not only the disordered, the emotional,
and the irrational, but also something associated with the protected and
nurturing world of the mother and child in the home. In contrast, skepticism and science are not for women, children, or wimps: they epitomize
objectivity, rationality, and the adult world of harsh realities and battles
for survival.

   That skepticism is both a discourse of men and a masculinist discourse
receives some confirmation from the parapsychologist and engineer George
Hansen, who stated in a paper presented before the Parapsychological
Association that "CSICOP and its local affiliates have been perceived as
rather insecure and macho" (1987:322; see also Hansen 1992:28–30). He
goes on to state that in an article titled "Where Are the Women?" and published in the March 1985 issue of Basis, the Bay Area Skeptics' newsletter,
the skeptic Mary Coulman said that at the local skeptics' meetings there

were frequently only two or three women present, and sometimes she was the only woman in meetings of sixty to seventy men. Hansen adds: "In the September issue, Elissa Pratt-Lowe wrote a letter and noted, 'Finally, I think another aspect of organized skepticism that may deter women is the aggressive, "macho" attitudes held by some of the (male) participants'" (Hansen 1987:322; see also 1992:29). The martial imagery that skeptics so frequently invoke may be a masculine way of conceptualizing the entire relationship. Indeed, the "never-ending battle" between skeptics and their paranormal Other has overtones of what the anthropologist I. M. Lewis (1971), in his study of women and peripheral possession cults, has referred to as the age-old "sex war."

One finds similar aggressive, "macho" attitudes in a skeptical, backlash book on women and feminism, Nicholas Davidson's *The Failure of Feminism*. Although Davidson is not listed as a fellow of or consultant to CSICOP, his book was published by Prometheus Books, and at the time I was researching *Science in the New Age*, it was the only book available from that publisher that explicitly dealt with feminism.[16] Davidson maintains a virulently antifeminist stance that, although perhaps not representative of skeptics as a whole, defines a "skeptical" approach to feminism and the women's movement. The book ends with a call to replace feminism with a new "familism"—in which women abandon their careers with "dignity" and return to the home by "choice"—and it adds an appendix that gives lessons to men on "countering feminist verbal tactics," since feminists "are not interested in intellectual speculations or in acquiring new knowledge" (340, 343). That would, one would presume, leave the business of science—and skepticism—to men.

Conclusions

The question of gender in the paraculture is complex because it apparently brings out differences among the three discursive communities rather than similarities. Still, the differences reveal how the three communities provide complementary perspectives within a shared set of assumptions and meanings. To understand the latter, it is helpful to review first some aspects of the now extensive literature on gender and science.

Gender metaphors occur in modern science as early as in the writings of Francis Bacon, who constructed "natural philosophy" as a masculine enterprise that penetrated the mystery of a female nature (Merchant 1980). The neurophysiologist Ruth Bleier described the relationship succinctly: "Woman as a reproductive being embodied the natural, the disordered, the emotional, the irrational; man as thinker epitomized objectivity, rationality, culture, and control" (1986:6; see also Keller 1985:33ff.). The feminist critique of Bacon invokes a series of cultural meanings for Western scientific discourse that has some parallels to anthropologists' finding that the equation of "female is to male as nature is to culture" occurs in many cultures (see Ardner 1972; Ortner 1974). Although the universality of this equation may be debated (see MacCormack and Strathern 1980), one does not have to assume universality to maintain the narrow argument that the equation adequately depicts gender notions in most Western thinking, particularly in the context of scientific boundary-work: science is often represented as male, whereas nature is correspondingly female (see Jordanova 1980, 1989).

In the world of discourse on the paranormal and alternative spirituality, the problem of gender representations is complicated by the fact that nature is replaced by the paranormal ("supernature") and the spiritual. The question then emerges: does the paranormal/spiritual belong more to the side of nature or to that of culture? In the essay "Is Female to Male as Nature Is to Culture?" the anthropologist Sherry Ortner offers one point of departure when she argues that because the female is a mediating category, it is often viewed as ambiguous and sometimes polarized. For example, one frequently encounters "subversive feminine symbols" such as witches and castrating mothers as well as "feminine symbols of transcendence" such as mother goddesses (Ortner 1974:86). Although Ortner's point is directed more toward the double meaning of "subversive feminine symbols," her example suggests that the paranormal may be opposed to the cultural and therefore marked as feminine in much the same way that nature is marked as feminine.[17] Thus, her argument is consistent with my general argument that the paranormal Other is characterized as the feminine: the New Agers' goddess, the parapsychologists' psi phenomena, and the skeptic's paranormal Other.

Is there also some general evidence that supports my argument that the division between experimental parapsychology and spontaneous case research is gendered? One might expect the opposite: that the "natural" sciences would be associated with the feminine (because nature is frequently associated with the female, particularly in Western cultures), and the humanities (linked to the human and therefore to culture) would likewise be associated with the masculine. However, the terms are in fact reversed. As scholars such as the anthropologist Clifford Geertz (1971:ix) and the STS researcher Evelyn Fox Keller (1985:77) have argued, the natural sciences are masculine as the humanities are feminine, a division that is still obvious on most American college campuses in the relative sex ratios in science and humanities departments.[18] Furthermore, as the geneticist

Marion Namenwirth notes, in Western society the values associated with masculinity—for example, being "intelligent, logical, objective, independent, forceful, risk-taking, and courageous" (1986: 19)—tend to correspond with those associated with what are sometimes called the "hard" sciences, as opposed to the "soft" fields of the human sciences and the arts. Likewise, Keller notes that "scientists are perceived as not only more masculine than artists but simultaneously as less sexual" (1985:78). It is therefore reasonable to argue that experimental parapsychology, as a "hard" science, is culturally masculine relative to spontaneous case research, with its frequently qualitative, "soft science" methods.[19]

Distinctions marked for hierarchy and gender therefore play themselves out at a variety of levels. Among the cultures, skepticism is relatively masculine, the New Age movement relatively feminine, and parapsychology somewhere in between. Within the cultures, the internal Others may be marked for gender as well. The gendering of internal Others is clearest in parapsychology, but there are suggestions of it in the other two cultures. Within the New Age movement, goddess religion is much more explicitly feminist and women-oriented than Ferguson's Aquarian conspiracy, and in some ways the martial metaphors of debunking mark it as more masculinist than the erudite critiques that Kurtz calls "neutrality." Finally, each culture conceives of its paranormal Other (the skeptics' world of the paranormal, the parapsychologists' paranormal phenomena, and the New Agers' goddess) as feminine. All sides agree that orthodox science and skepticism, no matter how they view it, is a relatively more masculine category.[20]

Our Bodies, Our Souls: A Coda

The three communities therefore construct a gendered world that makes sense in terms of what we know about gender, science, religion, and Western culture. But as they build a disputed paraculture with its undisputed doxa (science is to masculine as the paranormal is to feminine), they also remake some of the relationships in these cultural domains. Perhaps nowhere are the transformations more clear than in their construction of what has emerged as a crucial site for cultural studies of gender and power: the body. I therefore end this chapter with a round-robin coda on the reconstruction of the body in the paraculture.

Even a superficial sample of New Age books, magazines, therapies, and so on reveals how far they have come from the puritanical cultural legacy that casts suspicion on "the old Crazy Rotten house of the body" (cited in Bellah 1975:67). Circling back now to the opening lines of Diane Stein's *The Women's Spirituality Book*, the feminist goddess worshippers seem to sanction the sensuality and diversity of their bodies of "all ages, sizes, colors, [and] styles" (1986:xiii). The women use their bodies and their clothing — casual blue jeans or "skyclad" (naked), which is "natural and accepted here" (xiii) — to inscribe an antipatriarchal ethic, one which rejects a standard of female beauty against which all women may be measured and judged. They celebrate the female body as something "natural," not in the sense of nature as opposed to culture, but in the sense of the good and the spiritual as opposed to the evil and the material. By its very physical nature part of the material order, the body is transubstantiated into an icon of new spiritual order.

More generally, New Agers tend to emphasize the sensuality of the body as a means of spiritual transformation, a rather unpuritanical approach to spirituality that is probably a legacy of the sixties-era sexual revolution. For example, Shirley MacLaine writes how she had neglected her body for fifteen years, but after this long hiatus she began to pay more attention to her body because "the process of connecting with my body put me more in touch with the real me inside of that body" (1983:4–5). Her comment implies again the latent dualism of Western constructions of the body: a division between the "real me," which is spiritual or psychological but not physical, and the body. Although MacLaine's discussion here does not go beyond Western dualism and American puritanism, she does establish a way out. By paying attention to the body and feeding the sensual needs of the body, she moves toward a closer equation of self and body.

Michel Foucault has described the development of techniques for disciplining and controlling the body in the nineteenth century (1979); in contrast, some of the twentieth-century New Age writers describe a parallel but inverted set of techniques for liberating the body and, through it, the mind or soul. At the more rationalized end of the spectrum of New Age discourse, the techniques are part of holistic medicine, which Marilyn Ferguson believes has made possible "the rediscovery of bodymind" (1987: 424). In *The Aquarian Conspiracy*, she discusses how "over the years our bodies become walking autobiographies, telling friends and strangers alike of the minor and major stresses of our lives" (255). To break the cycle of embodied autobiographies, she names a whole series of "bodywork" therapies that act directly on the body to "affect the whole bodymind loop," from Rolfing and structural integration to orthomolecular psychiatry (a megavitamin therapy) and acupuncture and acupressure (255–56).

In different ways, then, the Aquarian Age links the mind's true liberation to a renewed sensuality and appreciation of the body. Liberation can come under the sign of dancing skyclad goddess worshippers, a movie star jogging on the beach of Malibu or taking a sauna in the Peruvian Andes, or middle-class consumers experimenting with the new psychotechnologies of holistic medicine and brain-mind gyms (see Dumit 1991, Ross 1991). The common thread in these diverse experiences is that the road to spiritual knowledge inverts the path of Western, monastic asceticism, which denies, disciplines, and even tortures the body in order to awaken higher awareness. It is true that the New Age movement is diverse enough to include more classical forms of awakening awareness, particularly Eastern meditation techniques, but these techniques become the ascetic counterpoints of a broader cultural system that tends to celebrate the sensuality of the body. Furthermore, even among adepts of Eastern meditation techniques there may be an elective affinity toward the more corporeal side of these spiritual disciplines, such as hatha yoga, Buddhist walking meditation, tai chi, and tantrism.

In contrast to the sensuous, accepting attitude toward the body, experimental parapsychology adopts a relatively puritanical attitude. Parapsychologists have developed a rich array of experimental protocols that operate on the body in ways which they believe make it more "psi-conducive." For example, in a review of experimental research on "psi and internal attention states," the parapsychologist Charles Honorton (1977) includes studies of meditation, hypnosis, and induced muscular relaxation, all of which focus on a quieted body or one in which there is an optimal combination of relaxation and arousal.

Perhaps the best known of the corporeal techniques of parapsychology is the Ganzfeld procedure. A number of ostensibly successful experiments in different laboratories has even led parapsychologists to ask if this protocol might be the repeatable experiment for which the discipline has been searching, but skeptics have also been quick to challenge such claims.[21] The theory behind the Ganzfeld protocol is intuitively appealing: by reducing external "noise" or sensory input, attention is more readily focused on possible extrasensory sources of information. Honorton, who developed the protocol, describes Patanjali's *Yoga Sutras* as his source of inspiration (Honorton 1977). The protocol for inducing a light altered state of consciousness works by placing the subject in a relaxed position with modest instruments blocking hearing and sight: body covered, if necessary, by a blanket; headphones hissing white noise into the ears; half a ping-pong ball taped over each eye; and a red light shining in the face to create a homogeneous visual field.

The picture of the Ganzfeld technique, if somewhat monstrous, is also more than the "sliced-ping-pong-balls-over-the-eyes bit" that meets the skeptics' eyes (Gardner 1981b:302). Viewed culturally, the Ganzfeld also encodes the oppositional nature of mind and body in the culture of parapsychology: the psi-conducive body erases the physical body with white noise and sensory deprivation. One might argue that this interpretation overstates the case because parapsychologists believe that quieting the body is appropriate for receiving information, for extrasensory perception, although it is not necessarily appropriate for the psychokinesis mode. However, even for the latter mode, experimental subjects generally sit in quieted positions and attempt to concentrate or relax. There are few, if any, experiments that attempt to measure psychokinesis during, say, jogging, dancing, saunas, massage, or the four F's: feeding, fleeing, fearing, and — what some of the more tantric corners of New Age thought would lead one to expect as a very promising protocol for a psychokinesis experiment — fornication.

Regarding a second area of parapsychology that involves an explicit construction of mind/body relations, research on the out-of-body experience, again parapsychologists tend to adopt a relatively ascetic approach to the body. For example, recall how Janet Lee Mitchell imagines the body as a machine (an automobile), and the self-freed-from-the-body as the outdoors and nature (1981:128). Even if the out-of-body experience is ultimately only a kind of lucid dream or vivid hallucination (as most parapsychologists believe), the subjective experience provides a narrative in which mental or spiritual liberation is linked to a denial of or escape from corporeal experience. Mitchell's strict dualism also suggests a continuity with J. B. Rhine, in contrast with the New Age notion of "bodymind." However, Mitchell shares with the New Agers a concern with psychological growth and even spiritual liberation. Both therefore articulate a very American value — freedom and self-realization — but they do it in opposing ways: New Age sensuality versus parapsychological asceticism.

Differences notwithstanding, at least some parapsychologists assume that changes in the body (either via Ganzfeld protocols or out-of-body induction techniques) can help bring about changes in the mind, so they share with New Agers a concern with relations between mind and body. What about the skeptics? Alas, they have not developed a psychocorporeal technology; after all, they are skeptics. Although skeptics have published a thorough critique of holistic medicine (Stalker and Glymour 1985) that challenges the mind/body connections that both parapsychology and the New Age movement seek to affirm in their different ways, the critique does not really constitute a third point of comparison. When skeptics wax eloquently, it is not likely to be about techniques, embodied or disembodied, for achieving extrasensory knowledge or spiritual liberation. Isaac Asimov, for example, explained his vision of mind/body relations through reference to the castle analogy. (Asimov apparently had a proclivity for castle metaphors. As we have already seen, he described "pseudoscience" as the "castle" that Randi assailed, 1982:xv.) In a critique of the possibility of life after death, the science fiction writer argues that life is more than just an ensemble of tissues and molecules; the tissues and molecules must be ordered in a "complex arrangement" (1981:157). If the arrangement is upset or destructured, the "body dies." To make his point, he compares the body to a "medieval castle," with its intricate structure of towers and crenellations that is ultimately made up of "thousands of small bricks" (157). He then imagines death in the form of a "giant hand" that knocks down the castle. The bricks are still there, in a pile of rubble. "But where is the castle?" he asks. The castle, he argues, "existed only in the arrangement of the bricks and when the arrangement is destroyed the castle is gone" (158). So it is for the mind, which, as the skeptic would argue, disappears when the body dies.

Nevertheless, the contrast between parapsychological and New Age formulas for disciplining the body is stark enough to warrant asking if their different psychotechnologies also coincide with conceptions of gender. To the extent that Western cultures associate control with masculinity, parapsychology corresponds to a more traditional notion of mind/body relations that encodes the domination of the mind (culture) over body (nature) through a technology of corporeal discipline. In the process, this drama plays out a set of symbolic oppositions — mind/body, culture/nature, and, implicitly, masculine/feminine — that encodes the predominance of the first term and therefore, implicitly, the patriarchal order. In contrast, the New Age emphasis on the needs and desires of the body as "natural" aligns it to some extent with the nature side of a nature/culture dichotomy, a dichotomy which it simultaneously attempts to supercede with terms like "bodymind." Two contrasting images emerge from this comparison: the naked, female bodies of the earth goddesses and "womyn" in the glen as portrayed in *The Women's Spirituality Book*; and the covered, unmarked bodies of the Ganzfeld percipients, in which the body of the percipient is hidden, or the body of the out-of-body voyager, who simply leaves it behind.

6

Skepticism and the Paranormal in Hollywood

T H E present chapter moves into a slightly different arena: Hollywood films, which represent and comment on the dialogue among the various defenders and debunkers of the paranormal. It would be tedious and probably re- dundant to discuss all Hollywood films in the paranormal genre — in 1990 alone at least seven ghost movies were released — so I focus instead on a few of the best known and most popular movies of the 1970s and 1980s that portray ghosts, haunted houses, or possession. By examining these movies culturally, I provide a check on the analysis presented in the pre- ceding chapters. If the by-now-familiar aspects of American paranormal culture turn out not to be evident in the Hollywood movies, then my argu- ment would be less compelling. Instead, I shall show how Hollywood is also part of this emergent paraculture.[1]

Hollywood in the Context of American Culture

By no means a static genre frozen in time, Hollywood horror movies have undoubtedly changed dramatically from the old horror and science fiction movies of the 1950s and early 1960s, when the memory of World War II was still vividly etched on the popular imagination and the threat of a fascist invasion had shifted to that of the communist menace. The popu- lar concern with invasion helped make audiences readily receptive to the numerous portrayals of invading aliens, monsters, or, in the case of *Night of the Living Dead*, zombie-like ghouls (see Walker 1986: chs. 7, 8). While invasion at this larger, societal level does occur in some of the more recent Hollywood movies (as in *Ghostbusters* or the remakes of *King Kong* and *Invasion of the Body Snatchers*), the theme of invasion of the postdétente (and now post–cold war) period is likely to be restricted to the domestic level, such as the household or the summer camp. As the cold war slowly eroded and space exploration became more routinized, Hollywood's horror themes have shifted away from the hysteria of national invasions by Nazis, communists, and extraterrestrials to the more proximate fear of domestic invasion, perhaps reflecting increased concern with street crime and domestic security in an era of economic decline.

The transitions of the horror and science fiction genres are therefore undeniable, as is what might be called the "Spielberg" effect: the sanitization of extraterrestrials and ghosts from the negative, horrific Other to the harmless merely exotic Other. Certainly the difference between the ghosts of *The Haunting* (1963), a movie discussed at the end of this chapter, and the ghost of *Always* (1989, directed by Steven Spielberg), is, even literally, one of night and day. Whereas the ghosts of *The Haunting* are unseen, occult forces that come to life at night and threaten to swallow up this world, the ghost of *Always* is the protagonist Peter Sandich (Richard Dreyfus), a human who has been killed. After death, Sandich finds himself not in some ghoulish netherworld but in a brightly lit heaven, remarkably similar to the forested glens of New Age relaxation tapes, where he chats with a benevolent, spiritual, New Agish earth mother played by Audrey Hepburn. She explains to the former pilot that his fate is to return to this world, not to haunt the living but instead to provide them with inspiration, to serve as a guardian spirit in a task that will allow him to develop spiritually by "letting go" of his earthbound tie to his former girlfriend Dorinda (Holly Hunter). The ghost of *Always*, then, is a very human figure who, like his counterparts in the New Age movement, is engaged in a spiritual odyssey.

Much the same is true for the transformation of extraterrestrials over the last twenty years. In *ET* and *Close Encounters*, the subhuman invaders of previous generations have been transformed into higher life forms. The "there and then" of the Other is no longer backward or atavistic but instead an exotic higher civilization, not unlike the Atlanteans, Incas, or Mayans of New Age lore. Furthermore, in these more recent extraterrestrial movies the official powers – the government and the scientists – now pattern their contact with the Other on the cultural forms of top-secret diplomacy, not unlike secret missions to China, rather than on the older rites of national security and defense.

Like the ghost of *Always*, the extraterrestrials of more recent movies bring with them promises of rejuvenation, redemption, and rebirth. The theme is perhaps most clearly articulated in *Cocoon* (1985, directed by Ron Howard), which develops the idea of literal rejuvenation that Spielberg had explored two years earlier in an episode of "The Twilight Zone" (1983, directed by John Landis and starring Scatman Crothers). In this redemptive vision, the other world is a source of wonder and revelation rather than of fear. The transition in movie mythology is comparable to the change in the popular imagination and bookstore labels from the dark world of the "occult," with its emphasis on Faustian forces and magical powers, to the bright light of the New Age, with its emphasis on spirituality and self-development. Even when the films are comedic, as in *Beetlejuice* or *Ghostbusters*, Hollywood's paranormal seems somewhat less Other, and often much less scary.

That is, of course, one way to read Hollywood's construction of the paranormal in historical and cultural terms, and the reading has the benefit of recognizing a changed thematics that might be tied to routinized space exploration, eased East-West tensions, an increasingly globalized economy, and, to return to the question of postmodernism raised in the second chapter, the culture (or multicultures) of a globalized "late capitalism." While this domestication-of-the-paranormal reading certainly has its truth, I wish to tack here in a different direction, one which finds a paranormal Other that is still threatening, still ostensibly antisocial, and consequently still a "horror." In exploring this more savage paranormal, it is easier to locate a critical discourse, one in which the powers of official science and official government do not embrace the paranormal Other—as in the final scene of *Close Encounters*—but instead deny it, fight it, and are often defeated by it. Thus, Hollywood's horrific, paranormal Other combines some of the qualities of both the skeptics' and New Agers' paranormal Other. As for the skeptics, the Hollywood paranormal Other is negative and evil, but as for the New Agers, it is endowed with true paranormal powers that are located in an exotic there and then.

As dramas about the threat posed by the paranormal Other, Hollywood movies are also morality tales with heroic protagonists. We learn that the official forces of science and society—usually marked as skeptical and male—do not have the power to battle the evil, paranormal Other. In their place emerge paranormal heroes, often somewhat marginalized or exotic figures not unlike the new Agers' shamans, Atlanteans, and mediums. These paranormal heroes must save the family and society in a double battle against both the evil, paranormal Other and the skeptical forces of official science and society. In the process, the paranormal heroes play leading roles in movies that also serve as popular social commentary on gender, class, ethnicity, power, and hierarchy.

The Power of Possession: *The Exorcist* as Cultural Drama

The Exorcist (1973 directed by William Friedkin) is the quintessential horror movie of the 1970s and 1980s, even if its technology now seems out of date in the rapidly changing world of computer-generated special effects.[2] The film begins by portraying the discovery of a mysterious icon uncovered during an archeological dig in northern Iraq. The setting locates the paranormal Other in a spatiotemporal logic of maximal distance: the other side of the planet; the most ancient of civilizations; and even, to return to the imagery of depth encountered in Louisa Rhine's mining metaphors, a site hidden beneath the earth. Thus, the identification of the paranormal Other with exotic spaces and times — a consistent theme in the discourse of skeptics, parapsychologists, and New Agers — is continued in the spatio-temporal code of this Hollywood movie. To anticipate my argument some-what, in the "Poltergeist" series the source of the paranormal energy is at first a graveyard and then a nineteenth-century catacomb hidden deep be-neath the surface of the earth; in the *Amityville Horror* series, it is Salem witches or an ancient Indian burial ground, accessible through a deep hole in the floor of the house's basement; and in *Ghostbusters II*, the source of the paranormal slime is an abandoned subway, again located deep be-low the big city. In contrast with the serious and romantic alchemy of Louisa Rhine, the abandoned subway with its river of slime is comedic and gro-tesque, but both are located deep beneath the surface of the earth, and therefore "occult" in the original sense of the word: hidden.

The Exorcist also inscribes paranormal culture by dramatizing a transi-tion across discursive boundaries, from what I call the "skeptical baseline" of the beginning of the movie to the paranormal world that encompasses all secular and skeptical discourse at the movie's end. The transition is, in many movies, a gradual process that, like hypnotic induction, helps the viewer gradually to achieve and then deepen the willing suspension of dis-belief required to experience the effects of horror and the uncanny. In *The Exorcist*, the skeptical baseline is established by portraying the mother, Chris MacNeil (Ellen Burstyn), as engaged in a series of this-worldly ac-tivities: she works as an actress who is being filmed at a political demon-stration, and later she goes home to an apparently ordinary household to be with her children. She is also a woman head of household (Chris's estranged husband is away in Europe). Perhaps for the early 1970s this situation may be interpreted as a sign of weakness that makes the home vulnerable to demonic infestation, but it is also a sign of Chris's indepen-dent, progressive, and secular position in life and therefore one more marker of the movie's skeptical baseline.

The voice of the skeptic, then, is first sounded through a woman, a de-velopment that my discussion of gender in the previous chapter would not lead us to expect. However, Chris is a woman with a career, and she is also the head of the household; thus, in some ways (and perhaps some-what more anomalous for 1973 than it would be twenty years later) she plays a role generally marked as masculine. When the first signs of the possession appear, Chris seizes upon a naturalistic explanation — rats in the attic — but when the bed of her daughter Regan (Linda Blair) begins to shake, Chris decides to seek help. The trajectory of help-seeking behavior sketches out a continuum from the scientific to the spiritual, with several mediating categories. At first, the neurologists diagnose Regan with temporal lobe seizures, but after they run a series of painful tests with the most modern equipment, they admit they cannot find anything wrong. Several seizures later, the doctors give up and recommend a psychiatrist, who hypnotizes Regan and calls for the person inside of Regan, and the paranormal Other — the devil — promptly appears and dispenses with the psychiatrist. The next character is the detective Lieutenant Kinderman (Lee Cobb), who now broaches the possibility that there may be some kind of connection between the desecration of the local Catholic church and the murder of Burke Dennings (Jack MacGowran), Chris's boyfriend who had been watching Regan but was found dead on the sidewalk outside their home.

Thus, a series of transitions takes place as the skeptical, materialistic explanations gradually shift toward paranormal and otherworldly discourse. The underlying commonality of the etiologies — neurological disease, psychiatric condition, satanic murderer — is a construction of the paranormal Other in an idiom of pathology. In suggesting that there may be some kind of Satanic murderer on the loose, the detective opens up the possibility of otherworldly explanations, although his explanation remains this-worldly. He makes his suggestion in a conversation with Father Karras (Jason Miller), a priest whom Chris eventually asks to perform an exorcism. As a psychiatrically trained priest, Karras mediates between this-worldly and otherworldly explanations. At first Karras is skeptical, but he is slowly convinced that Regan is suffering from genuine possession. After being satisfied that the signs of true possession are present, he talks to his superiors, who in turn call in Father Merrin (Max von Sydow), an elderly priest who has performed exorcisms all over the world, including, most recently, northern Iraq. The paranormal hero has no doubt about the validity of the possession, and he proceeds immediately to undertake the rite of exorcism, thus completing the trajectory of explanations that began with the rats-in-the-attic theory.

In addition to marking a series of discursive boundaries from skeptical to paranormal belief, Chris's trajectory from the doctors to the priests unfolds as a drama of gendered social relations. The reader has probably noticed that the helpers (doctors, psychiatrist, detective, priests) are all men, whereas the possessed household is a home of a mother and two daughters, with an absent father and a boyfriend who is quickly killed. Chris's journey from the doctors to the priests therefore confirms their power just as it puts into question the skeptical theories of the men to whom she turns for help. Toward the end, she must even convince the skeptical priest, Father Karras, that Regan is indeed possessed; in other words, this very secular woman must reawaken recognition of the other world that the priest, the custodian of the other world, at first denies.

In a similar way, the gendered relations involving Chris's daughter Regan both confirm and put into question the patriarchal order. As the anthropologists John Burton and David Hicks (1976) point out in a cultural analysis of *The Exorcist*, Regan embodies the contradictions of gender and power: innocent, female, human, and child, she utters animal noises and speaks obscenities in an adult, male voice. Father Karras, who is a boxer and therefore a strong adult male, cannot subdue the powers of the possessed Regan, who is still only an adolescent girl. In short, older men do battle with the younger girl, whose possession transforms her voice into that of an older man and gives her the power of several men.

Although the gender/paranormal relationship in this movie is complicated, it is consistent. Chris suggests true possession long before the men do, and thus the dialogue between skepticism and belief is, in several episodes, marked with the skeptical position as male. Furthermore, the power of the paranormal (the demon) and the power to overcome it (the priests) are associated with the masculine: a powerful, male demon afflicts a disempowered female household who turn to powerful, male doctors and priests for help. In a sense, then, the movie confirms the patriarchal social order by portraying power as a battle between two sets of male characters (demon versus doctors and priests). Nevertheless, the viewer is constantly led to question the validity of the men's explanations and the efficacy of their solutions. Thus, *The Exorcist* may portray and represent the gendered power relations of the broader society, but at the same time it puts them into question. Similar patterns are also evident in some of the other movies.

"They're Here": The *Poltergeist* Series

In many ways, the *Poltergeist* series tells a similar story to that of *The Exorcist*, but there are also some significant variations. One similarity involves the dimension of gender and social hierarchy: both movies make a little girl the locus of paranormal power. In the first movie in the three-part series (*Poltergeist*, 1982, directed by Tobe Hooper), the disturbances center on five-year-old Carol Anne (Heather O'Rourke), an angelic child of a white, middle-class family that lives in a quiet, suburban home in southern California. At first Carol Anne's mother, Diane Freeling (Jobeth Williams), believes that her daughter is afflicted with "nocturnal somnambulism" (sleepwalking). We learn that Diane herself suffered from this illness as a child, and therefore Carol Anne's problem is implicitly depicted as a hereditary or biological disorder. Like the rats-in-the-attic explanation of *The Exorcist*, the skeptical baseline is established through a naturalistic explanation: a skeptical, scientific discourse encompasses the paranormal.

However, the events soon get out of hand, and the parents decide to call in a parapsychologist, who in turn brings a medium. Thus, one difference from *The Exorcist* is that *Poltergeist* substitutes the role of medical professionals and priests with a parapsychologist and medium. *Poltergeist*, released nearly a decade after *The Exorcist*, is in a sense more up-to-date. (I have also been told that the movie *Poltergeist* actually distinguishes between the parapsychologist and medium because a parapsychologist served as a consultant and insisted that the two roles be kept distinct: Hollywood boundary-work.) One of the assistants to the parapsychologist Dr. Lesh (Beatrice Straigh) proudly tells the family that he once saw an object move seven feet, a statement that is consistent with the relatively mild events that are recorded in most poltergeist studies and also with the rarity with which parapsychologists report firsthand observations of apparently unexplained object movements. However, when the assistant opens the door to Carol Anne's room, the viewer looks over his shoulder and is treated to a paranormal smorgasbord: many of Carol Anne's toys are circling the room, as if they were on a giant mobile operating without strings or wind.

The parapsychologist Dr. Lesh explains to the family that they are experiencing a poltergeist (person-centered and of short duration) rather than a haunting (place-centered and of long duration). However, it is like no poltergeist Dr. Lesh has ever seen before, and, as could happen only in Hollywood, the case soon seems to be a mega-poltergeist/haunting. Later that night, when the parapsychologist sets up a night watch with her team and the family, Dr. Lesh ("Lush") sips from her hip flask and begins to talk like a Spiritualist. Unlike parapsychologists, who generally believe poltergeists to be products of a person's "recurrent spontaneous psychokinesis" (Carol Anne as a child Carrie), Dr. Lesh talks about death, the white light, and the problem of earthbound spirits. The "poltergeist" is beyond the reach of science, even parascience, as Dr. Lesh recognizes. This is a job for a psychic: Tangina Barrons (Zelda Rubinstein), the paranormal hero.

With the transition from Dr. Lesh to Tangina, the movie marks a second discursive boundary. Just as the original skeptical discourse of nocturnal somnambulism and bad genes ceded to the semiskeptical discourse of parapsychology and psychokinesis, now the latter cedes to the psychic's explanation: some souls are not at rest, and there is also an evil force which Tangina refers to briefly and ominously as "the Beast." Science — both the orthodox biomedical form and the heterodox parapsychological form — has now proven unable to deal with the strength of the paranormal Other. However, unlike in *The Exorcist* the alternative offered by the paranormal hero is not the conventional rite of Catholic exorcism. Instead, in a movie that appeared nearly a decade after *The Exorcist*, the psychic's explanation weaves an odd course between fundamentalist Christianity (belief in the Beast) and Spiritualism (wayward souls), a religion that generally does not accept the reality of the Evil One.

There is still a skeptical holdout, Stephen Freeling (Craig Nelson), the father of Carol Anne and husband of Diane. As the skeptic and the man, he now finds himself opposed to three women: Diane, Dr. Lesh, and Tangina. As an every-American, Stephen is worried about what the neighbors will say, and furthermore he does not like Tangina, whom he believes is a fake. However, his skepticism rapidly fades when Tangina telepathically reads his mind. Only Stephen's boss, the developer who chose to build his houses over a graveyard (he removed the tombstones, but not the graves), remains as a skeptical voice. But the boss is not part of the home and its moral universe; instead, he is part of the profane outside world, what the anthropologist Roberto DaMatta calls the world of the street (1985), or, in the parlance of suburban southern California, the development. Stephen's boss belongs to this world, a world of commercial materialism that does not honor the dead: a kind of this-worldly beast.

Poltergeist therefore tells a story that fractures along age and gender lines very similar to those of *The Exorcist*, just as it articulates a similar trajectory from this-worldly to otherworldly explanations. In both cases the paranormal is associated with an innocent girl, and although the anxious mother at first adopts a medical explanation and turns to doctors, she soon finds herself advocating a paranormal explanation against skeptical males. Likewise, the two movies trace out a trajectory of graded positions from the scientific/material to the paranormal/spiritual, from the five steps of *The Exorcist* (neurology, psychiatry, criminology, pastoral counseling, exorcism) to the three steps of *Poltergeist* (medicine, parapsychology, Spiritualism).

Both *The Exorcist* and *Poltergeist* also play out a moral drama of good and evil around the issue of respect for the dead (and with them the otherworldly). In *The Exorcist* the paranormal emerges because of the hubris of modern archaeologists who have apparently not respected the buried dead of an ancient civilization, whereas in *Poltergeist* the hubris is that of the developer, who has neglected to rebury the dead before building his homes. The paranormal thus operates as a sanction guarding a moral system that places honoring the dead above what amounts to grave robbing. The comparison also makes it possible to associate two forms of materialism: the commercial materialism of Stephen's boss and the scientific materialism of the archaeologists. In both cases, the protagonists of the stories end up believing in the world of the paranormal and rejecting that of their materialistic, skeptical Others.

Poltergeist II (1986, directed by Brian Gibson) develops the theme of honoring the dead, but it drops the Christian imagery of the Beast and instead moves toward Native American knowledge, therefore giving the poltergeist an even greater New Age flavor than its predecessor. The problems begin when Grandma (Geraldine Fitzgerald) dies, an event which puts the domestic order into question. Tangina's friend Taylor (Will Sampson), a Native American shaman who seems to have stepped out of one of Carlos Castaneda's books, comes to the rescue. As Tangina cedes her role as hero to this more powerful paranormal hero, she explains that the paranormal Other is more powerful as well. The problem of the house is much deeper, so to speak: beneath the graves of the cemetery are the catacombs of a group of American pioneers who left for California in the nineteenth century to found a utopian society, but instead were massacred by Indians. However, Carol Anne's mother, Diane, also has a vision of the massacre, and she corrects Tangina's explanation in one crucial detail: the head of the cult in fact led his people into the catacombs to await the end of the world, but when the end of the world did not arrive, he resolved to bury them all alive: a nineteenth-century version of the Jonestown fiasco. The forces unleashed from this unfortunate history are terrible, and only family togetherness (which includes Grandma's intervention from the spirit world) is able to save them.

From a cultural perspective, *Poltergeist II* is interesting because it further confirms the basic argument I have been making about the location of the paranormal Other and the paranormal hero in the "there and then." This movie extends the imagery of depth from unremoved graves to hidden catacombs, a deep cavern that is even closer to the mine metaphor of Louisa Rhine. The paranormal Other is also located further back in time, the nineteenth century, and the hero shifts from the mildly Other Tangina — a somewhat eccentric woman but still located in contemporary, middle-class American society — to the strikingly Other Taylor, who brings with him the ancient wisdom of Native American shamanism. Thus, *Poltergeist II* exaggerates and magnifies some of the patterns already evident in *Poltergeist*.

Poltergeist III (1987, directed by Gary Sherman) also revolves around the question of family love, but it adds to the cast of characters a bona fide skeptic who could belong to CSICOP: Dr. Seton (Richard Fire), the principal of the school in Chicago where Carol Anne is studying. Carol Anne is now staying with her uncle, Bruce Gardner (Tom Skerritt), who loves her, and her Aunt Patricia (Nancy Allen), who seems to resent her sister's daughter's invasion of the household. Dr. Seton believes that hypnosis can explain all of Carol Anne's powers; in other words, the paranormal phenomena attributed to Carol Anne are nothing more than the result of her ability to suggest hallucinations to people. Carol Anne does not agree, and when Dr. Seton attempts to hypnotize her in order to ask her to remember what she sees when the anomalous events happen, she resists. Her protests notwithstanding, Dr. Seton insists, and the spirits come back. As viewers, we "know" that Carol Anne is right and Dr. Seton is wrong, since we can see, at least sometimes, the world through the young girl's eyes. As a result, we are led into a complicity with her, and our sympathy is reinforced by her underdog position as the helpless little girl who is resisting the skeptic: an older, confident, well-educated male, a figure who belongs to the outside world (the school) rather than the home.

Similar gender-coded dialogues occur first between Uncle Bruce and Aunt Patricia and then between Tangina and Dr. Seton. Regarding the first exchange, Bruce is skeptical, whereas Patricia thinks that Carol Anne may have psychokinetic powers like those of Uri Geller. Later, after Bruce is converted, the afflicted couple call in Dr. Seton. Tangina also shows up, called by her psychic intuition, and the ensuing conversation between her and Dr. Seton provides yet one more example of the dialogue between the psychic (female) and the skeptic (male).

Both psychic and skeptic are eventually killed by the terrible forces that have been unleashed in this haunted high-rise, a poltergeist variant on the *Towering Inferno* in which the viewer is treated to a barrage of special effects that are ambiguously perched between the real and the hallucinated. Tangina, however, and not Dr. Seton is the one who eventually plays the paranormal hero who saves the day. She reappears as a spirit in order to pass her amulet on to Bruce and Patricia, that is, a material object which transgresses the boundary between the two worlds and reveals that the other world is not all hallucination. In the end, the family is reunited, and any hints of Dr. Seton (the male, skeptical discourse) have disappeared, as both Bruce and Patricia have been won over to the reality of love, family, and paranormality, three cultural categories that finally come together at the end of the movie.

Skepticism is never a very serious option in the *Poltergeist* series, and even in *Poltergeist III*, where many of the events are apparently only the characters' hallucinations, the general impression is that the dead are causing the quick to hallucinate. The skeptical Dr. Seton and his explanation of hallucinations are literally engulfed by—or, to use Louis Dumont's (1980) term again, "encompassed" by—the paranormal world. As the opposition between paranormality and skepticism is transformed into a hierarchy, a series of social oppositions is also transformed into hierarchies. In other words, the viewpoint of the female child whose place is home, sweet home eventually wins out over that of the male adult whose place is outside the home in the cruel, cruel world.

This structure of alignment also carries over into the domain of ethnic and class stereotypes. For example, in *Poltergeist II* the paranormal hero is a Native American, just as more recently in the movie *Ghost* (1990, directed by Jerry Zucker), the paranormal hero is a poor, African-American woman named Sister Oda Mae Brown (Whoopi Goldberg). Like the white, middle-class family of *Poltergeist II*, this white, middle-class, yuppie couple —the protagonists Sam Wheat (Patrick Swayze) and Molly Jensen (Demi Moore)—must reach out to an ethnic Other who is endowed with the paranormal powers that are capable of saving them. The process of identification is ambivalent and complicated rather than straightforward: the paranormal hero's powers allow the yuppie protagonists to value the hero, but at the same time Oda Mae Brown returns to her world at the end of the drama. Thus, although the power of the paranormal hero is equated with the popular, that power can only be an ambivalent concept of the popular in a cinematic tradition aimed at middle-class consumers (predominantly "white") who identify themselves with the "underdog" but who also distance themselves from social categories "below" them in the social pyramid.

A Nice Home in the Suburbs: The *Amityville* Series

Like the first two *Poltergeist* movies, *Amityville Horror* (1979, directed by Stuart Rosenberg) takes as its baseline the nice home in the suburbs, the scene of family values and domestic tranquility that is transformed into a zone of terror, death, and destruction: the threatened family and invaded home.[3] This movie dramatizes the same gender pattern of skepticism and belief that was seen in the *Poltergeist* series, first between George and Kathleen Lutz (James Brolin and Margot Kidder) and then later between George's business partner, who is a skeptic, and his wife, who believes that the house was built on ground formerly occupied by a witch from Salem and that there are people buried in the basement.

In addition to reproducing the gender structure of male debunkers and female defenders, *Amityville Horror* has several novel features. For example, one dialogue between skeptics and advocates occurs between Father Delaney (Rod Steiger), a Catholic priest who knows the history of the house, and his superiors, who do not want to hear about haunted houses. When his superiors suggest that the problem may be hysteria, Delaney snaps back that he is a trained psychotherapist and that he knows the difference between hysteria and the paranormal. His superiors retort, in not particularly godly language: "Who the hell do you think you are? Do you think your secular education gives you a right to question the Church?" They obviously do not, and they decide to send him on a "vacation."

The exchange between the two positions in the religious hierarchy is instructive on several grounds. It is not marked for gender, nor is the exchange a clear confrontation between science and otherworldly experience. Father Delaney appeals not only to the authority of his experience, which is firmly rooted in his deep religious faith, but also to his scientific training. He therefore draws on both religion and science to oppose skepticism, which is associated with his superiors. Skepticism here is corrupt and authoritarian, and one archetype of corruption and authoritarianism in what remains a Protestant culture is still the Catholic church hierarchy. Again, the skeptic/advocate dialogue reveals a social conflict involving relations of power, here articulated as the power of superiors over their subordinates in a hierarchical institution. The increasing power of the evil spirits in the haunted house serves to confirm Father Delaney's position, and while his superiors do not change their minds, the evidence for the paranormal leads the audience to side with this underdog and his paranormal interpretation.

Amityville 3-D (1983, directed by Richard Fleischer) is a tragedy that serves as a warning to the middle-class, white, male skeptic, and thus it dramatizes similar power issues. The movie begins on a skeptical note: a district attorney, a parapsychologist, and two journalists attend a séance in the Amityville house, which is now used by a phony psychic whom they proceed to bust. Although contemporary parapsychologists are not in the psychic-busting business — in "real life," psychic busting and debunking are more the work of CSICOP — the opening episode establishes the skeptical baseline that aligns the parapsychologist with the skeptical journalist John Baxter (Tony Roberts), who decides to buy the house.

The first of the four skeptics to be converted is Baxter's journalist partner, who is significantly a woman. A photographer, Melanie (Candy Clark) develops some pictures she took in the house and discovers that the Realtor's face is marred in an uncanny way. The Realtor (John Harkins) dies in the house, ostensibly of a heart attack, and Melanie suggests to Baxter that this tragic event has some kind of connection with her anomalous photograph. Baxter does not agree, so Melanie takes her photographs to the parapsychologist Dr. Eliot West (Robert Joy), who expresses his own, more open-minded, skepticism: he says it may have a normal explanation, as, he believes, do 97 percent of the reports he investigates. "What about the other 3 percent?" she asks. "I guess that's why I'm here," he replies.

At this point, the film begins to reveal the awful power of the horrific, paranormal Other and the hopeless delusion of skepticism, even in the mild form exhibited by Dr. West. Melanie eventually dies in her car, where the evil force traps her and burns her alive. The dialogue between skeptical and paranormal belief continues (again in gendered terms) between Baxter and his former wife (Tess Harper). Like Melanie, she is more of a believer and certainly enough of one to forbid their daughter, who is in her guardianship, to go near the house. Here, the gendering of the dialogue between advocates and skeptics breaks down somewhat, perhaps because their daughter identifies more with her skeptical father on this issue. Disregarding her mother's orders, Susan (Laurier Laughlin) visits the house with her girlfriend Lisa (Meg Ryan), who is also a skeptic—that is, until they go on a boat ride and Susan mysteriously disappears into the ocean.

Baxter is left paying an unfathomable price for his skeptical hubris: Susan is sacrificed. Converted by this tragedy and by other experiences, he calls in the parapsychologist Dr. West, who arrives with a team of investigators and proceeds to set up his equipment for an all-night vigil. Baxter's is the last fully skeptical voice in the movie, and when he converts, the only character approximating skepticism is Dr. West, who as a parapsychologist still believes he can domesticate the paranormal with his equipment and scientific knowledge. For his hubris, Dr. West also pays a big price. First, however, he discovers the source of the psychic forces, which —as is almost predictable at this point—come from deep below, more specifically, a hole in the floor of the basement. The explanation that surfaces in *Amityville 3-D* is that the house is built over an ancient Indian burial ground. In other words, the Salem witchcraft idea of *Amityville Horror* is now dropped in favor of this relatively New Age theme—a move similar to the transition from Tangina in *Poltergeist* to Taylor of *Poltergeist II*. Eventually, the forces swallow up the parapsychologist, who emerges from the pit just long enough to tell Baxter to get out, and, as the house comes crashing down around him, Baxter barely manages to escape with his life.

The plot moves by slowly breaking down the alliance among the skeptics: first by converting and then destroying Melanie, then by swallowing up Susan, and finally by consuming Dr. West. Dr. West does not suspect his fate when he arrives; instead, his team of researchers and their machinery hold out the promise of naturalizing the supernatural, domesticating the paranormal, and rendering the irrational rational. As he is swallowed up into the depths of the pit and his team is lost in the ensuing fire and destruction, so science — represented here as parapsychology — is encompassed by the paranormal and the unfathomable. Only Baxter lives to tell the story, but he lives reborn as a believer who has lost his family and friends. His skeptical hubris has cost him his family and home.

Once again, the Hollywood movie reveals a trajectory that can be described as a transition from a materialistic, skeptical baseline to an otherworldly, paranormal conclusion. Likewise, the paranormal Other is constructed in terms of culturally based notions of alterity: depth (the pit below the basement) and temporal distance (Salem witches or an ancient Indian burial ground). Finally, the dialogue between defenders and debunkers is generally situated in a gendered relationship in which skepticism is masculine.

Ghostbusters, the Paranormal, and the Popular

The *Ghostbusters* series takes place largely against the backdrop of New York City, and consequently it brings into play the question of social hierarchy in somewhat more explicit terms than the other movies, which are more domestic in orientation. For the sake of brevity, I will focus on the second of the two movies in the *Ghostbusters* series, since it more clearly articulates the social hierarchies of class and civic relationships.

Ghostbusters II (1989, directed by Ivan Reitman), like *Amityville 3-D,* begins by establishing a skeptical baseline of discredited and fraudulent paranormal belief. The famous ghostbusters who have saved the city in the first movie are now reduced to making paid appearances at the birthday parties of "nine-year-old yuppie larva," who appear bored by the passé act. In other words, skepticism is so widespread that even the children are skeptics. Like the opening scene of *Amityville 3-D,* where the psychic is exposed as a commercial huckster, the opening scenes of this movie play out with exaggerated humor the skeptical association of the paranormal with commerical materialism.

While two of the former ghostbusters are reduced to playing ghostbuster clowns for wealthy children, another of their number, Peter Menkmin (Bill Murray), is even further demeaned. The cynical Menkmin (after H. L. Mencken?) is now hosting a psychic TV show, one that is so discredited that even self-respecting psychics refuse to appear as guests. Instead, he is reduced to inviting the worst kind of cranks, including a man who is prophesying that the world will end in a short time. Peter cynically asks his guest if it would not be better to predict that the world will end in a few more years, so the prophet could make more money on book royalties, not to mention film rights. In short, the skeptical baseline is so strongly established that the parapsychologists begin as skeptics, and the whole discourse of the paranormal, not to mention the former ghostbusters themselves, is mired by commercial materialism.

However, the return of the paranormal works through dramatic irony; the movie establishes the secret conspiracy between the viewer and the one believer, Dana Barrett (Sigourney Weaver). As in *The Exorcist* and the *Poltergeist* series, the paranormal Other enters the secular, materialistic, everyday world through the vulnerability of a young child, this time a baby, and the mother-daughter relationship. Like Barrett, the viewers witness the uncanny motions of her runaway baby carriage, which takes off down the sidewalks of New York and maneuvers busy street crossings as if it were guided by some kind of hidden hand. When Barrett reports her experience to Egon (Harold Ramis) — a professor and former ghostbuster who seems to have gone on to other, more mundane, research topics — he seems skeptical, although he promises to look into the case.

Gradually, the skeptical, male ghostbusters reunite and are swayed over to the position of the female advocate, Dana. They then discover the menacing slime that is accumulating in a location that, once again, reveals the cultural logic that locates the paranormal Other in the "deep" and the "past": the abandoned and haunted subway line hidden beneath the city of New York.[4] When the police catch the ghostbusters illegally working on the abandoned subway line, they arrest the cranks. The role of the skeptic now shifts to three new personae: the judge, who begins the case by saying that the court does not recognize the existence of ghosts; the mayor's assistant, Jack Hardmeyer, who has the ghostbusters committed to the psychiatric ward at Parkview Hospital; and the psychiatrist, who decides that the ghostbusters are crazy when they explain their theory about the menacing paranormal slime that gains power from New Yorkers' bad vibes. Thus, the ghostbusters and their paranormal discourse are repressed by three representatives of official discourse and society: the court, the government, and the medical profession. Once again, the dialogue between skeptics and advocates is encoded in a social drama between the underdogs and the representatives of the official powers of society.

The reversal of terms occurs through the actions of the mayor, who as the elected leader of the city is both a servant of the people and their ruler, a mediator between the underdog vision and that of the muckety-mucks (or, as the movie's imagery would suggest, the "slimeballs") at the top of the social hierarchies. In the first movie, the mayor became convinced that the ghostbusters could save the city, and consequently in the second movie he is quickly swayed to the side of the people and their paranormal heroes. His decision is facilitated by an hour-long chat with Fiorello LaGuardia, the ghostly, long-dead, populist mayor. When the current mayor finds out that his assistant, Jack Hardmeyer, has had the ghostbusters committed, he fires Hardmeyer and demands to see the underdogs, whom he now transmutes – albeit somewhat reluctantly – into potential superheroes.

Thus, the ghostbusters first suffer rejection as criminals and mentally ill patients, that is, as sociopaths and psychopaths. In the process, they are set apart from society – or, in the language of rites of passage, they undergo a period of separation (see V. Turner 1974) – which enables them to reemerge in a liminal status, in which they remain until they do their job and are reincorporated into society as superheroes. As an indication of their liminal status, the mayor listens to them but not with much patience; however, he does promise to cooperate with them. The heroes soon realize that all their high-tech equipment is not enough to conquer the malicious forces that have been set loose on the Big Apple. As a last resort, they loosen Lady Liberty from her moorings in the harbor, a marvelous feat which they accomplish by spraying her insides with slime and then singing songs of good cheer. They then bring the female icon onto the streets of New York, where she rallies her fellow citizens to the spirit of cooperation, neighborliness, good citizenship, motherpie, applehood, and all that – all of which is made easier because it just happens to be New Year's Eve, a time of forgiving, forgetting, and, in short, good vibes.

Ghostbusters II may pastiche other horror and science-fiction movies with its ridiculous humor, but this spook spoof nevertheless translates the moral message of the *Poltergeist* and *Amityville Horror* series – family love – onto the broader stage of good neighborliness, good citizenship, and other community-oriented values that it ambiguously embraces. The movie also extends the identification of the paranormal hero with the popular from the informal structures of social organization – such as male and female, parent and child, professional and layperson, European and non-European, and superior and subordinate – to the formal institutions of contemporary social control: the police, courts, elected officials, and medicine. In doing so, its message has a hint of countercultural political critique, one made more palatable – or slimier – to its middle-class consumers by all of the clowning around. In short, in *Ghostbusters II*, the equation of the paranormal hero and the popular is even more evident and framed in more social terms.

An Anthropologist and a Haunted House:
Further Variations on Class, Gender, and the Paranormal

The question of class and the paranormal is posed somewhat more directly
in an older horror movie *The Haunting* (1963, directed by Robert Wise
and based on the Shirley Jackson novel *The Haunting of Hill House,* 1959).
In this movie, the anthropologist Dr. John Markway (Richard Johnson)
decides to spend some time attempting to observe apparent paranormal
phenomena in a haunted house that is owned by a rich spinster who lives
in another home in Boston. Markway invites as guests two "sensitives" who
happen to be single, young women: Theodora (Claire Bloom), who ex-
celled in ESP tests at Duke University, and Eleanor (Julie Harris), who was
a poltergeist child and is somewhat unstable psychologically (again bringing together the female, the pathological, and the paranormal). To make
sure that there is no hanky-panky between the professor and his research
assistants (and perhaps to suggest to the viewer that it will occur later),
the rich old woman decides to send her nephew Luke (Russ Tamblyn) as
a chaperone.

Luke, who is slated to inherit the house, is both an aristocrat and a skeptic. The rich nephew does not believe the house is haunted; instead, he
agrees with the mayor of the town, who thinks there must be subterranean
currents or some other natural phenomena that could explain the reports
of mysterious noises. The mayor, of course, is worried about keeping his
town attractive to home and business investors, just as Luke is concerned
that if his future estate gains a reputation as a haunted house, its property
value could plummet. Somewhat cynical about life, Luke also reveals himself to be somewhat sleazy: he cheats in a game of poker with Theo, and
he is not above flirting with the women whose virtue he has been sent
to guard. Thus, a discourse of material gain is associated with a materialist world view and a cynical if not sleazy outlook on life. These values
in turn are associated with the mayor and the scion, that is, two men who
occupy positions of power in the social order and whose skepticism is portrayed as a veiled ideology that serves their material interests.

The movie leaves unresolved the question of whether or not the skeptical theory of the mayor and the aristocratic Luke is indeed the valid explanation of the apparent ghostly activities in the house. It is possible that
the servants have engineered some of the phenomena in order to keep the
house to themselves, and likewise much if not all of the phenomena may
have been hallucinatory. By leaving open the question of the nature of
the uncanny events as hoax, hallucination, or hobgoblin, the movie ren-
ders itself open to multiple interpretations to an even greater extent than

does *Poltergeist III*. What the movie does suggest, also like *Poltergeist III*, is that even if the haunted house is only a case of haunted minds, the hallucinations may nevertheless be very dangerous ones, for they lead the psychologically unstable Eleanor to take actions that eventually result in her death.

Unlike the deaths in *Amityville 3-D* and *Poltergeist III*, Eleanor's death is caused by her belief and not her skepticism. Because the movie leaves open to interpretation the question of whether the force that leads Eleanor to her death is her own imagination or something from beyond, the story does not move from the skeptical baseline through the sacrifice of the skeptic to the triumph of the paranormal hero. Instead, it operates by enmeshing the conflict between debunkers and defenders in one coded for class and gender. At one extreme are the skeptical scion and mayor, whose skepticism is associated with their positions of wealth and power in society, and at the other extreme are Theo and Eleanor, the two middle-class women who are credited with being psychically sensitive.

Between the two extremes is Dr. Markway, the anthropologist. According to the cultural logic that I have been elaborating, this position could have been filled by a parapsychologist. Markway, however, is an anthropologist who is well-read in psychical research and parapsychology; thus, structurally, he is a parapsychologist. Still, the film's association of the two professions merits some reflection, for it suggests some parallels in the cultural meaning of the two sciences.[5] As an anthropologist, Markway is a custodian of ancient and non-Western knowledge, and his access to other ways of knowing allows him to adopt an attitude of critical and questioning skepticism toward the materialist values of official science. His skeptical attitude toward skepticism — yet one which is framed within the confines of scientific discourse — is not unlike that of the parapsychologist, whose study of claimed paranormal phenomena provides a basis for a similarly critical attitude toward orthodox science. Anthropologists occupy a position at the borderland between Western science and non-Western knowledge, just as parapsychologists occupy a similar position of mediation between the scientific and the nonscientific, between skeptical and paranormal belief. One marginal discourse therefore encounters another.

Conclusions

In a number of cases, then, Hollywood movies confirm the existence of elaborate and multiplex boundaries between skeptical and paranormal discourse that I have discussed in the preceding chapters. Skeptical, materialistic discourse usually marks the beginning of the movie, which often be-

gins with what I have called a skeptical baseline that is established by
marking the paranormal Other in metaphors of pathology or commercial
materialism. For example, the first explanation in *The Exorcist* or the *Poltergeist* series is that the paranormal can be understood as a neurological
disorder, and when that is discredited, the slightly less materialistic explanation of a psychiatric or hypnotic condition emerges as a second candidate. The alternative pathway is through a skeptical baseline of commercial materialism, where the paranormal is discredited not through official
science but through its own commercialism, as appears at the beginning
of *Amityville 3-D, Ghost, Ghostbusters II*, and *The Haunting*. However,
this is only a skeptical baseline. In general, skeptics do not fare well in
Hollywood; to the extent that their voice is heard, it is at the beginning
of the movies. Although the movies may begin with a skeptical voice, they
usually end with a position closer to that of New Agers.

One example of convergence with the New Age position is how the
movies generally construct the paranormal Other through cultural markers of the "there and then." The paranormal Other frequently emerges from
an exotic time or place, and sometimes it is buried and hidden beneath
the surface of the earth. True, there are some apparent exceptions, such
as the high-rise apartment of *Poltergeist III*, which, like the skyscraper at
the end of the first *Ghostbusters* movie, may appear not to fit into the
general pattern of locating the paranormal in a hidden or buried region.
However, even in the haunted towering inferno of *Poltergeist III* the paranormal phenomena at first appear in the hidden parts of the building: its
ventilating pipes, electrical circuits, and elevator shafts.

In a similar way, the paranormal heroes, too, tend to be marked as exotic Others: the almost otherworldly Father Merrin, the eccentric woman
Tangina, the Native American Taylor, the African-American huckster Oda
Mae Brown, the marginalized ghostbusters, and the elusive and psychologically unstable poltergeist child Eleanor. Those paranormal heroes who
belong to and to some extent represent the institutions of authority in
society — the universities and the churches — are set up in ambivalent relationship to their own institutions. For example, the parapsychologist in
Poltergeist explains that while she occupies a position in the university,
her work in parapsychology is more of a hobby; Father Karras is wracked
by guilt and doubt about his faith; and Father Delaney must battle with
his superiors in the Church. Without the backing of the institutional infrastructure, they become Davids facing the paranormal Goliaths, that is,
underdog heroes who are set apart from society, do battle with superior
paranormal forces, and finally save the social order.

The heroes, however, are not the only characters who signify the triumph of the individual in the Hollywood dramas. It is interesting and possibly of cultural significance that although the entire family is threatened by the paranormal invasion, the attack usually focuses on one member of the family, and usually not the person of authority in the household, such as the father or mother. Rather, the attack focuses on a relatively helpless and innocent young female or child, such as Eleanor, Regan, Carol Anne, Susan, or Dana Barrett's baby. The choice of the frequently least powerful family member may dramatize the power of the paranormal Other; as in the case of Regan, the powerless becomes the superpowerful. However, in a culture of individualism, the entire social order is also put into question when even one member of the domestic unit is subject to paranormal attack. It would be possible to resolve the dramas by sending the young girl away from the family or letting her be swallowed up by the dark forces.[6] The Hollywood solution, however, is for the family to close ranks and do its best to protect its most innocent member. Thus, rather than sacrifice the weakest member of the community for the good of the community, the individualistic drama works in the opposite direction and puts the entire family at risk in the defense of one member.

One figure, however, does tend to get sacrificed in the Hollywood movies: the skeptic, who is generally male and often associated with a higher position in the scales of social power and hierarchy. Dr. Seton, for example, is a successful (*materially* well-off) and well-educated school principal. In general, skeptics seem to be associated with positions of power in society: the Catholic church's superiors in *Amityville*, the press and the district attorney in *Amityville 3-D*, the judge and mayor's assistant in *Ghostbusters II*, and the aristocratic scion and mayor in *The Haunting*. However, their possession of social power is undone by their lack of paranormal power, whose very existence they deny. For their hubris they are frequently sacrificed, and sometimes fairly early in the movies. The drama then shifts to a struggle between the paranormal Other and the paranormal hero. In a formula — and Hollywood movies, like neolithic myths, sometimes can be expressed in formulas — the paranormal is the popular.

To argue that the paranormal is the popular is to take advantage of an ambiguity in the language. On the one hand, Hollywood movies equate paranormal heroes with the underdog, the victimized, and the common people: the "everyviewer" of the movie theaters. On the other hand, paranormal horror movies are popular in the sense of box-office sales, enough so that they often lead to sequels. These two aspects of the popular — the cultural sense of popular as opposed to elite and box-office success — are closely connected. As viewers, we sense a certain justice when the skeptic is sacrificed. The director has already let us in on the secret, the reality of the paranormal Other, so as viewers we have not fallen prey to the same hubris. Instead, we side with the underdog paranormal hero, who while socially disempowered is able to muster the power of the right to overcome the double (and doubly wrong) mights of skepticism and the evil, paranormal Other. There is, indeed, an almost biblical flavor to the drama of the righteous individual who stands alone against the overwhelming forces of mammon and the devil in the land of milk and money.

It would be possible to produce a movie in which the skeptic played the underdog against a paranormal conspiracy of cranks and charlatans who somehow threatened a domestic, neighborhood, or national social order. Here, the public would be deluded by the paranormal beliefs, and the elites (probably the corporate media but maybe a few government officials) would be in cahoots with the conspiracy because it made for good business or good politics. Nevertheless, the viewer would be let in on "the secret" and therefore side with the underdog skeptical hero against the overwhelming odds of corruption and charlatanism. Such is, more or less, the script played out by real-life skeptics in their never-ending struggle against the forces of the paranormal. But why, we might ask, is this script not the formula of the successful Hollywood horror movies? I would suggest that the Hollywood equation of the paranormal and popular (rather than an alternative equation of the skeptical and the popular) is itself popular because it reflects — even as it reproduces, distorts, and alters — the same equation in society. Thus, at the popular level, there is still a widespread mistrust of official ideologies of any kind: a widespread skepticism of skepticism that in turn is channeled — or, depending on one's perspective, mischanneled — through Hollywood horror movies and the texts and rituals of New Age consciousness.

My concept of the "popular" includes a variety of positions that are marked supplementary with respect of any given cultural hierarchy. Although class, ethnicity, and occupational level are key markers of hierarchy in these movies, gender is arguably even more salient. Consistent with the general pattern found in the readings of the skeptics' and New Agers' texts, the skeptics tend to be male. Although the pattern is clear enough, it would be an oversimplification to argue that the skeptical voice is always male and that the paranormal voice is always female. To mention just one counterexample, in *Poltergeist III* Uncle Bruce at first plays skeptic to Aunt Patricia, but the roles are reversed later, where Aunt Patricia plays skeptic to Uncle Bruce's belief. The reversal is interesting, since it is also accompanied by a delineation of their attitudes toward Carol Anne: Uncle Bruce loves her, whereas Aunt Patricia would rather not have her niece around. The reversal to gender in the dialogue between advocates and critics is therefore revealing, since it is also accompanied by a reversal of conventional parenting roles: Uncle Bruce becomes the warm, nurturing parent — that is, a role conventionally marked as feminine — at the same time that he adopts the feminine-coded voice of the paranormal. Eventually Aunt Patricia must overcome both her skepticism and her lack of love for Carol Anne in order to bring her family back together, which also restores the destabilized reversal of gender meanings.

The Hollywood dramas, then, are continuous with those of the real-life heroes — psi cops, pararevolutionaries, Aquarian conspirators — who battle official science, popular mysticism, or both. Hollywood both confirms and elaborates the emergent paraculture, with its referent points of Self/Other distinctions in terms of pathology, materialism, exoticism, science, mysticism, individualism, morality, gender, and so on. The movies also devote a great deal of attention to showing how paranormal culture is sharply divided along a spectrum of positions similar to the boundaries in which real-life skeptics, parapsychologists, and New Agers invest so much energy to maintain. However, as I shall now discuss in more detail, the work of constructing and deconstructing boundaries is rendered even more complex by yet one more voice, one suggested in the movie *The Haunting*. What role do we human scientists play in these real-life dramas, and why is our role important?

Part III

Conclusions and Implications

7

Theoretical Conclusions

A curious similarity among New Agers, parapsychologists, and skeptics is that they are all divided by internal discursive boundaries: "neutral" skepticism versus debunking, experimental parapsychology versus spontaneous case research, and the relatively scientific and erudite writing of Marilyn Ferguson versus the mystical discourse of channelers, goddess worshippers, and crystal healers. Consideration of these internal boundaries makes it possible to extend somewhat the concept of "boundary-work" as developed by the sociologist Thomas Gieryn (1983a, 1983b, Gieryn and Figert 1990).[1] Gieryn argues that "'science' is no single thing" and that the "boundaries of science are ambiguous, flexible, historically changing, contextually variable, internally inconsistent, and sometimes disputed" (1983a:781, 792). Moreover, he argues that boundary-work should be situated in specific historical and cultural contexts in which communities of scientists distinguish science from other discourses or cultural domains. Boundary-work, he also argues, is not a mere rhetorical exercise or a purely intellectual activity; instead, it is rooted in the "interests" of or social conflicts between science and other institutions, such as religion, that also seek to have a special legitimacy in society.

I see one of the main theoretical contributions of *Science in the New Age* to be an expansion of the concept of boundary-work by examining how in a concrete case study it can operate in complex and multiple ways. My analysis shows not only how scientists engage in boundary-work to distinguish science from nonscience, but also how a variety of other groups construct boundaries (and consequently themselves as groups) not only with respect to more orthodox scientists and skeptics but with respect to each other. In short, scientific boundaries are recursive, nested, and multiple; there are layers of scientificity that become clearer as one unfolds levels of skepticism and "pseudoscientificity" both within and across discursive boundaries. Boundary-work therefore is going on in all directions, not just in the direction of orthodox science toward religion and "pseudo-science."[2]

To be able to see these multiple and recursive boundaries, it is necessary to adopt a cultural perspective, that is, to understand the world from the viewpoint of the communities and writers in question. The cultural perspective makes it possible to see how the science/nonscience boundary usually becomes equated with a distinction between the Self and the Other (although the polarities sometimes shift, and consequently the discourse of the Other may become equated with the "scientific"). Thus, I also extend and develop the study of boundary-work in a second way by treating it as meaningful "social drama" (to invoke the old phrase of Victor Turner, 1974), or, perhaps better, as meaningful cultural dialogue. More than a cognitive activity, boundary-work takes place in a group of related idioms that are themselves part of the surrounding cultural context.

The question of boundary-work becomes considerably more complex when one's own discourse and disciplinary frameworks are included as part of the analysis. In other words, one of the boundaries in the ideological arena of debate and dialogue on skeptical and paranormal belief is the one with my own discourse of the human sciences. In the remainder of this chapter I will consider some of the implications of boundary-work with respect to this issue of reflexivity.

Boundary-Work and Reflexivity

Readers of this book may themselves end up occupying a spectrum of positions from skepticism to belief about the argument that I have defended. As appears to be the pattern from the reactions of some of the people who have read earlier drafts of the book, the closer readers are to one of the three communities, the more likely they are to question my argument that the community to whom they have allegiances is similar to the other two and that the three (or more) cultures of borderland science are in many ways one paraculture. Their reaction is not surprising, for I have put into question the boundaries in which representatives of these different communities have frequently invested substantial time and resources to defend. To a certain extent, then, I am questioning their legitimacy, first by showing how each community has some similarities to the others and then by arguing that these similarities are made possible by their shared cultural context. In the process, I have also set up an alternative discourse, that of the human sciences, which encompasses the other discourses within its own framework.

Thus, while the contested cultural space of the paraculture is a crowded one, there is yet one other community that is an active and important contestant in that space: the human sciences, specifically anthropology, history, sociology, literary/cultural studies, feminist studies, and science and technology studies (STS). To consider our role in this arena implies adding a small chapter to the sociology of sociology, the anthropology of anthropology, and the criticism of criticism.

The reflexive venture opens up new and welcome complexities, but it is fraught with difficulties, perhaps the most outstanding being the following reflexive paradox: not only is the knowledge of the observed scientist, usually a natural scientist, socially constructed, but so is that of the observing human scientist. The question then emerges of how to examine the socially constructed nature of one's own discourse. I shall begin by reviewing some strategies already under development in the STS literature, and then I shall consider an alternative way of discussing the place of the human sciences in the broader ideological arena.

Previous discussions of the reflexivity question within the social studies of science and technology have tended to focus on epistemological issues and the inscription of knowledge paradoxes in the human scientists' texts. The result has been some occasionally ingenious, occasionally bothersome, and always unusual tinkerings with the genre conventions of humanities and social science writing.[3] One example of this version of reflexivity would be to turn my analysis back on my own text by deconstructing the metaphors in *Science in the New Age*. The project, however, would be somewhat disingenuous since I could easily add or delete metaphors to fit whatever argument I wished to make. Furthermore, if I were to take the task more seriously, I would give it up as impossible because it would be so difficult to recognize my own moments of blindness and insight.

An alternative would be to develop a chapter on the metaphors and symbolic language of human scientists who have written on the paranormal. Rather than approach the reflexivity discussion at the individualistic level of my own text, it would involve a more sociological and cultural analysis of a discursive community. However, the social sciences literature waxes on erudition and wanes on metaphors, as does the erudite literature by skeptics and parapsychologists on experimental and philosophical issues. Without the concomitant popular literature that would explain the social studies of the paranormal to a mass market, there is little room to apply to human scientists' discourse the kind of analysis developed here for the popular scrivenings of New Agers, parapsychologists, and skeptics.[4]

Yet another alternative, one also used by the reflexivists (and sometimes to the annoyance of their readers), would be to include secondary voices, generally in the form of an imaginary dialogue with an imagined Other who interrupts the text and utters ostensibly disquieting critical comments. The strategy provides a way of "reflecting" on one's own text and discourse, albeit in a way that readers may find bothersome. However, the secondary voice remains that of the author, and as a result the technique does not fully recognize the dialogical nature of the social scientist's text. (Nor does it recognize that secondary voices are always already "present" in the text, particularly in footnotes.) Anthropologists have come up with a parallel but more "realistic" solution: to open up part of the text to the voices of one's informants or Others (as, for example, I have done here to a small extent by making room for the Others' voices via quotations, although of course within legal limitations). However, as the historian and ethnography critic James Clifford (1988) has pointed out, despite the advantage of letting the Other's voice into the text, the anthropologists' solution can be manipulated almost as easily as the secondary voice device.

Despite the evident shortcomings of the anthropologists' approach, it is part of an agenda and framework that broaches the question of reflexivity from a somewhat different perspective than that of the STS reflexivists. Consequently, the anthropologists' approach may help move forward the discussions on reflexivity in science and technology studies. In anthropology, discussions of reflexivity and textual construction have been much more explicit about the connection with issues of power. More than intellectual exercises that inscribe the paradoxes of constructivism, experimentation at its best is part of a move toward the critique of institutional arrangements that have led to asymmetries of power, a research question that the STS constructivists and reflexivists have largely ignored. For example, the program of anthropology as cultural critique requires culture critics to pose alternatives to the institutions and discourse that they are questioning, and consequently their perspective is critical and transformative rather than merely reflexive.[5]

Regarding the relations between human scientists and our paranormal Others (skeptics, parapsychologists, and New Agers), a critical, reflexive perspective begins with the assumption that the human scientists are part of the same ideological arena of debate and dialogue as their Others. The perspective is still reflexive, but it is recast in the more critical space of institutional and power/knowledge relations. A double question emerges: To what extent do human scientists legitimate the positions of their Others and under what circumstances? and To what extent do human scientists stake out their own, independent position in this arena? I shall begin with the first question, for which the answer, as I shall demonstrate here in a brief way, is far from evident. My discussion will focus on sociologists and anthropologists, who are in this area the most prominent of the human scientists and the most easily identified.

The Position of Social Scientists in the Ideological Arena

Beginning with the skeptics, inspection of the partial list of about fifty of the CSICOP fellows that appeared in the winter 1991 issue of the *Skeptical Inquirer* reveals three anthropologists (John R. Cole, Eugenie Scott, and Thomas A. Sebeok) and one sociologist (Dorothy Nelkin). Three other anthropologists (Robert E. Funk, Laurie Godfrey, and Stuart D. Scott, Jr.) and one sociologist (William Sims Bainbridge) were listed as scientific and technical consultants.[6] In addition to lending their names to the CSICOP cause, sociologists and anthropologists occasionally contribute an article to the *Skeptical Inquirer*, such as pieces on archeology (Feder 1980, see also 1990; and McKusick 1981).

Regarding parapsychology, there seems to be more support from anthropologists than sociologists, probably because anthropologists are more likely to be exposed to ostensibly anomalous phenomena during their fieldwork experiences. Consequently, anthropologists have shown an interest in psychical research since at least the nineteenth century, as in the case of Edward B. Tylor, one of the founders of anthropology, who observed Spiritualist mediums.[7] In the twentieth century, perhaps the most prominent anthropologist to have supported psychical research was Margaret Mead, who in the 1940s was a trustee of the American Society for Psychical Research. Later in life she is said to have been instrumental in winning acceptance for the Parapsychological Association as a member unit of the American Association for the Advancement of Sciences in 1969.[8] In addition, a number of anthropologists, some of them prominent, have at different points in their careers shown some interest in psychical research or the utility of parapsychology as an analytical framework for interpreting shamanism and related phenomena.[9]

In two of the member units of the American Anthropological Association, anthropologists occasionally express interest in parapsychology or belief in psychic phenomena. The Society for the Anthropology of Consciousness lists "psychic (psi) phenomena and [its] possible role in traditional cultural practices" as one of its research interests, along with a variety of psychological phenomena having to do with shamanism and altered states of consciousness. Likewise, in the informal, first-person accounts of field experiences that are often published in *Anthropology and Humanism Quarterly*, anthropologists occasionally narrate accounts of anomalous phenomena that they believe they have encountered in the field setting.[10]

There are also some cases of sociologists and anthropologists whose writings and statements might be interpreted as more aligned with the New Age movement than with either parapsychologists or skeptics. For example, the anthropologist Michael Harner, who distinguished himself as an ethnographer of the Jívaro and a student of hallucinogens and shamanism, subsequently resigned his post at the New School for Social Research and began a foundation dedicated to the study and sponsorship of shamanic voyages.[11] Likewise, in *The Aquarian Conspiracy* Marilyn Ferguson frequently mentions the work of the social scientist Willis Harman, and she calls the book *The Changing Image of Man*, which Harman helped write, a "remarkable document" that helped lay the "groundwork" for the paradigm shift she was advocating (Ferguson 1987:61; see Markley and Harman 1982).

In short, there are instances where sociologists and anthropologists side with each of their three Others, but because they do not do so in a monolithic way, it is not possible to argue that as communities they legitimate one of the three positions at the expense of the other two. Furthermore, there is a substantial body of sociological and anthropological work that does not fit into one of the three explicitly aligned positions. That observation leads to the second and more complicated question: is it possible for human scientists to be staking out their own position in the ideological arena, and if so, what is its nature and how does it interact with the Others?

Many human scientists do not openly advocate the validity of the positions of skeptics, parapsychologists, or New Agers. Drawing on the Durkheimian tradition of "social facts" or the Boasian counterpart of "cultural relativism," they bracket the question of whether the beliefs and practices under study are in some sense true or false. I would put into this group most of the survey approaches to paranormal beliefs (e.g., Emmons 1982, Greeley 1975) as well as most anthropological and sociological accounts of New Age beliefs (e.g., Danforth 1989, Tipton 1982, and this study) and most sociological studies of parapsychology. Perhaps the most sophisticated example of the latter group is the work of the sociologists and STS researchers Harry Collins and Trevor Pinch. A more detailed consideration of their "relativist" position will make it possible to discuss some broader theoretical issues.

Boundary-Work, Reflexivity, and Capturing

Stated briefly, the relativist position brackets the discussion of whether or not paranormal phenomena exist; as Collins and Pinch put it, they remain "neutral" regarding this question (Collins and Pinch 1979:263; 1982). Instead of attempting to settle truth claims, they view and represent their work as "that of the participant observer building up the background for good sociological fieldwork" (1979:239), a methodological position that they elaborate further in their book, *Frames of Meaning* (1982). Thus, their approach is more or less the same as that adopted by hundreds of anthropologists in studies of non-Western religion, magic, and medicine. The work of Collins and Pinch, however, has suffered from some criticism within the science and technology studies community. These criticisms warrant discussion because they involve general theoretical issues to which, I believe, the approach to boundary-work that I have outlined above may make a contribution.

In a footnote to their 1979 article, Collins and Pinch note how one skeptic criticized their paper, whereas parapsychologists were more "complimentary" (1979:263). The STS researchers Michael Mulkay, Jonathan Potter, and Steven Yearly develop this point by arguing that the two sociologists' relativist position caused them to develop an analysis "from the point of view of (some) parapsychologists" (1983:187).[12] The result, according to the three critics, is that Collins and Pinch privilege the parapsychologists' account over that of their critics, and in turn the sociologists fail to maintain their own goal of "relativism," a term which appears to mean "neutrality" on the issue of the validity of paranormal claims.

However, if one takes seriously Collins and Pinch's methodological stance of doing participant observation and fieldwork, then as good ethnographers they should be expected to tell the story "from the native's point of view" (Geertz 1983). Indeed, relativism in the sense of "cultural relativism" may be taken to mean merely that one tells the story *relative* to the culture of one's informants. Thus, from an anthropological viewpoint, to some extent the criticisms raised by Mulkay, Potter, and Yearly may be taken as compliments: if their argument is right (cf. Collins 1983:106–7), then Collins and Pinch did their job as good cultural anthropologists or interpretive sociologists. As Collins comments, "In general, using actors' categories does not necessarily lead to bias unless actors' epistemological evaluations are also taken over" (Collins 1983:106).

Whatever one's view about who is "right" in the debate, Mulkay, Potter, and Yearly do raise a problem of general theoretical importance, a problem that the STS researchers Pam Scott, Evelleen Richards, and Brian Martin (1990) have called "capturing." Reviewing several other cases similar to that of Collins and Pinch, Scott and colleagues argue more generally that scholars who attempt a symmetrical analysis of both sides of a controversy will almost always be "more useful to the side with less scientific credibility or cognitive authority" (1990:490).[13] Given this dilemma, the social scientist may be tempted by the positivist option and side with scientific orthodoxy rather than pursue a balanced and symmetrical analysis. Scott, Richards, and Martin describe the situation by invoking a sustained set of martial metaphors, complete with underdog heroics that should by now be familiar to the reader: "The analyst is at the front lines of the battle. It is so easy to be caught in the cross fire that many prefer to don positivist camouflage and seek shelter in the best-fortified trench, rather than venture out into the no-man's-land (which is even more a no-woman's-land) of sustained symmetry. The combatants have a good deal at stake in the sociologist's interpretation and presentation of news from the war zone. Both sides to a dispute have opposing and unshakable convictions as to who are the heroes and the villains involved and where truth and justice lie" (1990:490).[14]

I have little disagreement with the general lines of their argument against the myth of the neutral observer and the probability that ostensibly "neutral" accounts by social scientists will be captured.[15] However, there are some ways in which the argument of Scott, Richards, and Martin might be extended and amplified, especially when taking into account the cultural perspective that I have been defending and employing. To begin, it is likely that at least in some cases the options for the human scientist are not restricted to siding with the orthodox position or being captured by the heterodox one. To make the point by example, let us return to the Collins and Pinch case, this time to the reception of their book *Frames of Meaning* (1982). Unlike the article published in 1979, the book focuses on claims of psychokinetic metal bending, which both skeptics and many parapsychologists have rejected as fraudulent. Nevertheless, Collins and Pinch maintain their relativist position. Does this imply that they will be captured by the parapsychologists?

The question may be answered empirically by examining the way skeptics and parapsychologists reviewed the book. In a review titled "Fool's Paradigms," the skeptic Martin Gardner constructs Collins and Pinch as dupes of the parapsychologists; whereas on the parapsychology side, the psychologist Douglas Stokes questions the skeptical arguments raised by the two sociologists.[16] Furthermore, opponents Gardner and Stokes appear to agree with each other when they both reject the sociologists' radical formulation of relativism that emerges out of Kuhn's argument for the incommensurability of paradigms (1962). These reviews confirm the main argument of Scott, Richards, and Martin (1990): that human scientists are drawn into the debate and that they cannot remain neutral in practice. However, regarding their subargument that symmetrical analysis tends to result in being captured by the heterodox position, the reception of *Frames of Meaning* suggests a different case from what they report: that in some situations human scientists may be perceived as opponents by *both* the more and the less orthodox scientists. In other words, the possibility emerges that human scientists may be perceived as playing, and may actually play, a role as an independent voice with its own agendas and interests.[17]

The second way in which the argument for capturing may be extended requires some cultural critique that problematizes the dyadic assumptions that may be built into the argument. American culture (and probably most of the other Protestant, Anglophone cultures, including those of Australia and Britain) tends to operate in terms of sharp dyadic categories. The cultural pattern is easily seen when the Protestant, Anglophone cultures are contrasted with their Mediterranean and Latin American siblings, where sharp dyadic categories are frequently blurred by interstitial, mediating categories (DaMatta 1991). The American racial classification system, for example, categorizes people as either black or white, rather than admitting a whole series of mediating and flexible categories such as mulattoes and mestizos, as is the case of Brazil and other Latin American countries (Degler 1986). Likewise, the Protestant religious heritage leaves a legacy of dualistic categories, such as God and the believer or heaven and hell, rather than a world of mediations constructed around the cult of the saints and the dogma of purgatory. Today Hollywood movies tell and retell the same moralistic story of good guys versus bad guys, or, as they say in Brazil, the repetitive struggle between the "white hats" and "black hats" that sometimes has led my Latin American colleagues to comment that Americans can produce only an endless series of variants of the same basic movie. The question emerges, then, to what extent is the division of groups into the dyad of the capturing and the captured perhaps an oversimplification, or, at the minimum, just one of the possibilities?[18]

One of the theoretical implications of my argument in favor of a multiple and complex understanding of the boundaries between science and nonscience now becomes evident. In cases where there are multiple gradations of more or less cognitive authority (or orthodoxy) and multiple boundaries, both within and among groups, it is not easy to determine which social category is the one with less cognitive authority and therefore the one that is going to capture the discourse of the analyst. If, for example, spontaneous case researchers have less cognitive authority within parapsychology, but more than New Agers, then it may be possible for capturing to occur in multiple and contradictory ways.

Neutrality—or better, as the STS researcher Sal Restivo has suggested to me, "bracketing strategies"—might also be rethought as similarly complex and multiple. Thus, while at one level I may, like Collins and Pinch, bracket claims on the paranormal and risk being captured by one or more of the social categories with "less" cognitive authority (ah, but according to whom?), at another level I may do some capturing of my own. As actors who are not just observing the ideological arena but who are a part of it, we human scientists also have a perspective, a position, and a discourse. As a result it is possible to engage these other discourses in open and frank ways, particularly on issues for which as scholars we have a degree of expertise or as citizens we have a degree of authority. In other words, I argue in favor of a critical sociocultural perspective *in contrast to* the discourses of parapsychologists, skeptics, and New Agers, or in favor of critical elements within each of their own discourses.

Reflexive Critique

The sense of multiple and complex boundaries among discourses in a shared ideological arena has implications for the reflexive and critical examination of one's own disciplines and discourses. One example is the method developed in my essay "Disobsessing Disobsession: Religion, Ritual, and the Social Sciences in Brazil" (1989a), where I showed how debates among religious groups played themselves out as debates among social scientists, but transformed into the idiom of methodological and theoretical issues. I would suggest that we look for similar processes in the science and technology studies community. For example, at one level Mulkay, Potter, and Yearly (1983) present their critique of Collins and Pinch (1979) as a theoretical debate framed in terms of the superiority of the former's discourse analysis over the latter's program of relativism. Thus, the disagreement appears to take place on purely methodological grounds and with reference only to theoretical concerns within STS. Still, it is curious that the argument against Collins and Pinch hinges on the fact that they constructed their analysis "from the point of view of (some) parapsychologists" (1983: 187). If the discourse analysts had studied Collins and Pinch's *Frames of Meaning* (1982; see also Pamplin and Collins 1975), which exposes fraudulent metal bending, they might have had to argue that the sociologists had constructed their story from the point of view of the skeptics or orthodox scientists. Yet, that argument might not have carried the same weight as one that Collins and Pinch had been captured by parapsychologists. Even among the constructivists and post-Mertonians in the science and technology studies community, which is largely composed of white males who first studied the sciences, there is a widespread belief that orthodox science and existing technologies are "right."[19]

The horror, then, is that two colleagues in the human sciences might be seen as falling under the spell of "pseudoscience." Indeed, Collins and Pinch note that the taboo nature of parapsychology is so great that they "quickly discovered the importance of telling [their] sociologist colleagues" that they were doing participant observation and fieldwork (1979:239). In other words, the "boundary dispute between discourse analysts and Bath relativists" (Scott et al. 1990:490) — that is, a debate within STS that is framed in methodological and theoretical terms — might reproduce the debate between orthodox scientists and parapsychologists, which in turn plays out the conflict between science and religion for legitimacy in society.[20]

The reproduction, within the domain of social studies of science and technology, of conflicts between orthodox scientists and parapsychologists may or may not have occurred in the case just described, and I give it here only as an example of how such an analysis might proceed. In more general terms, however, the disciplinary hierarchies of the world of science and technology are reproduced in the sociological, anthropological, historical, literary, and other studies of science and technology. Thus, a human scientist who studies parapsychology may become polluted merely by having contact with the taboo science, and one way in which sanctions against this polluted status may operate may be through a critique of the polluted human scientist that is formulated in an ostensibly neutral or methodological idiom. At the other end of the spectrum, my "native informants" in the STS community tell me that the most prestigious and exciting areas of science and technology are also the most prestigious for science and technology studies. Causality is admittedly bidirectional. Science and technology studies legitimates the hot (or "sexy," to invoke the masculine metaphor, see Traweek 1990) areas of science and technology even as it follows them. However, the human scientists probably are doing more following, particularly those who belong to what is sometimes called the "hooray for science and technology" school.

Thus, in order to extend critical perspectives in anthropology and STS, I am advocating a form of reflexivity that goes beyond textual experimentation to a critique of the social, cultural, and political assumptions of both the discourse of the Self and that of the Other. In a postmodern and postfoundationalist world, the critique of the Other will be accompanied by a return motion directed toward one's own discourse, but in a postconstructivist world there are no neutral positions and therefore one must eventually articulate a position lest someone else do it instead. (And, of course, even articulating a position does not prevent the Other from capturing it or making use of it.) In this chapter, I have outlined some ways in which a critical, sociocultural perspective might lead to changes in contemporary conceptualizations of reflexivity within the social and cultural studies of science and technology: to move reflexivity from questions restricted to epistemological and representational issues to a critique of the political and ideological assumptions of one's own discursive community. In the next chapter, I will direct this critical perspective toward skeptics, para-psychologists, and New Agers.

8

Practical Implications:
Toward Dialogue

Let us test and examine our ways.
— *The Lamentations of Jeremiah* 3:40

THIS BOOK, *Science in the New Age*, might be described as "dialogical" rather than "reflexive," since I recognize that my interpretations are not only influenced by social contingencies but also situated in an arena of debate and dialogue with my Others. I therefore conclude the book by making that dialogue explicit, asking some at times pointed questions, and making some recommendations for changes.[1]

I am aware that my analyses, as well as the recommendations and criticisms about to be presented, may undermine the authority and interests of each community and therefore invoke a hostile response. I have already met Spiritualists and New Agers who have labeled me a materialist, parapsychologists who decided I was a skeptic, and a skeptic who called me "irrational"—all when I dared to give my own interpretations! However, to believe that dialogue is fruitless and change is impossible would be as great a mistake as wholesale cynicism. The three communities are far from monolithic or stagnant, and indeed there is a diversity of positions within each of them that, as I showed in the first chapter, is one of the sources of their historical dynamism. It would therefore be a mistake to assume that the critical questions raised here will be uniformly rejected. Rather, the questions may help some actors, even if they represent a minority position within their own discursive communities, to articulate and think through arguments that they may have already formulated in somewhat different ways. Indeed, I hope that the analyses and critical questions that follow, whatever their shortcomings, may play a small role in the ongoing process of the historical development of paranormal culture in the United States.

Before moving on to a specific discussion of each of the three communities, the most obvious and broadest critical question should be mentioned at the outset: yet one more common ground among the three discourses is their representation of "science" as "natural science." What is lost in this definition of science? When skeptics, parapsychologists, and New Agers talk about science, they almost invariably mean physics, chemistry, geology, biology, and other natural sciences, and then they go on to exaggerate "science" to support one pole or another of a metaphysical opposition between materialism and mechanism on the one side and dualism or holism on the other side. Rarely does "science" ever include or mean the social sciences or humanities, and in fact any discussion of human science perspectives is suspiciously absent. Does the repression of social and cultural discourse allow the three communities to hide from themselves a self-conscious inspection not only of their hidden values, politics, and potentials but also of their position to society? Such a possibility points to a way in which the dialogue between the human sciences and its three Others might take place in a constructive manner.

Some readers might think that my ordering of the chapters from New Agers to parapsychologists to skeptics means that I implicitly see a progression or hierarchy. I would not want to be interpreted as endorsing any such hierarchy. I do think that in many ways parapsychologists are located betwixt and between the other two, but I decided to discuss the New Age texts and writers first only to give a clearer point of reference for the parapsychologists' and skeptics' critiques. To make the point, let me begin with skeptics in this final chapter.

Skeptics

Without a doubt, skeptics have performed a useful social function by exposing the numerous cases of charlatanism and fraud associated with paranormal beliefs. Like tens of thousands of other people, I read with interest the *Skeptical Inquirer*. However, the world of paranormal beliefs and practices cannot be reduced to cranks, crackpots, and charlatans. A large number of sincere people are exploring alternative approaches to questions of personal meaning, spirituality, healing, and paranormal experience in general. To the skeptic, their quest may ultimately rest on a delusion, but debunking is hardly likely to be an effective rhetorical device for their rationalist project of getting the Other to recognize what appears to the skeptics as mistaken or magical thinking. Instead, if skeptics were to understand the world more from the perspective of their Others, then their attempts to educate and enlighten them might be more successful. By adopting this alternative perspective – essentially a cultural perspective – skepticism could become more sophisticated and ultimately more effective.

Consider, for example, the case of crystal healing, which to the skeptics certainly has to be one of the most questionable of New Age beliefs and practices. To the skeptic, the idea of crystals as quasianimate beings with healing powers may be patently ridiculous, as it is to many other people. However, crystal healing is not ridiculous to its clients and practitioners, and perhaps because some people believe in the healing power of crystals, they sometimes may feel better and may in fact get better in some cases. The cause may not be magical crystal powers, but it may also be considerably more complicated than a placebo effect. For example, my own experience with a local crystal healer, who volunteered to do a free session with me to demonstrate her work, is that the idiom of chakras and crystal diagnosis enabled a rather sophisticated psychotherapeutic dialogue to take place, and this general pattern is documented in innumerable ethnographic studies of alternative and non-Western healers (e.g., Crapanzano and Garrison 1977, Kiev 1964, McGuire 1988). A question of methodology is at stake: the skeptic might take a clue from cultural anthropology and develop a more sophisticated skepticism by understanding alternative belief systems from the perspective of the people who hold them and by situating these beliefs in their historical, social, and cultural contexts. As a result, the world of the paranormal may appear less as a silly turn toward irrationalism and more as an idiom through which segments of society express their conflicts, dilemmas, and identities.[2]

Rather than attempt to situate alternative belief systems in social, historical, and cultural contexts, skeptics instead tend to belittle them. When religious beliefs are involved, the strategy immediately raises not only questions of bigotry but also of rhetoric that may be self-defeating for the skeptics' own goal of public education and enlightenment. On this point, one critic of the skeptics' hidden religious polemics, the religious studies scholar J. Gordon Melton (1988), encouraged skeptics to drop emotive terms like "claptrap" and "drivel," to avoid characterizing New Age thought as "emotional," "mystical," and "subjective" in opposition to scientific thought, to avoid broadsides against easy targets such as Shirley MacLaine, and in general to be more careful with their analyses of issues and events within the movement.[3] Whether skeptics take such criticisms to heart is doubtful – sociological and cultural analyses may not sell as well as debunking exposés – but it remains a challenge for skeptics if they are to have their work taken seriously both by the human scientists who are studying and writing about the same movements and by the very members of the public whose minds they are attempting to change.

To the extent that skeptics have a psychological or sociological theory of New Age beliefs, it tends to be very simplistic: paranormal beliefs are "comforting" to people who cannot handle the reality of an atheistic universe, or their beliefs are the product of an irresponsible media that is not encouraging the public to think critically. Certainly, neither of these theories is necessarily wrong, but I have been arguing for a more sophisticated approach: to analyze paranormal discourse as cultural discourse, to take what New Agers say seriously, if not in the right/wrong sense then in the right/ left sense. Whatever their shortcomings, as New Agers articulate alternative spiritual visions, they are also expressing the dilemmas of the current social order and attempting to define alternatives to that order.

Another, perhaps even more important, way in which the human sciences may help lead to a more sophisticated skepticism is to challenge skeptics to think more culturally about their own discourse. I have pointed out several ways in which skeptics' construction of the paranormal resonates with the surrounding culture, but I wish to reemphasize the point about the implicit dualism in the sharp oppositions skeptics often draw between the scientific and the paranormal. As in American foreign policy, with its frequently disastrous constructions of evil menaces abroad, skeptical constructions of the paranormal Other can have violent implications. The implications are perhaps less evident in the United States, where first-amendment freedoms make state repression of advocates of the paranormal more problematic, but as organized skepticism spreads to other countries that do not have these same traditions of civil liberties, skeptical discourse could easily legitimate state repression of alternative religions, as has occurred in the past in Latin America (see Hess 1987a). Even in the United States, I have gathered many horror stories from parapsychologists, psychologists, and other scientists who have attempted to do ESP research in academic settings and, as a result, have had their careers ruined by skeptical colleagues (Hess in press a). Rather than belittle and debunk the paranormal Other, a much less violent and perhaps ultimately more effective form of skepticism would be to recognize and attempt to understand the significant plurality of voices within the field that skeptics tend to construct as a monolithic paranormal Other.

In addition, a sociocultural perspective could lead to critical self-reflection about the meaning and nature of skepticism as a social movement. Such a project would involve multiple levels, but a good place to start would be the professional or philosophical roots that some of the leaders of CSICOP have in secular humanist/atheist groups and the magicians' fraternity.[4] Like parapsychology and New Age thought, skeptical discourse is based on assumptions that have not been scientifically tested and may not be testable. Consequently, skeptics' assumptions may sometimes play themselves out in a kind of religious zeal to defend a materialistic and atheistic world view that smacks of what has been called "scientific fundamentalism" or "irrational rationalism," as New Age and parapsychology critics have called it respectively (Wilson 1986, Rockwell et al. 1978). When skeptics actually tried to test some of their assumptions empirically through experiments, their results were not what they expected, and subsequently skeptics have chosen, perhaps shrewdly, not to challenge the claims of experimental parapsychology via experimental research, which may not turn out in the skeptics' favor.[5]

For skeptics to recognize that they, too, speak from a position of untested assumptions would be the first step in a project that would involve inspecting their assumptions from a more sociocultural and historical perspective. One example would be to inquire into the ways political and philosophical ideologies have influenced and shaped the skeptical program. Such inquiry would have to be sophisticated enough to take into account the diversity of positions within the skeptical community. To give an example, consider the differences, and the underlying similarities, between two of the most prominent skeptics: Martin Gardner and Paul Kurtz.[6]

At first glance, Gardner and Kurtz bring to the skeptical movement opposing political and philosophical baggage, and thus they represent an apparent diversity of political views. Kurtz, for example, is an atheist who in 1983 described himself as a "libertarian democratic secular humanist" (1983a:266). He notes that in the 1930s and 1940s "the influence of Marx was very strong," and he was at one point a democratic socialist (266). However, since that time he became more of a libertarian, and although his libertarianism cannot be reduced to neoconservatism, there are points where Kurtz's writings converge with conservative agendas, such as his critique of the welfare state and unions and his defense of free-market ideology (1983a:48–49, cf. Kurtz 1988: 189–90). Thus, while as a libertarian Kurtz shows a great deal of concern for human rights such as property and free enterprise, he does not grapple with new forms of human rights abuses engendered by late-twentieth-century capitalism, such as the rights of local communities when faced with the problem of corporate hegemony. In contrast, those questions are addressed more directly in the scrivenings of the democratic socialist Martin Gardner, who — unlike his atheistic, libertarian colleague — proclaims himself a theist and a "democratic socialist" in the tradition of "democratic socialists" Norman Thomas and John Dewey (Gardner 1983:152, 155).

Differences notwithstanding, Kurtz and Gardner apparently share an Old Left background from which they have disengaged to differing degrees. Both also have a shared respect for Sidney Hook, who is difficult to situate politically but sometimes is labeled a neoconservative.[7] Gardner and Kurtz also converge on their rejection of the New Left and counterculture, or at least important aspects of it, and in doing so political persuasions may intersect with anti–New Age and antiparanormal stances. Listen to Gardner, for example, writing in 1983: "The entire counterculture scene of the sixties, with its weird mixture of kinky sex, pot, rock, zen, astrology, obscene language, and fusty anarchist theory, always struck me as a prime example of how quickly angry rebels turn into other-directed conformists of the most extreme sort. After telling everybody over thirty that each person has a right to do his or her own thing, millions of youngsters proceeded to do identical things. . . . A few became so mentally disturbed that they bombed and murdered those who wanted to do their own but different things" (1983:124–25). Kurtz, writing in 1969, expressed similar sentiments about the counterculture (and also drew on American cultural values of individualism and freedom), although in the more sedate tone of a college professor:

The way to meet the radical is on his own ground in a dialogue on values . . . Yes, we may say, there has been an overemphasis on achievement and work, and . . . we must be committed to freedom of the individual – sexual, moral, and social.

But we may also say in response that personal liberty and creativity without balance becomes chaos, and that passion without moderation or reason is a form of madness. . . . If the young radical has something to say to us, we also have something to say to him. And along with our vices – which we are all too prone to recognize – we should be prepared to defend our virtues (1969b:1).[8]

In the next issue of the *Humanist*, Kurtz wrote a critique of Herbert Marcuse's *An Essay on Liberation* (1969), contrasting this *"enfant terrible* of revolutionary students" with Sidney Hook, "their *bête noire*" (Kurtz 1969a: 33). While a student at Columbia, Kurtz had taken courses from both Marcuse and Hook, but he sided with the latter. Unlike Marcuse, Kurtz attempted to defend a "radical center" against the New Left and New Right (1970), and likewise Gardner defended a moderate, democratic socialist viewpoint. Both parted ways with the radical ideas of a younger generation.

To discuss the politics of these leading skeptical intellectuals should not be taken as an attempt to discredit them. On the contrary, their concern with politics reveals a laudable ability to think socially and culturally, an ability which is often absent in the debates of the paraculture. However, their explicit political ideologies and philosophies may be intersecting with generational diacritics in ways that lead to distortions of their paranormal Other. To what extent is the skeptics' dismissal of the New Age and the paranormal just an epilogue to the old drama of the generation gap? Is this, in cultural terms, the story of "slightly geriatric" and "predominantly white" men (Anderson 1987:51) reacting to a younger generation that grants a greater space to other voices and, through its mysticism and to some extent its membership, recognizes the emergence of a society that grants an increasing role for multiculturalism and feminist perspectives?

Whatever linkages there are between individual skeptics and social or political visions that may be interpreted to be in some sense "left-" or "right-wing," organized skepticism may represent a more general kind of conservativism: a conservative vision of what is scientifically and socially possible, a vision that has derived much of its historical energy and momentum in reaction to the more radical visions of the sixties and its transformations in the seventies, eighties, and nineties. However, even that appraisal is not complex enough. Organized skepticism emerged historically not only in the wake of the sixties and the development of the New Age movement, but also in the wake of the reactionary movements of fundamentalist Christianity and the Christian New Right, to which skeptics have directed their critical gaze as well. A whole series of interesting possibilities emerge. To what extent, for example, is contemporary skepticism shaped by the Old Left heritage of some of its leading figures, and to what extent are its rhetorical tactics — directed at New Age, New Left, New Right, New Everything — shaped by an Old Left generational experience that came of age in a time of McCarthyist rhetoric?

The underlying politicophilosophical presuppositions as well as the social and historical position of the skeptical movement therefore merit more reflexive self-questioning. I have only pointed at one direction in which this questioning might go. Another direction is to ask what the consequences are for a self-proclaimed scientific movement that seeks a large popular following and local skeptical "chapters." The apparent growth of organized skepticism suggests that it may be increasing at a rate directly proportional to the growth of New Age organizations, and skeptics might do well to view with suspicion and concern the linked history. Furthermore, the growing popularity of local skeptical societies, particularly overseas, may in turn transform CSICOP in ways that contradict the goal of "scientificity" it sets for itself. How will skepticism be redefined as it moves into Africa, Brazil, and other parts of the world where widespread belief in spirits and sorcery may lead to deviations from the CSICOP orthodoxy? Likewise, what are the contradictions inherent in a magazine- or book-publishing company that attempts to have a widespread popular appeal but also to maintain scientific rigor? For example, the backlist of Prometheus Books, an independent publishing house directed by Kurtz that in 1989 was celebrating its twentieth anniversary, includes self-help books on sexuality and psychology that, had they been published by another publisher, might have themselves come under the critical gaze of an Amazing Randi or fringe-watching Gardner. Thus, issues related to the very popularity and growth of the skeptical movement constitute yet another case in which a critical sociocultural perspective might help skeptics to examine their own movement: a skeptical skepticism.

Parapsychologists

Because parapsychologists are heterodox scientists who attempt to win acceptability within the academy and among orthodox scientists, their problems are somewhat different from those of skeptics, who represent scientific orthodoxy and are more concerned with winning support among the general public. Still, parapsychology could benefit as much as skepticism from a sociocultural perspective that analyzes critically not only its efforts to win greater legitimacy but also its methods and theoretical frameworks. As with skeptics, there are already people within the parapsychological community asking questions similar to the ones asked here.

At the 1990 Parapsychological Association conference, which I attended, there was considerable recognition of and discussion of the economic and political crisis of academic parapsychology, a situation which the 1991 Parapsychological Association president, Stephen Braude, subsequently described as "limping toward the millennium" (1991). It may be too early to write a requiem for American parapsychology, but it is true that during the 1980s several major laboratories in the United States and in Europe closed due to loss of funding or the retirement of their directors, and by 1990 the graduate program in parapsychology at John F. Kennedy University was also moribund. Parapsychologists openly recognized that CSICOP and a skeptic-controlled National Research Council report had taken their toll (see Palmer et al. 1989). They were also finding it difficult to recruit new scientists into their field, which in fact had suffered a decline in membership during the late 1980s (White 1990:8). As one potential recruit said to me during the meeting, he was interested in the field, but after attending the conference he was not sure he wanted to climb aboard a sinking ship, "especially one that has so many holes in it."

The final session of the 1990 conference was devoted to brainstorming for ways to make parapsychology more viable and less stigmatized. Thus, the parapsychology community itself recognizes its current state of crisis, and it is attempting to find solutions (see Braude 1991). I will argue here that the experimentalists' evaluation of the crisis and solution is sociologically naive, and they could benefit from a more sophisticated understanding of the politics of legitimation. Many parapsychologists still seem to believe that their struggle for scientific legitimacy depends on ever greater experimental controls and increasingly sophisticated analyses that show general trends over many experiments, so much so that it becomes possible to speak of replication. The general culture of parapsychology today, then, is one of dedicated experimentalists who perform increasingly complicated experiments and speak an increasingly technical discourse that is accessible to fewer and fewer people. To some extent, this trend may be viewed as "progress," but it may also have deleterious implications for the future of parapsychology as a field of inquiry.

In chapter 5, I discussed some of the cultural meanings of the division within parapsychology between experimental and case study methods. I argued that to some extent the experimental approach inscribes masculine values when it transforms the amorphous "stories" of psychic experiences into the "hard data" of laboratory experiments in which ostensible paranormal phenomena can be controlled, named, quantified, and domesticated. I do not wish to argue that such an approach is wrong; certainly, Western science has brought about many benefits via its masculinist project of the domestication of nature, and if experimental parapsychologists are successful at "harnessing" the paranormal phenomena that they believe exist, their research could potentially lead to new breakthroughs in medicine or communication. However, I wish to question the political and cultural implications of the experimental approach for the field of parapsychology as a whole.

The experimental approach is based on an idea of replication or repeatability, and many parapsychologists believe that greater levels of replicability will lead to greater acceptance of their discipline. However, the definition of replication or repeatability is itself a complex problem, and furthermore even if replication were achieved, we know from a number of sociological studies that demarcation conflicts over science and pseudoscience are considerably more political and social than merely intellectual debates over replication (e.g., Collins 1985, 1987; Pinch 1979). Thus, one might question the parapsychologists' sociological appraisal that better experimental replicability will change the legitimacy of their field in the broader scientific community.

Comparison with the Brazilian case is instructive. In Brazil parapsychology lacks the professionalism, secularism, methodological sophistication, and even, for the most part, the interest in empirical research that characterizes the academic parapsychology of North America and Western Europe. Nevertheless, in Brazil parapsychology enjoys higher prestige and wider acceptance than it does in the rich, Western countries. In part there is greater acceptance of parapsychology in Brazil because Brazilians believe more in supernatural phenomena. Spirit mediumship religions attract tens of millions of followers and folk Catholicism sanctions miracles. To the point, the movie *Ghost* sold more than ten million tickets in Brazil and was the biggest film in a decade.[9] Also contributing to the prestige of parapsychology in Brazil is the Catholic church's use of the heterodox science as an ideological weapon to combat the spirit mediumship religions, and therefore in a predominantly Catholic country parapsychology has the official sanction of the church. However, there is an additional difference that suggests an important lesson: the term *parapsicólogo* in Brazilian Portuguese often refers to a kind of psychotherapist; or the term may refer to an educator, often a Jesuit intellectual, who gives popular courses on parapsychology.

The higher prestige of parapsychologists in Brazil may therefore be related to the fact that, despite their "less scientific" outlook relative to North American and European parapsychologists, they perform therapeutic and educational services for the general public and therefore are socially valued. In Brazil the parapsychologist is frequently a therapist who has many patients or an educator who gives large public classes; that is, the clinical and educational applications are more professionalized and also capable of generating income. The Brazilian case (like that of psychoanalysis and other psychotherapeutic and self-help psychologies) suggests the following social and cultural pattern regarding enhanced legitimacy for heterodox sciences: it is applicability, and with it financial and professional power, rather than replicability, and with it strategies of sanitization, that enables heterodox sciences to win greater acceptance, both among the general public and in the scientific community.

Unlike the Brazilians, the leaders of the Parapsychological Association do not devote much of their resources to research that would produce clinical and educational applications. It is true that there are occasional papers and sessions at Parapsychological Association conferences on clinical issues, and many parapsychological research organizations and laboratories provide public outreach by answering phone calls and letters. There are also public lectures at the American Society for Psychical Research and summer courses at the Foundation for Research on the Nature of Man. Nevertheless, only a fraction of parapsychology research is devoted to potential clinical and educational applications. Furthermore, although it is true that some psi researchers have advocated generating applicable knowledge (e.g.,

Jahn 1983), they seem to hope for applications to flow from their experimental work, which in turn would require much more reliable and replicable — and less controversial — results than is presently the case. Thus, the experimentalist program remains more or less intact, notwithstanding an increasing number of critics from within the parapsychology community (e.g., Stevenson 1987b, White 1990).

In following the experimentalist program and attempting to win legitimacy by providing convincing experimental evidence, American parapsychologists are confronting the legitimation issue based on a relatively naive sociology of science. It is not entirely clear that any amount of evidence will ever change the minds of their critics, as some members of the parapsychology community are beginning to recognize (e.g., Braude 1991). Furthermore, as I have shown "repeatedly" in this book, the whole issue of the boundary between science and nonscience in this area is thoroughly invested with cultural meanings and rather stereotyped constructions of the Other. Parapsychologists are the skeptics' Other, and almost by definition there is little in the way of intellectual arguments or experimental evidence that will persuade the skeptics to change their minds, notwithstanding skeptics' protests that they are open-minded and "neutral." It is always possible to find a loophole in an experimental protocol, and if the critics are philosophically opposed to the project of parapsychology or the existence of extrasensory perception and psychokinesis, then they are certain to find that hole.

Thus, the battle over whether or not skeptics and orthodox scientists will ever accept research on extrasensory perception and psychokinesis as part of the proper purview of science may ultimately rest on cultural assumptions about the nature of the world — whether it is materialistic or dualistic, reducible or holistic, etc. — rather than on experimental evidence. Cultural assumptions, however, can be shaped; and if skeptics are publishing a mass-market magazine that is widely circulated among the general public (not to mention within the scientific community and the academy), while parapsychologists continue to publish academic journals with miniscule circulations and extremely technical discussions, the latter are not likely to achieve their goal. In an area of research where data are elusive and questionable, power and financial resources will be at least as important as experimental evidence.[10]

Having political power and greater financial resources, however, hinges on generating socially useful and applicable knowledge. How could parapsychologists accumulate applicable knowledge that does not suffer from the replicability problem? At the 1990 meeting of the Parapsychological Association, there was some further discussion of potential clinical applications. For example, one researcher was applying experimental protocols first developed for psychokinesis research to problems involving more conventional psychosomatic healing processes. Likewise, at other conferences there was some interest in developing an applied branch of parapsychology that provided counseling services for people who experienced trauma related to psychic experiences (e.g., Roll 1986). Applications in the sense of counseling and clinical work have an important ideological advantage: they need only assume that some people have troubling subjective psychic experiences, a social fact that not even skeptics would challenge. Such applied research does not have to make the more controversial claim that paranormal phenomena exist objectively.

By bracketing the issue of the reality or nonreality of paranormal phenomena in field and clinical settings, where — as the skeptics justifiably point out — the issue would be extremely difficult to resolve convincingly, parapsychologists would be able to focus on new research questions such as the relative efficacy of different intervention strategies and the way cultural meanings are evident in different interpretations of psychic experience.[11] Parapsychological research could then begin to break down the walls between it and orthodox science by contributing to existing research programs in medical/psychological anthropology, transcultural psychiatry, clinical psychology, the psychology and sociology of paranormal belief, and pastoral and cross-cultural counseling. Their work would also make it possible to generate socially useful knowledge that could help clinicians, clergy, and social workers who must work with people who present their personal and family problems in an idiom of paranormal experience.

Some kind of clinically oriented research would therefore provide one way to the door of orthodox science and medicine from the corner of heterodoxy into which parapsychologists seem to have painted themselves. It would help put a discourse that has become increasingly obscure, quantitative, and experimental back in contact with the society from which it ultimately derives its vitality. About two-thirds of the American population report having psychic experiences, so understanding these experiences from psychological, sociological, and cultural perspectives would mean addressing an important aspect of the contemporary culture (White 1990). Furthermore, the argument that a social need is being left unfulfilled is given some support by the number of new organizations that have emerged in recent years in a social space that could have been shared with a field of "clinical parapsychology" or "counseling/therapy for psychic experiences": TREAT, or the Center for Treatment and Research of Experienced Anomalous Trauma; the International Association for the Study of Near-Death Experiences; and the International Society for the Study of Multiple Personality and Dissociation. More generally the growth of all sorts of New Age therapies suggests, again, that there is a demand for clinical approaches — as well as a need for critical scientific research and therapies — for people troubled by psychic experiences.

Despite some interest in the topic during the mid 1980s, most parapsychologists seem to have rejected the clinical option, at least as defined in these terms. When I asked one leading parapsychologist why they were allowing this opportunity to slip away, he told me that they had looked into clinical work a few years ago (when there were some panels on the topic at the annual meetings), but the insurance costs were prohibitively high. Furthermore, most academic parapsychologists have a background in experimental psychology or the natural sciences, and therefore they lack the training and legal status to do clinically applied work themselves. Still, alternatives in this area could be considered, such as an option discussed at the 1990 annual convention of the Parapsychological Association: rather than get involved in clinical work directly, experimental parapsychologists and affiliated clinicians could provide seminars and training for the benefit of professional clinicians who wanted to know more about the psychology of psychic experiences.

As with the clinical option, parapsychologists have also largely abdicated the role of public education and criticism that psychical research once held. In the nineteenth century and early twentieth century, psychical research was a very different field of inquiry that brought to the public relatively skeptical or psychological interpretations of claims of mediumship, apparitions, poltergeists, hauntings, and other kinds of "spontaneous" psychic experiences. The debate between skeptics and advocates frequently took place within the confines of the psychical research societies, not, as is the case today, between two divided and hostile organizations (CSICOP and the Parapsychological Association). Paradoxically, parapsychologists' sanitization strategy of developing a professional organization, moving into the laboratory, and developing experimental methods may have hurt the prestige of their discipline, given that this move entailed surrendering the social function of critically examining popular claims of paranormality.[12]

The fact that CSICOP was able to emerge at all, and then to do so successfully, indicates the extent to which parapsychology abdicated what was once an important social function. The role of social criticism and public education is still widely practiced today by Brazilian parapsychologists, both Jesuit and Spiritist, as well as by American skeptics. However, unlike the psychical researchers in the past, parapsychologists today rarely concern themselves with exposing or debunking psychics, mediums, healers, gurus, and so on. Whatever criticisms parapsychologists have of CSICOP, they might recognize that the skeptical organization is occupying a space that psychical research once held.[13]

Like the problem of developing a clinically applied knowledge, the possibilities of public criticism and public education return us to the question of disciplinary boundaries. Parapsychologists today seem to have accepted the boundary between their field and orthodox science in the terms defined as long ago as 1900 (as in Jastrow's work), rather than continue to contribute to research in a more general area of the psychology of psychic experiences and altered states of consciousness, as was the case at the turn of the century. There are some exceptions — such as the Edinburgh University program directed by the psychologist Robert Morris — but in general parapsychologists have been content with the present definition of their field and unwilling to consider creative blends of research programs that would incorporate more orthodox questions raised in the related fields of psychology, sociology, anthropology, and psychiatry.[14] At the turn of the century, it was still possible to define psychical research as the scientific study of claims of psychic/mystical experiences and some altered states of consciousness. As parapsychologists recognize, many areas of research that were once within the purview of psychical research — hypnosis, near-death experiences, and out-of-body experiences — have become part of mainstream psychology as they have lost their status as anomalous phenomena. Because parapsychology is defined as the study of apparently anomalous organism-environment relations — a negative definition that inherently situates parapsychology in opposition to orthodox science — it loses research topics whenever they become understandable within the framework of orthodox science. As an alternative, some critics have suggested that parapsychology be redefined as an interdisciplinary field that would study paranormal beliefs and experiences from clinical, experimental, historical, and sociocultural perspectives.[15]

To conclude this discussion, the sociocultural perspective leads to a variety of questions about the position of parapsychology in society and the viability of its experimentalist research program. These questions suggest that the legitimacy of parapsychology is probably linked less to the achievement of replicable experimental results and more to the problem of generating socially useful knowledge — which would, I hope, include critical stances — in areas such as clinical practice and public education. Even if, as some parapsychologists argued to me at the conference, the advent of minicomputers in the 1980s has led to more efficient data gathering and better "effect sizes," the repeatable experiment remains an "elusive quarry," to invoke the phrase of the skeptic Ray Hyman (1989). In contrast, generating psychological and sociological knowledge oriented toward clinical or public education applications is an immediately achievable alternative. By moving in this direction, parapsychologists would also be moving toward a ground that could be shared with a more sophisticated skepticism. In other words, by moving away from debunking (on the skeptics' side) and evidentiality (on the parapsychologists' side), a door might be opened toward détente: both sides might be able to find a middle ground on which they study paranormal beliefs and practices in reference to the social and cultural contexts that shape them. Such a proposal might seem "Pollyannaish," as one reader called it, but in recent years we have seen the fall of greater walls.

New Agers

New Agers also have their hidden assumptions and values that warrant critical inspection. In many ways the emergence of the New Age movement was a reaction to the defeats of the political aspirations of the 1960s, especially the violence of the Democratic convention in 1968 and the failure of Senator George McGovern's presidential bid in 1972.[16] The turning inward of reformist and even revolutionary aspirations after external political defeat calls to mind the similar development of romantic and utopian socialist movements that emerged in Europe in the wake of the failure of the French Revolution. Those movements were often opposed to more "mundane," working-class struggles for social justice. Today, despite the flexibility with which the New Age movement is able to accommodate a wide range of new paranormal beliefs and spiritual traditions, one of the constants is its steady refusal to cast itself in right/left political terms or to welcome a working relationship with progressive political movements.

One area where the conservative side of the New Age movement has already been explored is the social organization of holistic medicine. While skeptics criticize holistic medicine for not being scientific enough (e.g., Stalker and Glymour 1985), a more sociological alternative has been to examine it as political discourse, an approach which in critical medical anthropology has already been developed for orthodox medicine (e.g., Taussig 1980). Critics have argued that holistic medical practices reproduce some of the structures of domination found in official medicine, among them "solo, fee-for-service entrepreneurial practice"; a commodity form of knowledge or skill; sexism and elitism (which would include holistic medicine in the United States as a middle-class, white phenomenon); an individual, not social, framework for examining the sickness; and the separation between practitioners and "those who are served" (Berliner and

Salmon 1980:143). Therefore, notwithstanding holistic medicine's opposition to orthodox medicine, it may also reproduce similar social hierarchies even as it provides alternative treatments and speaks an antiestablishment discourse. Thus, whereas skeptics and parapsychologists would both approach holistic medicine by determining which practices are more or less scientific, a critical sociocultural perspective provides an alternative and complementary division: which practices reproduce and which challenge existing social hierarchies.

Critical questions put to the New Age movement range from narrow issues such as the inscription of social hegemonies in holistic medicine or the impact of crystal mining on the environment to the underlying values of the broader political programs of the Aquarian conspirators.[17] To the Aquarian conspirators who follow Marilyn Ferguson, the values of their new society—a heightened voluntarism, a new community spirit, renewed spirituality, and more decentralized government—may not be as radical or as different from those of the old society as they believe. That these values are accessible to the mainstream of American society can be seen when one realizes that a very similar list of values became central to the rhetoric not only of the 1984 "yuppie" candidacy of former Senator Gary Hart but also of the Reagan/Bush revolution itself. If the Aquarian vision has correctly fathomed its potential to have a powerful, mass appeal in response to its call to create a profound political "revolution," it also appears to have underestimated the power of existing social arrangements and right/left polarities to appropriate similar values and rhetoric for their own interests. Although the New Age movement does not have to stand the test of presidential elections (fortunately enough), it might take a clue from the history of American presidential politics in the 1980s and examine the extent to which its apolitical, "yuppie" discourse is convincing, justified, or ultimately even the most effective way of bringing about the kind of society it intends to create.

Although aspects of New Age discourse are ostensibly antipolitical and even arguably conservative, this is not true for all aspects of it. Crystal mining notwithstanding, New Agers do seem to be concerned with the environment, particularly through ecofeminism, and it may be possible to link this concern with more conventional programs of local empowerment. On this possibility, Bantam New Age executive editor Toni Burbach promises future directions when she notes, "We've been wanting to take the New Age back toward the idea of community action and social responsibility since our imprint first came out" (Jones 1989b:22). Concern with the environment or the romanticism of the Native American Other has, in some cases, even resulted in some recognition of the problems of ethnic injustice, as in the book *Rolling Thunder* (Boyd 1974). Here, the New Age quest for spiritual wisdom and paranormal experience intertwines with a description of contemporary Native American culture and the politics of land development, treaty violations, and racism. *Rolling Thunder* therefore provides a step toward a socially conscious, critical New Age discourse that might be applied to the struggles of working people and underrepresented ethnic groups in the First and Third Worlds. The book also moves away from an almost exclusive concern with the so-called green issues such as ecology toward the "red" issues of economic and ethnic injustice.[18]

This problem is particularly evident in the New Age economic vision spelled out by Marilyn Ferguson, who carefully distances her Aquarian revolution from the leftist tradition in American politics. She writes that she is opposed to the "old paradigms of politics and power"—which were paternalistic, centralized, right/left, and win/lose in orientation—and in their place she advocates a new paradigm of decentralized, win/win government. The new paradigm of politics emphasizes "freedom for positive, creative action"; she calls this a "radical center"—a term also used by Kurtz (1970)—that transcends "old polarities" (210–11). She cites approvingly a British position paper that backs away from leftist or even liberal political positions and instead labels the extremes of both the "right" and the "left" as "part of the old culture as the status quo they oppose" (39). The alternative "Third Way" is, as the position paper labels it, "radical" but not in a rightist or leftist sense of the word (39).

The Aquarian conspiracy is, in a sense, a revolution within the revolution of the 1960s, or, better, a reaction to the revolution. On this point, Ferguson cites Dorothy Healy, the former chair of the Communist party of southern California, regarding the failure of the New Left. Healy is said to have claimed that the classic Marxist model, which privileged the working class and economic issues, no longer works (1987:207). As a result of the "failures and partial successes" of the New Left, Ferguson argues that many leading leftists became disillusioned and "involved in their own transformative process" (207). Ferguson's quieter, internal revolution might therefore appear to have more to do with hippies and their communal experiments than radicals and political demonstrations, but at another point Ferguson also rejects the label of counterculture: "the new society within the old is not a counterculture, not a reaction, but an *emergent* culture—the coalescence of a new social order" (38).

Ferguson's rejection of both the New Left and the counterculture is more than a rhetorical maneuver to position her own Aquarian conspiracy as something new. It also rejects the human being as a social being, a view which both the New Left and the members of the counterculture shared.

Both political radicals and hippie communalists linked personal change to social change by arguing that effective strategies of social transformation must involve not only individual personalities but also, and even primarily, social institutions. The two movements diverged in their strategies of social change: refashioning the existing society versus leaving it to recreate a new society, a split that runs parallel to that between the detective and cowboy heroes, the seventeenth-century English revolutionaries and the Massachusetts pilgrims. Nevertheless, New Leftists and hippies shared a common vision of pursuing change at a social and institutional level as well as at a personal one. Consequently, there is a fundamental gap between the New Left and the New Age: as the New Left writer Michael Rossman says about Ram Dass in *New Age Blues*, the New Age guru is "constricted by a tradition which keeps him from integrating the strengths and potentials of most of his own cultural heritage, and furnishes him in exchange few tools or plans for working on the self as a social being, for working in the world" (1979:34; see also Ross 1991). Wedded as she is to her utopian individualism, Ferguson seems to think that changing values and vocations, rather than institutions and social structures, is enough to change the world (1987:323–60).

Another New Age writer, Mark Satin, does a somewhat better job of recognizing that the shift in values must be accompanied by fundamental institutional changes. In his book *New Age Politics*, the Canadian author addresses the problem of corporate hegemony by providing a vision of a "participatory economy" with worker- or community-controlled firms (1978:135). However, in his efforts to distance himself from socialists, Satin makes the (to my mind naive) argument that control can occur apart from ownership (136). Likewise, in his eagerness to distance himself from Marx (see his appendix, "Clearing the Ground: A New Age Critique of Marxism," pp. 203–20), Satin makes some rather questionable sociological decisions, such as replacing economic classes as an analytical instrument with a "psychocultural class analysis" based on a trichotomy of "life-oriented," "thing-oriented," and "death-oriented" classes (68–71).[19]

These comments on the New Age are meant to be critical but not negative. When one goes beyond the shortcomings of the New Age movement in terms of red/green polarities to the "rainbow" dimension of multiculturalism, it fares considerably better. The New Age movement is one way in which middle-class baby boomers can continue to question and rethink what the feminist scholar Barbara Ehrenreich (1991) has aptly called the "monoculturalism" of their patriarchal, Judeo-Christian, and Eurocentric cultural heritage. In a society that is increasingly characterized by a diversity of ethnic and gender perspectives, the white, male, Judeo-Christian

God, not to mention most of the biblical narrative, appears less and less as the universal truth and more and more as the gendered story of a segment of a particular cultural tradition. By opening up the faith of the fathers to the vast syncretic possibilities of Native American shamanism, Eastern mysticism, African-Latino *oricha* rituals, and pagan goddess worship — but at the same time by bringing these currents in contact with the discourse of modern science and the heritage of European rationalism — New Agers are thinking through the tremendous social changes that their society is undergoing, even if, to quote the French ethnologist/sociologist Roger Bastide on another syncretism, they "forge their ideology confusedly through the veil of a religion" (1967:16). For the middle-class American mainstream, which in the 1980s and 1990s is still overwhelmingly of European descent and Christian heritage, New Age religions may be one way to see the tremendous growth of new voices — African, Asian, Moslem, Latino, Native American, feminist, gay, lesbian, bi — not as a threat to be feared and resisted but instead as an opportunity to be treasured and welcomed, for after all these communities are now constructed as the custodians of the ancient wisdom and the bearers of a more promising global future.

More generally, I see the New Agers' search for alternatives in religion, science, medicine, and social organization not as an atavistic attempt to flee the modern or postmodern world, but instead as one additional modulation of the characteristic restlessness of Americans and our culture. As I have flagged on several occasions, this restlessness is rooted in the country's foundation myths of religious and other forms of social liberation and experimentation: in a sense, America was a commune from its first colonial (and in some cases pre-Columbian) moments. The restlessness of the American people is also an integral part of the country's cultural vitality and its ingenuity. If, for example, one listens to the medical doctor Bernard S. Siegel's (1986) relaxation and meditation tapes for exceptional cancer patients, echoes of New Age discourse reverberate in what may turn out to be a promising new approach to cancer treatment that has a voice within orthodox medicine via the emerging field of psychoneuroimmunology. Certainly Siegel has filtered out some of the metaphysical language (and music) that would be more objectionable to orthodox medicine and some mainstream patients, but the commonalities here suggest at least one case in which the charisma of the New Age may become routinized as innovations in orthodox science and medicine (see Tiryakin 1972). In short, even if the skeptically minded rightly reject the scientific solidity of much New Age discourse and practice, a far more productive strategy would be to recognize in them the kernels of potential cultural innovations and inventions: ingenuousness may sometimes be the mother of ingenuity.

Last Word, First Word

My goal, then, in raising critical questions for each of the three faces of the paraculture is therefore not a polemical one. Instead, I hope to encourage human scientists and members of the paraculture to reflect critically upon the cultural politics of each of the communities. For the most part, each community is good at seeing the social and cultural in its Others, but its boundary-work is obscured by a conviction that the Self possesses a transcendent, asocial knowledge. I have attempted to put the social, cultural, and political back into their discourse.

At the same time, I recognize the similar way in which my own voice is socially constructed. By ending with a critical dialogue rooted in a vision of the human sciences as a dialogical enterprise, I recognize our place as part of the same ideological arena. If New Agers, parapsychologists, and skeptics were to recognize a role for a critical sociocultural perspective in this arena of debate and dialogue, they might be able to find a common language in which they would be able — at least for part of the time — to bracket questions of the relative scientificity or pseudoscientificity of a given set of truth claims — agreement on this level is unlikely in any case — and instead to begin to discuss the cultural meanings and the sociopolitical implications of their paradigms, practices, and programs. To think that such a "sociocultural turn" is imminent would be to engage in a utopian dream about a dubious future; but, to end on a reflexive note, to call for it as necessary would be to join the reformist spirit that characterizes all four communities and our broader cultural heritage.

Appendix

Notes

Bibliography

Index

Appendix: Methodology

The Concept of an Ideological Arena

The approach I have adopted in *Science in the New Age* represents a continuation of the social constructivist project in science and technology studies, but it also represents a shift of emphasis. Hence, I prefer the term "cultural reconstructivism." Rather than ask how scientists construct facts by going into a laboratory and making observations, I ask how the public in general — intellectuals, writers, mediums, laypeople, but also scientists when they write for the public — reconstruct scientific discourse in a broader social context. As I and others pursue this "anthropological" approach, we may indeed begin to address the larger questions of the cultural meaning — and cultural politics — of modern science and technology in society.[1]

In my previous book, *Spirits and Scientists*, I used the term "ideological arena" to signal the domain of debate and dialogue in which religious, scientific, political, and other discourses encounter each other.[2] My goal was to interpret, for example, Brazilian Spiritist parapsychology by situating it as part of an onging *dialogue* with Spiritists' Others in the ideological arena: Jesuit parapsychologists, the medical profession, jurists, legislators, northern hemisphere parapsychologists, Umbandists, and so on. To some extent, in *Science in the New Age* I apply the same interpretive strategy to a similar (and connected) ideological arena in the United States. Brazilian dialogue, however, is often so subtle and indirect that it is often necessary to read between the lines to realize that a dialogue is going on; the culture of personalism and the political history of repressive authoritarianism have resulted in much less of a tendency to engage in blunt disagreement (see DaMatta 1991, Kant de Lima 1985). Americans, in contrast, are relatively blunt. Consequently, the juxtaposition of texts and positions that was necessary for the Brazilian case is less so for the American context, where skeptics and parapsychologists, for example, are very clear about what they think of each other.

In Brazil, then, the challenge is to show polemics and disagreements where they are frequently veiled; whereas in the United States, with its individualistic culture and political tradition of first amendment freedoms, the opposite is the case: one expects and finds disagreement, debate, and differing positions. The dialogue of the ideological arena is therefore much more out in the open, and there is less of a role for an interpreter to ferret out hidden polemics, since the polemics are frequently obvious to anyone who has some familiarity with the literature. Indeed, much of the writing is explicitly posed in opposition to other positions in the ideo-logical arena. For example, in the book *Science: Good, Bad, and Bogus,* Martin Gardner includes replies by parapsychologists, New Agers, and others whom he considers to be pseudoscientists, and he then provides his rebuttals. In this situa-tion of explicit polemics, the challenge is to show how there is any underlying agree-ment at all among all the competing, contrasting, and conflicting positions.

Thus, in *Spirits and Scientists,* I took only the first step by showing that a welter of different positions could be interpreted as a dialogue and then that the cultural interpretation of any given discourse or text depended on recognizing its position within a larger system of debate and dialogue. Since that is fairly obvious in the American case, I am able to take the analysis one step further by showing how the disparate communities are forging a new paraculture through their disputes, and how their disputed paraculture is situated in the broader cultural heritage that it simultaneously draws on and transforms.

Research Methods

To get at this question of "doxa," I turn to the resources of my home discipline: cultural (or symbolic) anthropology. One method for studying the dialogue would be through fieldwork; however, as a research method fieldwork runs into a prob-lem with the New Age movement. Unlike academic parapsychology and organized skepticism, the New Age movement is large, amorphous, and acephalous. Whereas skeptics and parapsychologists have clearly defined national organizations and con-ferences, New Agers tend to meet in a myriad of local groups and expos across the country. As a result, anthropologists and sociologists who have examined New Agers or similar groups have tended to focus on local communities.[3] Whereas that methodological choice provides a good sense of the relations between discourse and practice, it is somewhat restricted when one wishes to have a more national-level picture of the diverse New Age movement.

The cultural interpretation of texts therefore provides a somewhat better alterna-tive for the specific research problem of my study. Some social scientists may turn up their noses at textual approaches because, so they argue, textual methods bracket the question of what people actually do in New Age groups or at skeptics' and parapsychologists' conferences. Of course, textual studies advocates could turn the problem around and say other methods — surveys, ethnographies, life histories — ignore the importance of what people actually say in their texts, which indeed are central to any sense of a national New Age movement. My plea is for less disci-plinary boundary-work and more tolerance for methodological diversity: let a thou-sand lotus flowers bloom. I make no general claims; I only defend a particular methodological choice for a particular research problem.

In the case of skeptics, parapsychologists, and New Agers, there is an additional reason for focusing on texts. For intellectuals and writers, what they say (and write) is basically what they do: the scribes are the tribes, to borrow a phrase from the anthropologist James Boon (1982). Furthermore, in this area text-based interpreta-tion can provide a more synthetic description of the various positions within the

New Age movement as well as a picture of the broader context of the discourse of skeptics and parapsychologists. In addition, the symbolic world of the three cultures may be much more richly and imaginatively articulated in their texts.

Nevertheless, to interpret the texts from a cultural perspective I draw on my fieldwork among Spiritists in Brazil and on informal visits to New Age and Spiritualist groups in the United States. I also draw on my decade-long exposure to American and Brazilian parapsychology, which includes attending about a dozen national and international conferences as well as discussions, both informal conversations and formal interviews, with many of the leading figures in the two countries. Much of my background knowledge comes from this combination of fieldwork, interviewing, and informal visits. It is also rooted in my own "native knowledge" that emerges from the conversations that I constantly encounter with Americans who, once they learn about my research in Brazil, want to talk about their own psychic or spiritual beliefs and experiences.

SELECTION CRITERIA

To interpret the cultures of the three communities it helps to have samples that are in some sense representative of their discourse on society. Certain choices are fairly obvious, because the texts are written by leading figures — people like Paul Kurtz in skepticism, J. B. and Louisa Rhine in parapsychology, and Marilyn Ferguson in the New Age movement. I have also attempted to provide a sample of the diversity of positions within each of the three cultures, such as advocates of debunking and "neutrality" among the skeptics, and experimentalists versus spontaneous case researchers among the parapsychologists.

Because the New Age movement is so diverse and amorphous, it presented a more difficult problem of selection criteria. One colleague suggested that I construct a list of important New Age books by surveying ten or twenty prominent New Age writers and asking them each to come up with a list of the most important books. However, any list of "key" New Age texts would warrant some skepticism, because it might lead to the imposition of a canon on a movement that is, above all, decentralized and characterized by flexibility, variety, and change. Instead, I selected the texts after 1) seeing what is displayed prominently or frequently in New Age book sections and bookstores, 2) reading what is frequently mentioned in books or articles on the New Age movement, and 3) discussing what is familiar to friends and acquaintances who read New Age books. I then chose exemplars that are representative of some of the major tendencies of the New Age movement: crystal healing, neopaganism, shamanic studies, channeling, and so on.[4] In addition, I chose texts that involved significant elaborations of cultural meaning.

Interpretive Methods in the Context of Interdisciplinary Inquiry

My decision to focus on texts does not make the study a purely literary venture, if such a term has any meaning in the academy today. As an anthropologist who in this case chooses to focus on texts and discourse, I intentionally adopt an interdisciplinary method of research and a "blurred genre" of writing (Geertz 1983). My goal is a wedding—perhaps somewhat alchemical—of the methods of literary studies and the social sciences; in other words, my goal is to employ a discourse situated at one intellectual border (anthropology/criticism or the social sciences/humanities) to engage and interrogate another intellectual border, that of orthodox and heterodox sciences. Indeed, the three cultures of borderland science have their double in another triangle of cultures of borderland science—science and literature studies (SLS), science and technology studies (STS), and symbolic/cultural anthropology. At the level of methods, then, I attempt to find a common ground among the fields of SLS, STS, and symbolic/ cultural anthropology.

By pointing the way toward a common ground, I am also pointing toward changes that might occur in each of the three disciplines. For example, I wish to encourage the SLS side of the triangle to welcome more cultural studies perspectives into their field, particularly studies that examine representations of science in popular culture and, more generally, science and technology from a critical perspective that is rooted in an interpretation of their cultural meaning and an interrogation of their political assumptions. Most social or cultural anthropologists would probably take that position for granted, but I also believe that anthropology can benefit by a corresponding countermove toward literary studies, particularly a greater openness to and recognition of the fact that good anthropology need not be anchored in fieldwork. As anthropologists increasingly study literate peoples who write, we need to find a bigger place for textual studies and criticism in our methodological repertoire and to question our own "textual" taboo. Thus, I see this book as one example of the bridges that anthropologists are building between the closely related fields of criticism and cultural anthropology through the intermediary of cultural studies. I also hope to contribute to the field of science and technology studies by asking more questions about the meaning of science and technology to nonscientists, the representations of science and technology in popular culture, and the transformations of science and technology as they pass from the "producer" communities of scientists and engineers to the the general public.

In the twin fields of SLS and STS, previous scholarly studies have generally not examined scientists' texts for their cultural meanings and ideological valences, at least not in the sense pursued here, and thus cultural anthropology may provide a welcome extension of existing text-oriented analytical frameworks. Before considering the cultural approach, however, it may be helpful to do a little "boundary-work" among the available interpretive frameworks. I begin by delineating some of the roads not taken.

Of the several textual frameworks currently in use in SLS and STS, the one most distant methodologically to this study is quantitative content analysis. Content analysis can be useful for many practical questions, such as policy issues involving the appropriate content of textbooks, but it is not the best method for the kind of research problem addressed here. Still, since some readers may be advocates of content analysis and other quantitative research methods, it is worth making clear some of the claims that are not being made here, particularly regarding issues of selection and representativeness. Quantitatively oriented scholars (including experimental parapsychologists) may think I claim that the selected texts constitute something like a random sample that is representative of the beliefs of populations of each community. No such claims are made. I have taken no polls, nor have I counted pages to determine the relative frequency of the discursive structures, metaphors, representations, and so on that are discussed. Just as one does not read a novel by counting words, one does not interpret cultural meaning by counting frequencies.

Closer to my method are the approaches of the rhetoricians and ethnomethodologists. Unlike the content analysts, they adopt an interpretive method that belongs to the same family of methods as my own. However, while they have found valuable ways of addressing their problems, their methods and research questions remain complementary to my own. For example, while studies of the rhetorical devices or the *topoi* of science texts (e.g., Bazerman 1988, Prelli 1989) bring out one way in which the texts are socially constructed, in such studies the social is relatively limited to the domain of language and communication. Much the same is true for sociological discourse analysis and ethnomethodology, both of which relate textual strategies and rhetorical issues to problems of communication and persuasion among persons in specific contexts.[5] Although the focus on writers and readers in specific contexts makes the method of the discourse analysts and ethnomethodologists in a sense more sociological than the work of the rhetoricians, generally the former do not probe texts for broader ideological and cultural meanings. Thus, the methods of the rhetoricians, discourse analysts, or ethnomethodologists, interesting as they are, remain complementary to my approach.

The historical work of Donald MacKenzie on the relationship between the debates on statistics and their social context in early twentieth-century Britain is in one way closer to the kind of approach that I adopt (MacKenzie 1978, 1983; Barnes and MacKenzie 1979). At a general level, his interpretive strategy characterizes one of the more important advances in post-Mertonian STS: to take what may first appear to be a purely intellectual or scientific disagreement, and to show how it is part of a broader dialogue in the surrounding society. This method reveals scientific actors and discourses to be in diaogue with other, nonscientific (or ascientific) actors and discourses, and as a result scientific and intellectual discourse can be reread as social and cultural discourse. In the process, the distinction between science and ideology is collapsed, and science is instead interpreted *as* ideology. In somewhat broader (and more Durkheimian) terms, the method takes discussions that portray science and technology as in some sense "set apart" from society, and it reinvests them with their social, politicocultural, and even "profane" meanings.

The point in bringing up the fine research of the Edinburgh school is to acknowledge its contribution of a method that reveals links between scientific discourse and broader questions of culture and power. There are, however, significant differences between those historical studies and my own method. Barnes and MacKenzie have been challenged on possible problems associated with the imputation

of interests as a way of explaining scientific theories; and although they have defended their perspective and method, I think it prudent to sidestep the problem
by not imputing motivations, intentions, or interests (see Woolgar 1981a, 1981b,
Barnes 1981, MacKenzie 1981). Instead, I see the boundaries among groups as co-
constituted in the intellectual boundaries that they draw: skeptics, for example,
become skeptics precisely by characterizing their Others as nonskeptics. Furthermore, as I show, the way in which boundaries are drawn results in new, hybrid
discourses and communities.

To understand better how the intellectual/social boundaries are drawn, the literary approaches that examine networks of metaphors or images provide valuable
interpretive techniques. Relevant examples include Gillian Beer's *Darwin's Plots*,
Stanley Edgar Hyman's *The Tangled Bank*, Ludmilla Jordanova's *Sexual Visions*,
and several of the essays collected in George Levine's *One Culture: Essays in Science and Literature*. The method of these scholars was most useful and influential
for me when the text was more literary, as, for example, in the case of J. B. Rhine's
New World of the Mind or Louisa Rhine's *ESP in Life and Lab*. However, as with
MacKenzie's analysis of statistics debates, I borrow a bit from the literary method
without remaining restricted to it. I prefer to extend the literary interpretation of
metaphors and images by articulating it with a cultural interpretation of the construction of categories and codes, hierarchies and values, and mediations of symbolic difference. Here, then, is where anthropological methods become important.

The Contribution of Anthropology to the Question of Interpretive Methods

Some readers will have recognized that my language draws on the anthropological vocabularies inherited from structuralism and cultural interpretation, and it
is worth positioning myself with respect to the various interpretive methods associated with what is sometimes called "symbolic anthropology," the discipline that
I believe adds a new dimension to the various text-based approaches in science
and technology studies. For anthropologists, most of what I say in this section
will belabor the obvious, but given the historical situation in STS — where the "anthropology" of science and technology has been defined by nonanthropologists
and "anthropological" approaches are frequently misunderstood (Hess in press b) —
I think it is useful to situate my methods more specifically in the field of symbolic
anthropology.

In an era of posts, it may seem "retro" to be calling up French structuralism and
American cultural interpretation as points of reference, but their importance should
be recognized alongside their limitations, and certainly no discussion of contemporary symbolic anthropology can take place without reference to those frameworks. The way in which I have framed my research problem, the use of Pierre
Bourdieu's term "doxa" notwithstanding, might be seen as structuralist in the sense
defined by the anthropologist Claude Lévi-Strauss as the search for the "invariant
elements among superficial differences" (1978a:9) that characterized his *Mytholo-
giques* series (1973, 1975, 1978b, 1981). I read Lévi-Strauss as an ethnologist — or

better, a Brazilianist and an Americanist—rather than as a philosopher or psychologist, and it seems unfortunate that today so few anthropologists recognize either their intellectual debt to his work or its profoundly historical character.[6] Many of the elements of Lévi-Straussian structuralism—its ability to recognize similarity through difference, its development of a way of articulating codes through oppositional categories, and, as Boon (1982) reminds us, its resurrection of the comparative, Frazerian tradition in anthropology—are still influencing some of the bolder and more creative interpretive and critical projects in contemporary anthropology.

To pay homage to Lévi-Strauss is also to honor his critics, particularly those who have pointed the way beyond structuralism. Bourdieu (1977), for example, teaches us to be wary of the "synoptic illusion," and thus I focus on the fuzzy and fragmented structures as they appear in the specific statements (or discursive practices) of New Agers, skeptics, and parapsychologists, rather than attempt to build a synoptic system, or, to switch to the Foucauldian term, to view the discourses from a panoptical gaze. In addition to a wariness of the totalizing implications that have been attributed to some versions of anthropological structuralism, I follow some critics in placing a greater emphasis on the question of actors, change, and events. Thus, in different ways, the social theorists Michel Foucault (e.g., 1980) and Marshall Sahlins (1976, 1981) teach us to look more carefully at the relationship between structure and event, as well as the shifts and continuities of structures and practices over time.

Furthermore, French structuralism by no means has a monopoly on comparativism and symbolic analysis in anthropology; the project of finding similarities or patterns across ostensibly different domains and positions lies at the heart of almost any attempt to discuss society in terms of cultural patterns, values, or structures. In the Anglo-Saxon tradition, the project is often instituted less through an analysis of opposing categories articulated with reference to codes than through an interpretation of symbols and native terms that form nodes in interconnected networks of meaning. The latter approach is fruitfully employed by Victor Turner in his analysis of Ndembu ritual (1967) and by Clifford Geertz in his analysis of Balinese cocks and cockfights (1973). Turner, for example, follows out the meanings of color terms in the ritual, just as Geertz explores the multiple meanings of the term "cock" for the Balinese. Their approach focuses on the meaning of key terms and relations among them, an interpretive technique that, in the domain of literary studies and rhetoric, is similar to Kenneth Burke's explorations of terministic screens (1966:44ff.). It is also an approach that Geertz advocates for studies of contemporary thought, which I take to include science. In the essay "The Way We Think Now," he argues that the ethnography of thought can benefit from a "focus on key terms that seem, when their meaning is unpacked, to light up a whole way of going at the world" (1983:157).

The divide between the French and Anglo-Saxon approaches to the interpretation of social and cultural meaning may itself be related to broader cultural differences that articulate along the Protestant/Catholic watershed. To use the language of the French anthropologist Louis Dumont (1980), the Anglo-Saxon approach treats the symbol as an "individual," a key term that is, true enough, located in a web of symbols, but certainly not as submerged in the whole as the French signifier. The signifier is defined oppositionally and positionally and furthermore it is understood as having meaning in reference to a code. In a phrase, the French signifier is "encompassed" by the whole, by the code, in a way that the Anglo-Saxon key term or symbol is not: French *société* versus Anglo-Saxon individualism.

As discussed in the chapter on gender, Dumont uses the term "encompassment" to refer to a relationship in which two terms are in opposition at one level, but at another level one of the terms can be used to include both (1980). Privileging one side of an opposition in this way sets up a hierarchy, and thus the relationship of encompassment is crucial to understanding not only hierarchical thinking but also hierarchical societies, such as India and to some extent Latin American countries, where relative to northwestern Europe and North America hierarchical and holistic social forms predominate over more egalitarian and individualistic ones. From his analysis of the Indian caste system and its hierarchical arrangements, Dumont then returns to Western societies to examine the development of individualism and tensions between hierarchical and egalitarian thinking from the seventeenth century to the present.

Dumont's project is important as a point of transition from Lévi-Straussian structuralism and Geertzian cultural interpretation to contemporary critical methods.[7] Like one aspect of poststructuralist criticism (that is, challenging existing categories and undermining apparently clear oppositions), Dumontian analysis can be applied to apparent oppositions to reveal how they may in fact obscure hierarchical relationships. Upon recognizing a hierarchy, one can then challenge it by positing or finding alternative arrangements that contest the "supplementarity" of the unmarked term (see Derrida 1974, Culler 1982:213). By undermining hierarchies and positing alternative ones, the scholar's task slides from the scientific project of describing social hierarchies to the critical one of engaging and even challenging them. In Dumont's corpus, this shift is most evident in his later studies of Western ideology (1977, 1986), such as his controversial and not entirely convincing analysis of Marx as an individualist thinker.

Dumont's project of critiquing Western ideology from a comparative perspective bears some similarities to contemporary projects in cultural studies that return the critics' gaze reflexively back on their own discourse. Those projects include both the movement within anthropology to inspect the epistemological and political assumptions of ethnographies as historically situated texts, as well as the development of reflexively critical persepctives in science and technology studies. I have already compared those developments elsewhere and argued that there are some similarities between critical projects in anthropology and in STS (in press b). Both positions recognize that the discourse of human scientists is part of the ideological arena that they describe and interpret, and both make the return move of critiquing the political and cultural assumptions of human scientists.

Contemporary critical methods usually also grant some room for writing from an "engaged" or "critical" position with respect to society. For example, Marcus and Fischer explicitly argue that not only should critics include "an account of the *positioning* of the critic in relation to that which is critiqued," but they also "must be able to *pose alternatives* to the conditions [they] are criticizing" (1986: 115). In a similar way, Chubin and Restivo (1983) insist that the critic cannot achieve a position of neutrality, and in the essay "Modern Science as a Social Problem" Restivo (1988) gives an account of some of the ways in which he wishes to see the critique of science developed. As Restivo points out, feminists have frequently led the way in providing critical accounts of scientific ideology; subsequent to his article the historian/culture critic Donna Haraway's accounts of primatologists (1989) have provided one detailed and thorough example of a critical, feminist, and cultural studies perspective on scientific discourse as ideology.[8]

Perhaps the most relevant and, for this book, influential example of a critical, cultural anthropological approach to scientific texts is the work of the anthropologist Emily Martin, who examines science discourse in textbooks, lectures, popular writing, interview responses, and everyday conversation, and shows how immunology (1990, 1992), obstetrics (1987), and women's reproductive physiology (1987, 1991) construct the biological through images of race, class, and gender. In general terms my method is very similar to hers. Perhaps the key difference is that I stick somewhat more closely to the texts as integral units, in the tradition of the literary studies mentioned above, and I investigate in somewhat more detail dimensions other than those of race, class, gender and social hierarchy, as seen in chapters 3 and 4.

Part of the critical, cultural perspective of Martin, as well as Haraway, Rabinow, Ross, and others, is the historical dimension that allows them to situate newly emergent discourses in the context of what is variously called late capitalism, late modernity, or the postmodern condition. The historical dimension is also crucial to understanding what I have been calling the "paraculture." Although I have stressed continuities between the paraculture and longstanding discourses and practices, I have also found it necessary to inquire into the novelty of discourses and practices in which new hybrids tend to elide established boundaries between sacred and profane, science and religion, skepticism and faith, body and mind, and so on.

I therefore see this study as one expression of an intellectual movement that is beginning to bring together a critical perspective and an anthropologically rooted understanding of the culture concept into the interdisciplinary field of science and technology studies. I do not intend the interpretive framework that I develop here to be programmatic, nor am I proposing a comprehensive theory of the paraculture in the United States. Instead, I provide one map of the territory and one way of engaging in a dialogue with the people and positions we find there. In the process, I hope to add one more voice to the growing chorus of those culture critics who see themselves as socially situated and therefore a part of the ongoing public dialogue about the future of our society.

Notes

Chapter 1. The Three Cultures: New Age, Parapsychology, Skepticism

1. There may also be a continuity between the New Age movement and the tradition of American religious revivalism or revitalization movements in general (Wallace 1956). However, unlike the church-camp revivalism of previous generations, the New Age movement involves religious experience in a more secular key. The figure of sixty million unchurched Americans is commonly cited in the secular humanist literature, but recent polls indicate that church membership is at 65 percent, and therefore about ninety million people could be classified as unchurched (Goodrich 1990). A forthcoming study by the sociologists Benton Johnson, Dean Hoge, and Donald Luidens (*Vanishing Boundaries: The Religion of the Protestant Baby Boomers*) found an even greater number: 48 percent of their sample of Presbyterian baby boomers were unchurched (Associated Press report, June 5, 1992).

2. It is difficult to give New Agers, skeptics, and parapsychologists an unambiguous label such as "social movements" or "communities." Whereas parapsychology is organized as an academic discipline, skeptics are organized into local chapters under a national umbrella organization, and thus they might be classified as a club or voluntary organization. Because skeptics and parapsychologists both hold annual meetings and are fairly well institutionalized, their social organization might be classified as a community, but the label only applies loosely to New Agers, who constitute a community only in the sense of a "discursive community." With this caveat in mind, I use "communities" or "cultures" as the generic term when referring to all three social categories.

3. The statistic seems to vary somewhat; I have taken this figure from the well-titled article, "Has the Thirty- and Fortysomething Generation Passed its Peak?" (Shames 1990).

4. As I explain later, this is not an ethnographic study; however, I draw on my native knowledge as an American baby boomer and as a longterm observer of the parapsychology communities of Brazil and the United States. I have also attended some New Age groups and expos in order to get a better sense of the New Age movement in practice. Although nonanthropologists might call my visits "fieldwork," I think the term is better reserved for a systematic study of at least one year with a demarcated community of people, as I did among Spiritists in Brazil. Several anthropologists are now patiently engaged in such local studies of

the New Age movement (see appendix), and I view my book as complementary to their projects.

5. My decision to discuss the Rhines's texts brings about an asymmetry with respect to the skeptics and New Agers. The texts by Louisa and J. B. Rhine considered here were published between 1953 and 1975, whereas most of the texts by the skeptics and New Agers date from the 1970s and 1980s. However, while parapsychology has become both a target of skeptics and a source of legitimation for New Agers, it also existed long before they emerged in their present form. It therefore makes some sense to stretch backward in time for the parapsychologists. What is lost in symmetry is gained in an understanding of the parapsychological imagination, its historical context, and its transformations over time.

6. His independent and sometimes confrontational stance led to conflicts with the Foundation for the Research on the Nature of Man and the American Society for Psychical Research. For several years he was forbidden to publish in the *Journal of the American Society for Psychical Research*. Rogo once told me, and it is now common knowledge, that he got around this restriction by using the pseudonym T. C. Goodsort.

7. The literature generated by parapsychologists is tremendous, and consequently I leave out many leading figures, primarily because their writings do not address quite as elaborately the question of the cultural meaning of parapsychology and the paranormal. To mention only a few: the philosopher Stephen Braude; the physicists Helmut Schmidt and Russell Targ; the psychiatrists Jan Ehrenwald, Jules Eisenbud, and Ian Stevenson; as well as many other prominent figures in American parapsychology, most of whom were trained in psychology: William Braud, Charles Honorton, John Palmer, Robert Morris, Rex Stanford, K. Ramakrishna Rao, and Gertrude Schmeidler. Given the quantity of researchers and texts available, it would clearly be possible to write an entire volume on cultural aspects of American parapsychology, as would be the case for skeptics and New Agers.

8. The skeptics' voice is sometimes so strong and negative that parapsychologists have suggested that I refer to them as "critics" or even "hostile critics" rather than "skeptics," because parapsychologists see themselves as the true skeptics. It is clear, then, that the question of labels is already somewhat politicized. However, as part of my interpretive strategy anchored in cultural anthropology, I shall adopt the terms used by skeptics themselves, rather than their critics.

9. The original name of the organization was the Committee to Scientifically Investigate Claims of Paranormal and Other Phenomena (Kurtz 1976a).

10. See Weber ([1904–5]1958). The question is posed as a problem for those who believe in a secularization approach to religion, which has been soundly criticized by Douglas (1982) and, given the rise of various fundamentalisms throughout the world, remains quite problematic (see also D. Martin 1990). Church attendance in the U.S., for example, has held steady at about 40 percent since around 1940, and the primary shifts are from Catholicism and the mainline Protestant churches to the fundamentalist and charismatic churches (Goodrich 1990). For a related discussion of fundamentalism, creationists, and "resistance to science," see Nelkin (1982).

11. Kurtz defines the "transcendental temptation" as "the tendency for human beings to resort to magical thinking and to ascribe occult, mysterious, hidden, or unknown causes to events they cannot fathom" (1985–86:230). Asimov (1988:10) wrote of the similar "will to believe," which he saw, at least in part, as a reaction to an uncertain world, a "future-frightened public," and the fact of death. See also Frazier (1986:x–xi) and Zusne (1985).

12. This definition reflects my interpretation of "cultural relativism," which I believe can and should be distinguished from other relativisms. Cultural relativism is closely linked to linguistic relativism: languages (and cultures) cannot be arranged hierarchically on a unilinear evolutionary scale, and any aspect of language and culture must be understood relative to the broader linguistic or cultural context of which it is a part. Thus, cultural relativism does not necessarily imply moral relativism or antirealist epistemologies, and as my colleague the philosopher Deborah Johnson has pointed out to me, it may support just the opposite.

I use the term "culture" throughout the book to refer not only to the discourses and practices of a group, community, or society, but also to its unspoken and often unconscious values, principles, and assumptions about the world. The terms "culture," "discourse," and "practice" can be used recursively; for example, we may speak of "Western culture," then "American culture," the "culture of American parapsychologists," and even the "culture of American experimental parapsychologists." Likewise, cultures can be examined transnationally (e.g., the "international parapsychology community").

13. My use of the term "empirical" refers only to the ways in which religious questions are referred to passages in the scriptures rather than to the dogmatic statements of the church elders. In this way, debates become more "empirical." For a related discussion of Puritanism and empiricism, see Merton (1970:93–95).

14. See Kenny (1986), who raises this point in the context of the resurgence of the idiom of multiple personalities in psychotherapy.

15. I finished all but the final revisions of this book before seeing Ross's essay "New Age — A Kinder, Gentler Science" (1991). I decided not to change this phrase or any of my arguments in response to his often similar cultural critique. Ultimately, I develop a complementary analysis by focusing more on the religious/spiritual side of the New Age movement and on the broader paraculture of parapsychologists, skeptics, and Hollywood horror movies. I have, however, flagged the most significant places where we converge, usually "harmonically."

Chapter 2. The Historical Context

1. See Melton (1988:40–41). Mesmer was the founder of "Mesmerism," a mystical healing system that was the forerunner of hypnosis but which explained its efficacy by positing vital fluids rather than a psychology of suggestion. Swedenborg was a Swedish mystic whose hermetic philosophy was based on his visions of angels and otherworldly habitations. Swedenborg's visions and Mesmer's "somnambules," or hypnotized subjects, were two of the forerunners of Spiritualist and Spiritist mediums.

As can be seen in the epigraphs, the terms "Spiritism" and "Spiritualism" are used inconsistently in the literature of the period and even today. I use "Spiritualism" for the British and North American movement, and "Spiritism" for the more intellectual, reincarnationist French and Latin American movement associated with Allan Kardec.

2. Likewise, the British Society for Psychical Research dispatched one of its members, Richard Hodgson, to study Madame Blavatsky, and in 1885 he wrote a highly negative report that accused her of fraud (Gauld 1968:203).

3. A sustained, detailed cultural history of American spiritual groups in the twentieth century remains to be written. Starting points are Albanese's study of nature religion (1990); Ellwood's survey of various alternative spiritual groups in the United States (1973); his discussion of Theosophy and the transition to the Beatniks (1979); Adler's survey of pagan and witch groups in the United States (1979); and, for Britain, Luhrmann's (1989:32) typology and historical sketch of occult and New Age groups in London.

4. For an excellent, quasi-ethnographic, journalistic account of UFO cults in the United States and Canada, see Curran (1985). See also Ellwood (1973:131–56), who classifies the Spiritualists and UFO cults together in his categorization of occult and spiritual groups in the United States.

5. See Gauld (1968:141–42, 149) on Myers and the other British psychical researchers, Mauskopf and McVaugh (1980:131–40) on the Rhines, and Moore (1977: 157, 171, 185) on the religious backgrounds of the American psychical researchers. See also Cerullo (1982), Murphy (1990), and F. Turner (1974).

6. The American Society for Psychical Research was founded in 1884–85, but it was reabsorbed into the British Society for Psychical Research in 1889, then returned to the Americans in 1907 and reformulated as "Section B" of Hyslop's American Institute for Psychical Research. See Berger (1985a, 1985b), Mauskopf (1989), and Moore (1977:159).

7. Others placed more blame on Hyslop. William James, for example, thought Hyslop "crude and hot" and compared him to a "street terrier" (in Berger 1985b: 209), and Moore (1977:161–62) notes that Hyslop ran the ASPR like a "dictator" and that his critics thought he unfairly skewed the research toward a pro-Spiritualist perspective.

8. For historical sources on the ASPR from the "Margery affair" to the "palace revolt," see Mauskopf (1989), Mauskopf and McVaugh (1980:21), and Moore (1977: 176, 183). On Rhine and the institutionalization of parapsychology, see Mauskopf and McVaugh (1980:131–47, 304), and Rhine and Associates (1965).

9. Coon (1990:41) notes that by criticizing Mrs. Piper, Tanner and Hall were "battling the accumulated prestige, credibility, and authority of the leading lights of the Society for Psychical Research." Coon (1990:35) also uncovered an interesting letter written in 1920 by Hall to Jastrow, where Hall commends Jastrow on another anti-Spiritualist book and writes that he hoped Jastrow had the courage he lacked to criticize James for his role in legitimating the "medium-mad Bostonians."

10. Strauss (1991) has discussed yet an earlier forerunner of the skeptical magicians today: the British magician John Nevil Maskelyn. She argues that he and

other nineteenth-century magicians contributed to contemporary discussions about methodology and the natural sciences.

11. After I wrote the first draft of this section, I came across a book that lends support to the comparison made here. In the series introduction to *The Reenchant-ment of Science*, Griffin writes, "In some circles, the term *postmodern* is used in reference to that potpourri of ideas and systems sometimes called *new age metaphysics*, although many of these ideas and systems are more premodern than postmodern" (1990:x). Griffin's volume includes essays on postmodernism and science by the social scientist Willis Harman (1990), who influenced the New Age writer Marilyn Ferguson, and by the parapsychologist/humanistic psychologist Stanley Krippner (1990). Subsequent to that discussion, the culture critic Andrew Ross (1991) also raised the question of the connection between postmodernism and the New Age movement.

12. Jameson's political economy and periodizations are controversial (see Davis 1988), but questions regarding the accuracy of his political economy and the politi-cal assumptions of his characterizations of postmodern architecture are not rele-vant to the discussion here, which is restricted to exploring similarities and differ-ences between postmodernism and the New Age movement. My statements should not be taken as an endorsement of postmodernism but instead as an attempt to interpret it comparatively as part of the contemporary cultural landscape.

13. Examples of environmentally sound natural products and gadgets can be found in the catalog available from Eco Source of Sebastopol, California. Among the creative new technologies available are a garden dechlorinator, solar battery chargers, organic detergents, ozonators, energy-efficient lightbulbs, cotton coffee filters, and herbal pet collars. See also the *1991 New Age Sourcebook*, published by *New Age Journal*, and Ross's excellent discussion of brain machines and — no kidding — a New Age toilet (1991).

Chapter 3. Self and Other

1. I use the term "identity" to signal some commonalities with other colleagues doing research on science and popular culture, especially Downey (1986, 1988) and Layne (in press a).

2. See also Capra (1975) and Zukav (1984) as well as criticisms by Gardner (1981b:375–78). For a critique of the parallelist argument that there are meaning-ful similarities between Eastern metaphysics and Western physics, see Restivo (1985). For an alternative viewpoint, see Schumacher and Anderson (1970).

3. Here, Ferguson's optimism might be contrasted with the pessimism of Old World intellectuals, for example Baudrillard, who sees Los Angeles as a parody of cities (1988:104) and Reagan's "euphoric, cinematic, extraverted, advertising vi-sion of the artificial paradises of the West" as the Californian favorite son's exten-sion of the state's lifestyle to the whole country (108).

4. For a discussion of exotic Others that has influenced my own thinking, see Boon (1982).

5. Raphaell elaborates a complex grammar of crystal healing. At one extreme

are the dark crystals of obsidian, smoky quartz, and bloodstone; they correspond to the lowest chakra (body energy center) and are associated with "the cleansing [and] energizing of the physical vehicle" (156). At the other extreme, mediated by a stepwise progression through various shades of quartz and other stones, are the clear crystals of selenite, quartz, and diamond, which correspond to the seventh chakra and "the immortal part of one's self" (159).

6. See Gardner (1952) on the long history of the legend of Atlantis, which was brought up to date (and into the New Age era) by the medium Edgar Cayce (1968), who recorded spirit communications about the demise of that technologically and spiritually advanced civilization.

7. Andrews may be better known for her first book, *Medicine Woman* (1981), but I have selected *Crystal Woman* because it is more relevant to the topic under discussion. Sometimes called "witch doctors," shamans are the priests/healers of native religions. The relationship between Native American religion and the New Age spirituality of the urban middle classes has yet to be explored in a systematic and detailed way from a sociological, historical, or anthropological viewpoint. For beginnings, see Albanese (1990:163–71) and Michael F. Brown (1989). Adler (1979:340–45) also discusses the transformation of *Akwesasne Notes*, the Mohawk Nation newspaper that has chronicled Native American political struggles. She argues that articles in the paper have increasingly recognized convergences between Native American religions and other nature religions.

8. Readers familiar with Lévi-Strauss's *The Savage Mind* will undoubtedly enjoy the irony of Andrew's inversion of his famous discussion of the engineer and the bricoleur.

9. One might argue that accepting reincarnation means rejecting American-style individualism, because the uniqueness of a single lifetime and a personal identity would be relativized by a series of past lives. Indeed, the anti-individualist import of the reincarnationist beliefs of Theosophy and French Spiritism may be one of the factors behind American Spiritualists' reluctance to embrace these doctrines in the late nineteenth century. However, whatever the previous problematic nature of reincarnation to Americans, *Out on a Limb* makes clear that this belief is now part of the American search for identity: new personalities from past lives become resources for reconstructing one's present and future identity (see Kenny 1986).

10. For skeptical critiques of the extraterrestrial theory of South American archaeological sites, see Nickell (1986) and Story (1980). For skeptical commentaries on MacLaine, see Gardner (1988:32–37, 188–208; also in Basil 1988:185–201) and Gordon (1988). Ashworth (1980) compares the Atlantis myth to Erik von Daniken's thesis that ancient civilizations emerged from extraterrestrial colonization. The sociologist finds Judeo-Christian millenarianism more in the latter than the former, but Raphaell's version of the Atlantis myth also seems to resound with Judeo-Christian millenarianism.

11. How new is this new world? Although Rhine's parapsychology differs from Spiritualism and Spiritism in that it shows relatively little concern with the possi-

bility of postmortem survival and spirit communication, his discourse rearticulates some of the key structures of Spiritualism and Spiritism. For example, like Rhine but a century before him, the Spiritist Allan Kardec proposed that his doctrine represented a new science shorn of its materialistic superstitions (see Hess 1991b: ch. 3). Both Rhine and Kardec (as well as Hyslop) accepted the rationalism of science but discarded its materialism, just as they accepted the spiritualism of religion without its dogmatic faith. Spiritism and Spiritualism were to the nineteenth century what parapsychology was to the twentieth century: the new science of the future, the science of the soul.

12. She also invokes the river metaphor to describe the mind as studied by parapsychology, which she believes reveals "the human mind with all of its complexities and in one of its most subtle aspects. For one thing the mind of each person differs, for another, no person's mental content is ever twice the same. Like a river the mind flows forward. Like mercury it flits and changes, and gives no stable element for the test tube" (1967:5). These images of the mind — "no person's mental content is ever twice the same" and "no stable element" — recall what Burke in the *Rhetoric of Religion* (1970) called "God terms," the use of the negative (in the sense of "not" something) to express the ineffable.

13. For another example of the gold metaphor, see Rhine (1967:201). Her imagery of depth, with its alchemical associations, would probably best be characterized as romantic, in contrast with modernist constructions of depth, which are often linked to a future dominated by technology (see Williams 1990).

14. The argument might also be made at the level of methodology. To some extent, the categories of experimental and spontaneous case research also articulate with broader cultural divisions such as Snow's two cultures (1959) or, perhaps more to the point, Geertz's distinction between "an experimental science in search of laws" and an "interpretive one in search of meaning" (1973:5). Rather than try to predict paranormal phenomena by controlling variables, spontaneous case researchers tend to document psychic experiences that have already happened. Their research generally comes after the reports of psi (ESP and psychokinesis), rather than before them (with the exception of registries of premonitions). Furthermore, in at least some types of spontaneous case research (such as the psychoanalytic studies), psi is less a variable to be predicted than a text already written; and consequently spontaneous case research leads into the murky *verstehen* methodologies of the humanities, the *geisteswissenschaften* (literally, the "spirit-sciences"), and on to questions of motivation and meaning. Given the roots of hermeneutic methods in nineteenth-century biblical exegesis, one returns again to an implicit division between science and religion, with the interpretive forms of spontaneous case research having an elective affinity with the tradition of religious hermeneutics.

15. See also the presidential address of K. Ramakrishna Rao, who discusses parapsychology in light of ancient Indian metaphysics (1979).

16. Hyman is critical of some of the overstated claims made on behalf of orthodox science. In a subsequent publication, he writes, "[T]he pathology seems to be exhibited as much in the reaction of the scientific community as in the claims

of the offending scientist," because strategies to "discredit the offending claim by any means possible — *ad hominem* attacks, censorship, innuendo, misrepresentation, etc." may in the long run discredit orthodox science (Hyman 1989:245).

Other examples of the pathology metaphor include Kurtz's reference to the "current outbreak of psychic beliefs" (1981:viii) or Gardner's description of the psychic personality: "Over and over again history has demonstrated that there is a type of neurotic personality who thrives on being admired for psychic powers . . ." (1981b:318). Likewise, the psychologists David Marks and Richard Kammann talk about "Gelleritis," that is, "an extreme belief or conviction in the claims of Uri Geller, sometimes reaching pathological levels" (1980:140) See also "The Psychopathology of Fringe Medicine" (Sabbagh 1985–86) and, for earlier statements, Langmuir's discussion of J. B. Rhine in the context of pathological science (1953) and Houdini's claim that Spiritualism tends to be prevalent among "persons of neurotic temperament," to such an extent that the religious movement had become "a menace to health and sanity" (1972:xvi).

17. See also Schultz (1989:387), who emphasizes "material rewards" as one of the reasons why people become channelers, and Rosen (1989), who argues for parallels between the New Age movement and American consumer culture.

18. In another essay, Gardner seizes upon an analogy employed by Evan Harris Walker, a physicist who has advocated a quantum mechanical theory of psi. Gardner quotes Walker comparing himself to Martin Luther and arguing that his theory may provide a new scientific basis for religion. "The thesis he is nailing to our door!" Gardner replies scornfully (1981a:67).

19. For a parapsychologist's reply, see Stokes (1984). See also the discussion of humor and social structure by Mulkay (1988:152–77), who surveys previous studies including those of Radcliffe-Brown (1952) and Douglas (1975). Mulkay agrees with the anthropologists that humor may be related to ambiguities or contradictions in the social structure, but he also argues (against Douglas) that humor may be used to reinforce existing social arrangements. The case of skeptics' humor considered here would support Mulkay's argument.

20. On March 3, 1991, CBS's "Sixty Minutes" aired allegations that Erhard had committed incest. The show also claimed that Erhard had sold est a few weeks earlier.

21. I have also used the term "borderlands," but in a less pejorative sense because I include skeptical discourse and even my own interdisciplinary discourses in the definition of borderlands. That the term "borderland" may be used in a nonpejorative sense is evident in Still's *Borderlands of Science* (1950). On a usage closer to that of Frazier, recall the image invoked by Hall of the "dismal and miasmatic marshes" of Spiritism and Spiritualism (in Tanner 1910:xxxii).

22. Asimov invokes a similar analogy when he describes the child as a potential "field in which rationality can be made to grow." He contrasts the potential of training "new and fertile minds" with the less hopeful task of awakening "the deserts of ruined minds that have rusted shut" (1985–86:214).

23. J. B. Rhine also used recapitulationist imagery: long before parapsychology came "childhood religion," and after religion came "a new orthodoxy" of "the ma-

terialistic philosophy of a collegiate career," but now "the seeker will be wise to be prepared to adjust his older outlook to the new facts" (1953:321). J. B. Rhine also tells the story in more phylogenetic terms: "Man's first theories of what goes on in his world largely involved the supernatural, but later, as the effort to find the most rationally acceptable causes succeeded, science advanced into one area after another and supernaturalism had to give way before it" (1953:7). Likewise, Houdini discusses how the "full grown sense of the present generation" laughs at the "childish belief in demonology and witchcraft" or at the "mysteries of past ages" (1972:preface). See also the essay in *Time* by James Randi (1992), who criticizes "medieval thinking" and "childish notions of magic and fantasy."

24. On Reagan and space rhetoric, see Rushing (1986). For another, and slightly different, instance of an extended use of the "frontiers of science" metaphor, see the skeptics Abell and Singer (1981:2–3). For them, the "well-trodden region" behind the frontiers is the area of well-understood science, such as Newtonian mechanics, whereas the confusions and uncertainties of frontier science create the conditions of possibility for the media and nonscientists to delude the public with "pseudoscience." No doubt the book *Science: The Endless Frontier* (Bush 1960), which was commissioned by President Franklin D. Roosevelt and is sometimes given credit for having helped lead to the creation of the National Science Foundation, also contributed to the linkage between science and the frontier (on Bush and the NSF, see Reingold 1991:284–333).

25. To the extent that the features of American culture that I describe in this book are shared with other cultures, my argument is not specific to American culture. Thus, much of what I say may also hold true for a similar analysis for Britain, although it is certainly less so for Brazil, and so on as the cultural distance from the United States increases. I do not claim that the underlying cultural meanings are uniquely American, only that they are at the minimum American.

26. On the frontier or exploration metaphor in subsequent popular parapsychology texts, see Krippner, *Song of the Sirens: A Parapsychological Odyssey* (1975); Rhine and Pratt, *Parapsychology: Frontier Science of the Mind* (1957); McConnell, who writes, "Parapsychology cannot be evaluated without some feeling for scientific pioneering" (1983a:207); and Rogo, *In Search of the Unknown: The Odyssey of a Psychical Investigator* (1976).

27. The physicists and psi researchers Russell Targ and Harold Puthoff also invoke cyclical imagery when they trace the trajectory from "the dawn of humankind's recorded search" through "the mechanistically oriented concepts of materialistic science" to "our modern scientific paradigm" (1977:212). They go on: "Perhaps we have seen human evolution come full circle whereby explorations of outer space and inner space come together" (212).

28. In the authors' words: "It is ironic that the authoritarian approach has led many of *The Humanist*'s writers into the posture of the self-same 'true believers' they are criticizing. They are sustained by faith and argue by emotion. They want to save others from erroneous beliefs" (Rockwell et al. 1978:31). Likewise, they state: "When the charge of heresy no longer suffices, the final stand of the true

believer is to prophesy the apocalypse; like Socrates, the heretic is said to be part of a larger movement to subvert the minds of the young and destroy civilization" (33). See also Hansen (1992).

29. For example, in the book *The New Inquisition: Irrational Rationalism and the Citadel of Science*, which the writer Robert Anton Wilson describes as part of the "New Age Conspiracy" to raise consciousness against the "citadel" (his term for the "scientific-technological elite"), the skeptics are portrayed as irrational (34). For Wilson, orthodox science has priests, an inquisitional program, papal bulls (issued by Martin Gardner), a "propaganda department" (CSICOP), and a dogma of "fundamentalist materialism" (34–45; cf. Sheaffer 1989).

Chapter 4. Heroes and Sermons

1. Gardner (1981b:253). "Automatic writing" refers, in this context, to communications from spirits through the medium's hands without apparent conscious control over what the hands are writing. According to Montgomery, Ford was her friend when he was alive, but according to Melton, she overplays their friendship and in fact they were only acquaintances (personal correspondence, 1989).

2. The choice of this book may be faulted on the grounds that its publication date (1971) makes it somewhat early for the label "New Age." However, in the late 1980s and early 1990s, I often found Montgomery's books, including *A World Beyond*, in the New Age section of bookstores. Still, to be conservative it might be better to think of *A World Beyond* as representing a transition point between the longstanding American Spiritualist tradition and the contemporary New Age movement. I have chosen this text because its description of otherworldly existence is so richly detailed; the analysis here should be taken as an example of an interpretive strategy that could be applied to other New Age channeled texts.

3. The connection among psychical research, materialism, and morality clearly is one of the Ariadne's threads of parapsychological discourse. In addition to the work of Hyslop discussed previously, the British psychical researchers Myers and Sidgwick also hoped that their findings might help combat the potentially dangerous social effects of materialism (Gauld 1968:142).

4. Again, see Winner's discussion (1977) of the similar "technics-out-of-control" theme, including his discussion of Frankenstein.

5. Two qualifications should be made here. Like the early psychical researchers, Rhine builds no bridges to any specific religion. In contrast, in Brazil allegiances dramatically affect parapsychological discourse and even define the leading schools of parapsychology (Hess 1987b). In addition, many contemporary American parapsychologists are not interested in the religion question, and they may even consider themselves materialists.

6. These studies were later contested by the skeptical psychologist C. E. M. Hansel (1989:61–93). For a summary of the parapsychologists' responses, see Edge et al. (1986: 162–65). For a biographical background on Pratt, see Stevenson (1980).

7. See also McConnell (1983a) on Kuhn; Rogo (1983:183) on "cultural revolu-

tion"; and Edge (1990:140), who speaks of the "quiet revolution" in consciousness research and psychology that has occurred in cognitive science and related fields.

8. The psychologist John Palmer (1980) envisioned a somewhat less grandiose revolution at the same conference in a presidential address presented before the Parapsychological Association. In the second part of this lecture, "The Impending Revolution," Palmer employs Kuhn's work to apprehend what he sees as a "paradigm shift" within parapsychology from the "transmission paradigm" of J. B. Rhine to the new "correspondence paradigm" (205–6). The former is based on a communication model of extrasensory perception, that is, a model structured around a sender and a receiver. In contrast, the correspondence paradigm abandons attempts to delineate a mechanism for ostensible psi processes and instead "postulates some principle which causes events in nature to coincide to a greater than chance degree, given certain preconditions" (206; see Stanford 1978).

9. I am only selecting a few examples. Consider also Targ and Puthoff's *Mind Reach*, where the theme of nuclear Armageddon is implied when they call for the "peaceful uses of psychic energy" (1977: ch. 9). Likewise, the engineer and psychologist Dean Radin concludes his presidential address by noting that science can be good, bad, and ugly. He notes that "orthodox science systematically ignores the subjective side of human experience," and consequently it tends to make science a "value-less enterprise" (1989:168). The implications? "If we are no more than organic machines, then people will treat each other, and the planet, as machines" (169). The result is pollution, not only of the environment but also of "our own sense of purpose" (169). He implies that parapsychology can help avert this pollution of land and purpose.

10. Some parapsychologists may fault me for including Rogo and Mitchell, who never belonged to the inner circles of the Parapsychological Association, but higher status parapsychologists also sanctioned their books by writing forewords, such as Tart for Rogo's book and Schmeidler for Mitchell's book.

11. A review in the *Journal of the American Society for Psychical Research* shows that not all members of the parapsychological community agree with Mitchell's musings: "Moreover, I have difficulties with the basic premise; merely to know — even to know dramatically and existentially — that we are not just material objects is no guarantee that we will become better persons" (Grosso 1982:188).

12. See also White (1991) for another discussion of postmodernism in the context of parapsychology.

13. The skeptical psychologist James Alcock also argues that the spirit entities who communicate through channelers provide "hassle-free religion" (1989:384). Without the commitment of traditional religion, New Age channelers spout "hedonistic and narcissistic wisdom" that deemphasizes the moral rigors of avoiding sins and temptations. Furthermore, the "predigested" nature of the channelers' teachings means that New Agers face a "clear danger" of being "diverted from trying to grapple in a rational and realistic way with the difficulties of living" (384). Although Alcock suggests that many people lose little more than their money, some people come to channelers with "real problems and real distress," and for them

the fake wisdom of the channelers "may prove to be as deleterious for the psyche as the fake treatments proffered by medical quacks can be for the body" (384).

14. The relationship between the revolutionary and the Puritan may not be intuitively obvious, but let us return again to the parapsychologist J. Gaither Pratt's discussion of revolution. "The aim of a revolutionary development," he writes, "is to extend its influence" (1964:272). The result, he argues, is an inevitable "fight to the death" between the two ways of thinking. Any revolutionist worth his salt must, it goes without saying, believe in his cause and in its ultimate success" (272). Pratt's image of the revolutionary effort therefore bears some similarities to the Puritan divine: they both have an evangelizing mission, a deep dedication to the cause, and a dyadic concept of a world characterized by a confrontation between the preterite and the elect. As Walzer (1965) has argued, the Puritan saints of the seventeenth century were the first revolutionaries in the modern sense of being dedicated wholeheartedly and often ascetically to their cause of overthrowing and overhauling an existing social order.

Two possibilities emerge for remaking society: revolution or moving to the frontier and starting from scratch. Both are part of American cultural history, from the time of the Puritan "communes" and the Boston Tea Party. The same cultural logic characterizes the present era, with its division into the hippie and the radical, into Woodstock and Chicago, and later into the New Ager and political activist (or, to locate myself in this historically developing cultural logic, the critical intellectual).

15. Bercovitch also links the Puritan jeremiad to the revolution (1978:128–33) and the frontier (10–11, 163–65).

16. On magic and the seventeenth-century Puritans, see Thomas (1971). My interviews with parapsychologists (Hess in press a) also turned up one case in which a skeptical senior colleague burned the data of a parapsychologist, who was a junior colleague in the same department. Thus, as one of my readers noticed, there is at least one case that is quite similar to the Puritans' literal smashing and burning of artifacts.

Chapter 5. Gender and Hierarchy

1. I would also include in this category the physicist Fritjof Capra, who in *The Turning Point* builds his argument about major changes in society around a clash between the "Newtonian world-machine" and the "new physics." Thus, although he does not discuss Ferguson's work, he develops a similar kind of thematics between old and new ways of thinking. He also tends to avoid using the term "New Age," and instead he follows Roszak (1969) and labels the alternative social movement "counterculture," although it is true that Capra does occasionally use the term "New Age" (1982:46, 415).

2. However, see the skeptic Robert Basil's introduction to *Not Necessarily the New Age* (1988:17–19), where he discusses Ferguson's interest in Harmonic Convergence and trance channelers.

3. I find the styles of Andrews and Castaneda very similar, as well as the controversy over the validity of their work (see Adolph and Smoley 1989).

4. Ellwood (1973:187) defines neopaganism as a range of groups that share a belief in ancient gods. In addition to his survey of neopaganist groups in the United States (1973:187–213), see Starhawk on feminist neopagans (1979, 1982, 1987), the survey of neopagans and witches by Adler (1979), and the discussion by Albanese (1990:173–83).

5. I doubt many anthropologists or archaeologists would agree with this statement. For a scholarly anthropological account of the matriarchy question, see Webster (1975). The indigenous society that came closest to matriarchy was arguably the Iroquois, who have been held up as an example of a "tribal" society where men and women shared power on close to an equal basis, that is, a social order which is far from a straightforward inversion of patriarchy (Brown 1975).

6. For a more detailed statement of this thesis, see Achterberg (1990).

7. An earlier version of this section was presented as a paper at the 1988 annual meeting of the Parapsychological Association in a panel on women and gender in parapsychology (Hess 1988).

8. Some examples of members of the parapsychology/psychical research community who have advocated spontaneous case research include Carlos Alvarado, Stephen Braude, D. Scott Rogo, William Roll, Ian Stevenson, and Rhea White, as well as others who rely on the case-study method for discussions from a psychoanalytic or clinical perspective. See Alvarado (1987) and, for a sample of spontaneous case research, Rao (1986).

9. Likewise, as the skeptical philosopher Piet Hein Hoebens (1986) notes in his essay "Sense and Nonsense in Parapsychology," parapsychology is divided between the experimentalists and the relatively "less scientific" chroniclers of "spontaneous cases" ("less scientific" from the experimentalists' and skeptics' point of view, which on this issue converge).

10. Capra associates yin with the feminine, responsive, cooperative, intuitive, and synthesizing, and yang with the masculine, aggressive, competitive, rational, and analytic (1982:38).

11. The partial list of fellows appeared on the inside front cover. A similar list of scientific and technical consultants appeared on the inside back cover. The second list also included about fifty names total, of whom only four were identifiably women: Barbara Eisenstadt, Laurie Godfrey, Daisie Radner, and Sarah Thomason. There seems to be little or no change in the last few years, since the parapsychologist/engineer George Hansen (1987:322) noted the same pattern three years earlier. See also Hansen's subsequent study (1992:28–30).

12. There is, as yet, no local organization of skeptics in the Albany area, but I did attend a meeting of the Capital District Humanist Society, an organization of secular humanists that might be considered a close cousin of the skeptics. (One member explained to me that they had no direct connection to CSICOP, but Paul Kurtz was the president of their national organization, and during the course of the meeting several people mentioned with apparent approval books published by

Prometheus Books.) This meeting of about thirty-five people was more balanced sexually than the Bay area group described below, but only about 20 percent of those in attendance were baby-boom age or younger. In other words, the adjectives "slightly geriatric" and "predominantly white" would still be applicable.

13. See Albanese (1990: ch. 5) for a discussion of other women New Age writers not discussed here.

14. Randi (1986:157). The parapsychological account was, for this case, even more of a failure, since it consisted only of an attempt to validate the girl's abilities under observation outside the home (Stewart, Roll, and Baumann 1987). However, in general Roll's work has pointed to family conflicts and "repressed hostility" that would make possible a consideration of questions of domestic power and gender (Roll 1972; see also Fodor 1948).

15. Zusne (1985:687), citing Zusne and Jones (1982:186-90). Zusne goes on to argue that the data should be interpreted cautiously, but he also defends the same general image of the traits and characteristics of the occult believer.

16. I make this claim based on reading the Prometheus Books catalogue. Several other books were available on the topic of sexuality and psychology. I do not imply that the publisher or members of CSICOP endorse the contents of the book; however, it is also hard to image the book being published by a New Age press or imprint. In other words, I do not make the strong claim that the publication of the book reflects a conscious policy or endorsement, but instead I think only that there is an "elective affinity" between the approach of the book and the masculine culture of American skepticism. Another example of antifeminism is a brief comment in an article in the *Skeptical Inquirer* about Feyerabend and other members of the "intellectual revolt against science"; the skeptical author lists "'feminist' science" (with the word "feminist" in quotation marks) as one example of the intellectual revolt (Grove 1988:72). As this book goes to press, a new Prometheus Books catalogue announced a related book that, although apparently not antifeminist in the sense of the Davidson book, nevertheless critiques mainstream feminism from a libertarian standpoint (Taylor 1992).

17. I am also indebted here to my former teachers David Holmberg (1983) and Kathryn March, who examined the mediating role of the female in relations between the human and the divine.

18. Of course, these are relative distinctions, and within the humanities there are all sorts of other gendered arrangements and divisions that reproduce patriarchy.

19. Regarding my own home discipline, cultural anthropology, Dwyer has remarked how in several cases where husband and wife have been in the field in the same area and at the same time, the husband has written the more "objective" ethnographic monograph, whereas the wife has written the more anecdotal fieldwork account (1987:266).

20. Also, recall the parable of the spinster and the gambler discussed in the previous chapter. Here, the female medium (via the male spirit guide) marks the religious as feminine and the materialistic as masculine.

21. See the unprecedented joint publication by the skeptical psychologist Ray Hyman and the parapsychologist Charles Honorton (Hyman and Honorton 1986).

Chapter 6. Skepticism and the Paranormal in Hollywood

1. For a complementary perspective on horror films and fiction, see Carroll (1990), who focuses on the more psychological and aesthetic aspects of the genre.

2. On the history behind the story, see Travers and Reiff (1974).

3. For a skeptical view of the movie (one which, in a rare example of an ecumenical spirit, was written by a member of the parapsychology community, published in the *Skeptical Inquirer*, and anthologized in one of Frazier's volumes), see Morris (1981).

4. In the first movie, there are some interesting variations – the paranormal Other is associated with an ancient Middle Eastern religion (somewhat similar to *The Exorcist*), and the final scenes take the characters to the tops of buildings (as in *King Kong* and *Poltergeist III*) rather than down into pits – but the imagery of spatial and temporal distance for the paranormal Other is maintained.

5. The substitution of the anthropologist for the parapsychologist is perhaps the main reason why I have chosen to end this chapter with a discussion of the older film. It leads to the reflexive question of the meaning of the human scientist's discourse in the ideological arena, a question which I consider in more detail in the next chapter.

6. Incidentally, the former is similar to the solution that parapsychologists have sometimes recommended, and sometimes with success, in cases of families who believe they are troubled by a poltergeist. However, the family situation in these cases is usually very different from the Hollywood case, since in the real-life families that believe they are suffering from a poltergeist there is often a great deal of domestic tension (sometimes even domestic violence), so the isolation strategy may be to the benefit of the young victim. In contrast, the Hollywood families in these movies are usually not abusive or repressive, so the goal is reunification.

Chapter 7. Theoretical Conclusions

1. I also would argue that Barnes may have been premature when he made the announcement used as the epigraph for the introductory chapter. If one interprets the "sociological point of view" narrowly, then perhaps he is right that little remains to be said on this topic, but I would disagree if the sociological point of view is interpreted broadly to include the question of cultural meanings and politics. At least, from the anthropological/cultural point of view, much remains to be said.

2. Gieryn read an earlier version of this formulation and said he agrees with this notion of multiple and recursive boundaries; indeed, there is nothing in his formulation that would preclude the way I am elaborating it here. He is also exploring similar ideas in his most recent work, which involves the study of "roving

boundaries" and the interpretive flexibility of science (Gieryn and Figert 1990:91).

3. See, for example, the group of STS researchers I refer to as the "reflexivists": Ashmore (1989); Ashmore, Mulkay, and Pinch (1989); Mulkay (1991); and Woolgar (1988).

4. Exceptions are few and far between, one of which is a point where the language of a Pinch and Collins article compares the *Skeptical Inquirer* to *Fate*. Pinch and Collins describe the former as a magazine that, "sandwiched" between two covers, "feeds its readership a spicier fare than is normally served up in a technical journal," whereas *Fate* is a "pulp magazine sold at newsstands" (1984:528, 538). Their metaphors shift from the culinary to the "bestiary key," as Lévi-Strauss might say, when they describe *Fate Magazine*'s exposé of a *Skeptical Inquirer* story: "But big fleas have little fleas upon their backs to bite them!" (538). One might argue that such earthy metaphors indicate that these sociologists — like many of their colleagues — construct the social sciences as encompassing their Others, and perhaps the journal *Social Studies of Science* — where the Collins and Pinch article was published — stands implicitly at the apex of a hierarchy that runs from *Fate* at the bottom to the *Skeptical Inquirer* and on to the *Zetetic Scholar*, which they also mention. Likewise, one could also argue that my attention in *Science in the New Age* to metaphors, imagery, and cultural values — that is, to "literary" or "symbolic" dimensions rather than to referential or epistemological ones — implies that I have constructed my own discourse as encompassing the others by reducing them to the merely literary or symbolic. However, like Collins and Pinch I recognize the contingent and constructed nature of my own position, and thus any allegation that we are constructing "metadiscourses" may involve little more than the trivial observation that merely by writing about or studying other discourses one inevitably encompasses them with one's own framework. To use Bateson's term, everyone is constructing a "metalogue" with respect to everyone else (1972). Thus, to allege that someone has constructed a metadiscourse may amount to little more than recognizing that someone has constructed a discourse: a framework and body of statements for apprehending a piece of the world.

5. See Marcus and Fischer (1986:115). Perhaps Taussig (1987) is the best example of a conscious and reflexive linkage between writing and political critique. See also Clifford (1988), Clifford and Marcus (1986), and the more explicit linkages between text and power in the important criticisms raised by feminists (e.g., Mascia-Lees, Sharpe, and Cohen 1989). My argument is not against reflexivism per se, as perhaps is the case of Latour (1988), who has called for "infrareflexivity." Rather, my call for a more critical type of reflexivism comes closer to the interpretation of reflexivity by Downey (in press a), who argues that whenever one makes a theoretical argument one is in a sense being reflexive, since the argument constitutes a reflection on the assumptions of one's discursive community and it may indeed contribute to the ongoing development of that community's thought.

6. The lists appear respectively on the inside front and back cover.

7. Tylor admitted the possibility of a psychic force but remained unconvinced by most of the Spiritualist mediums he observed (Stocking 1987:191, 1971). How-

ever, he developed his theory of animism at least partly in response to his knowledge of the British Spiritualist movement (Stocking 1971:90–91). The folklorist/
anthropologist Andrew Lang was also very interested in psychical research.

8. For a skeptic's review of Mead's beliefs on the paranormal and religion, see
Gardner (1988:19–24).

9. Examples include Barnouw (1946); Elkin (1977); Locke, in Kelly and Locke
(1981); Winkelman (1982); and contributors in Angoff and Barth (1974) and Long
(1977). I, too, was at one point interested in psychical research and parapsychology. However, after completing graduate school in anthropology, I have partici-
pated in only two parapsychology meetings: the first to present arguments and
papers in favor of anthropological/cultural approaches (i.e., 1989b, 1989c, and 1988);
and the second to serve on a panel where I was invited to discuss my research on
parapsychology and Spiritism in Brazil, and also to complete interviews for a socio-
logical/anthropological study of the suppression of parapsychology in the academy.
Unlike some anthropologists, I have not found parapsychology very compelling
as an analytical framework for anthropological research, in part because my doc-
toral training was heavily influenced by the tradition of French and British social
anthropology. Unlike the American cultural anthropology tradition, social anthropology has little room for psychological anthropology, be it orthodox or
heterodox. As a result I tend to be more interested in social, cultural, and political
questions than in psychological ones, and, as should be obvious by now, I tend
to look at psychological discourses from a critical, sociocultural perspective. For
this approach, some parapsychologists have called me a skeptic, although my own
identification is with the human sciences rather than with skepticism, parapsychology, or, for that matter, with any of the schools of New Age thought.

10. Examples from the 1980s include Lee (1987), Owen (1981), Romanucci-Ross
(1980); see also Stoller and Olkes (1987). A well-known earlier account of an anthropologist's ostensibly anomalous experiences is Linton (1927).

11. See Harner (1980) as well as the popular books on shamanism by Halifax
(1979, 1982).

12. See the reply by Collins and Pinch in Collins (1983:106–7). Part of the debate hinges on the question of whether the term "orthodox" scientists is invented
by the sociologists or is a native term used by the parapsychologists and then picked
up uncritically by the sociologists. Collins and Pinch claim that the term is their
own, but I have heard parapsychologists use the term — maybe they picked it up
from the sociologists!

13. Their essay also resulted in a reply from Collins (1991) and a rebuttal by
Martin, Richards, and Scott (1991).

14. They go on to argue that their critique of the neutral observer bears some
similarities to the "weak program" of Chubin and Restivo (1983), who also argue
that human scientists are always part of the controversies they study and therefore
cannot maintain a "neutral" position. In subsequent work, Restivo has changed
the term from the "weak program" to the "critical sociology of science" (see Restivo
and Loughlin 1987).

15. Anthropologists may recognize the similarities to our own questioning of the myth of the Lone Ranger anthropologist (Rosaldo 1989) and the objectivist ideology of the holistic ethnographic monograph (Clifford 1988, Clifford and Marcus 1986).

16. Gardner (1988:184–87) and Stokes (1983). See also Gardner (1988:25–31) and Adelman (1983).

17. Such may, arguably, also be the case in Pinch's commentary (1975) in the issue of *Behavioral and Brain Sciences* devoted to the parapsychology debate (e.g., Adamenko 1987, Alcock 1987, Blackmore 1987, Rao and Palmer 1987). Here, Pinch criticizes the skeptics' criticisms, but he also offers suggestions for and criticisms of parapsychologists. I suspect that his position, like mine, will be satisfactory to neither camp.

18. Martin has pointed out to me that the cases he and his colleagues analyzed were all polarized, and in these cases capturing by the more heterodox position is likely. In contrast, the case of parapsychologists, skeptics, and New Agers reveals the complexities of capturing when the boundaries are not so neatly polarized into two opposing camps.

19. I owe this last insight to Restivo, who has proved a helpful sounding board for the discussion presented here. In comments on an earlier draft of this section, Brian Martin noted that ongoing structural factors may play an equally or more important role than the factor of socialization and life history.

20. As Culler has phrased it, "[C]ritical disputes about a text can frequently be identified as a displaced reenactment of conflicts dramatized in the text" (1982: 215). Thus, my reading represents one form of "deconstruction," although a more cultural and political version than that found in most previous applications of deconstruction in STS.

Chapter 8. Practical Implications: Toward Dialogue

1. One might even read this chapter as continuing the rhetoric of the jeremiad that I have found in my Others.

2. A similar point was made by a skeptic, who argued that his colleagues might do better first to accept that some paranormal beliefs work and then, from the skeptical viewpoint, explain why they are successful, rather than simply debunk the beliefs (Seckel 1986). See also the criticisms raised by Schultz (1989:378).

3. See also Anderson (1990), Shore (1989), Melton, Clark, and Kelly (1990: 417–27).

4. On secular humanism, see Kurtz (1983a, 1989a). Kurtz served as the editor of the *Humanist* magazine from 1967 to 1978, and during these years the magazine published many articles critical of paranormal claims. There are a variety of theological or philosophical positions within the humanist movement, and therefore one should not assume that all humanists are atheists or agnostics (Kurtz 1974). Some members of conventional religions think of themselves as humanists, and the first editor of the *Humanist* and secretary of the American Humanist Association, Edwin H. Wilson, was a Unitarian minister (Lamont 1975).

5. See Pinch and Collins (1984), Rawlins (1981); for an exception, see Hyman (1989:347–61). The magician James Randi has a standing offer to test any psychic and award the successful subject a large monetary prize, but like most skeptics he does not seem to be interested in running a series of experiments with large data sets, multiple subjects, and statistical analysis of the type routinely performed by parapsychologists. Furthermore, in the opinion I have heard from some parapsychologists, the tensions between skeptics and parapsychologists (not to mention psychics) are great enough that the latter perceive with suspicion the sincerity of the magician's offer.

6. Another example is Corliss Lamont. That influential member of the American Humanist Association, the organization that "first sponsored" CSICOP (Gardner 1983:57), was a well-known "fellow traveler" whose antireligious and procommunistic stances might be contrasted with the proreligious and anticommunistic stances of his contemporary J. B. Rhine. I am indebted to the parapsychologist George Hansen for pointing me in the direction of Lamont and commenting on my discussion of the political affiliations of the prominent skeptics. Subsequently, Hansen published an extended essay on the topic (1992).

7. For example, Gardner calls Hook a "democratic socialist who is occasionally branded a neoconservative by writers who should know better" (1983:396), and Kurtz, who lists Hook as one of his twentieth-century mentors (1983a:273), calls the former Hoover Institution fellow a "lifelong social democrat" who has denied the appellation "neoconservative" (1983b:x–xi).

8. Kurtz later wrote about the "assault of the New Left and the counterculture upon the intellect," and he suggested that the growth of "cults of unreason" might be one consequence (1976b:28).

9. CNN report, November 15, 1991. The movie also did very well in North America, but it did not achieve once-in-a-decade status.

10. This point is arguably true as a sociological principle for a much broader scope of scientific research, but I have restricted the claim here to parapsychology.

11. For an elaboration of this kind of alternative in the context of anthropology and transcultural psychiatry, see Hess (1989b, 1989c). See also Pinch (1987), who advocated building bridges to the orthodox sciences.

12. On this point, it is worth noting that at least one leading psychical researcher, the psychiatrist Ian Stevenson, is highly critical of the transition to experimentalism, and he has called for a return to the tradition of investigating claims of paranormal phenomena and spontaneous cases (1987a, 1987b). Stevenson's appears to be a minority position, but his call for a return to an investigation of issues closely linked to the public's experiences, and for linkages with the research agendas of the orthodox sciences — even to the extent of abandoning specialized parapsychology journals — merits consideration. He has resigned from the Parapsychological Association for these and related reasons. See also Stevenson (1984, 1988) and Braude (1986, 1991).

13. For example, the Parapsychological Association could adopt resolutions warning the public about potentially dangerous psychic claims, such as psychic surgery by untrained healers who physically operate on the body (as occurs fre-

quently in Brazil, where the Spiritist leadership has condemned such practices). Although parapsychologists might argue that resolutions of this type are not within the proper purview of a scientific organization, similar resolutions of public interest (generally on political issues) are standard practice in other scientific organizations, such as the American Anthropological Association.

At the opposite extreme, another form of public education that seems to be extremely popular in most American cities is the wide variety of classes on self-help topics such as training for psychic experiences, yoga, biofeedback, self-hypnosis, and so on. There is clearly a public demand for experiential approaches to altered states of consciousness as well as for acquiring frameworks to help make sense of these experiences, and this public demand provides another potential place for parapsychology to play a socially useful role. To some extent parapsychologists have recognized the possibility of developing an applied field involving experiential education, first in Charles Tart's "learning approach" to ESP (1976) and later in Jeffrey Mishlove's educational and evaluative approach to popular psi development systems (1983). Although it is true that such approaches have met with methodological criticisms within the parapsychological community (e.g., Stanford 1977, 1984, 1985; cf. Mishlove 1985), it may be possible to avoid these criticisms by developing a more conservative educational approach that again does not make claims about the reality or nonreality of paranormal phenomena. For example, parapsychologists could provide a sophisticated, critical alternative to the popular self-help classes by redefining the content toward psychological experiences — such as lucid dreaming, meditation, hypnosis, and out-of-body experiences — and by refocussing the educational framework to allow the public to explore altered states of consciousness in ways that combine an experiential component with a theoretical discussion of alternative explanatory frameworks, including skeptical, psychological, transcendental, and sociocultural approaches. Again, such an activity would help parapsychology to redefine itself as a broader field of study, such as the branch of the study of altered states of consciousness that focuses on the physical, psychological, and social correlates of psychic experiences.

14. See also the work of the psychologists Blackmore (1982), Irwin (1985), and Tart (1969).

15. See Blackmore (1983:142, 1987, 1988), Hövelman and Krippner (1986:4), White (1985, 1990); cf. Palmer (1988). One reader has misinterpreted me as urging parapsychologists to "abandon" the psi hypothesis or the quest for evidence for paranormal phenomena, as in most anthropological studies of related psychic experiences such as spirit possession and sorcery or the skeptics' psychology of the psychic. I suspect that such a move would be difficult for most parapsychologists to make, because the evidentiality question is the premise that their discourse and field is based on. At the minimum, however, the field could benefit from diversification, so that the study of psychic experiences becomes at least as important as the evidentiality question. In this way, parapsychologists could begin to break down the walls that divide them from the skeptics' project of the psychology of the psychic. Given the schismatic cultural logic that I discussed in chapter 2, I sus-

pect that such a development will occur through the emergence of yet another organization, one dedicated to the psychological and cultural studies of "exceptional human experiences" (White 1990), perhaps founded by disaffected parapsychologists, some social scientists, and even some skeptics.

16. On the relations to 1960s politics, see Restivo (1985), Rossman (1979), Tipton (1982), and Winner (1986:61–84).

17. On crystal mining and its deleterious impact on the environment, see the critical article "Crystal Diggers Mine Controversy," in *New Age Journal* (November/December 1989, pp. 16–17).

18. See also Adler's survey of the politics of contemporary American witches and pagans (1979). Adler argues that there is a wide spectrum of political positions among these groups, and that the politics of any group or person tends to reflect the community to which they belong rather than their occultist/New Age beliefs (1979:372–78). *New Age Journal*, whose readers are 37 percent "liberal" and 38 percent "very liberal" (May/June 1987, p. 46), also tends to be more political and more critical of some of the wilder claims to the New Age movement.

19. Satin's sociology and political economy therefore contrast with Gardner's considerably more realistic attempt to grapple with issues of economic and political justice (1983:116–76). In fairness to the New Age author I should point out that by the early 1980s Satin edited a newsletter, *New Options*, in which even he "questioned the New Age movement's utopian dreams, including many of those he had outlined in his book" (Clark 1990:323–25).

Appendix: Methodology

1. Thus, in contrast to the historically important laboratory studies by Knorr-Cetina (1981) and Latour and Woolgar (1979) as well as the Edinburgh and Bath schools, all of which to varying degrees make use of the anthropology metaphor, I find a closer affiliation with the work of anthropologists who examine the meaning of scientific discourse in broader cultural contexts. What I am calling "cultural reconstructivism" therefore approximates the work of several of my colleagues in American anthropology who have also been developing studies of science and technology in contexts other than the laboratory. Examples include Downey, who has contextualized science with respect to local and national political controversies involving activist groups such as the Clamshell Alliance (1986) and the Union of Concerned Scientists (1988; see also Downey in press b); Dubinskas (1988) and Zabusky (in press), who examine the meanings of scientific discourse in, respectively, private corporations and public bureaucracies; Forsythe (in press), Davis-Floyd (in press), Layne (in press b), Rapp (1991), and Suchman (1987), who are examining computer, obstetric, and reproductive technologies from users' perspectives; Martin (1987, 1990), whose work on women's reproductive sciences and immunology will be discussed below; Rabinow (1990, in press), who is developing historical/cultural frameworks on society and the genome project; Toumey (in press), who is studying science, creationism, and secular humanism; Traweek (1988, 1990), who has developed a long-term ethnographic and comparative study of high-energy

physicists, rather than just knowledge in the physics laboratory; and Weeks and Packard (1991), who are examining how ranchers and fishers in Texas appropriate science in their political and economic struggles. See also the volume edited by the sociologists Cozzens and Gieryn (1990), who advocate the related perspective in sociology of studying science *in* society.

2. The "ideological arena" bears some similarities to what Knorr-Cetina has called a "transepistemic field" (1981), but I am less interested in explaining how other positions influence or constrain the discourse under study and more interested in how any given position transforms and reworks the discourse of its Others. For similar reasons, I have also not adopted the term "contingent forum" of Collins and Pinch (1979, 1982).

3. On ethnographic approaches, see Badone (1991), S. Brown (1989), Danforth (1989), Luhrmann (1989), and Tipton (1982). Life history projects were underway by the anthropologists Michael F. Brown and Theodore Schwartz, as well as ethnographic studies by the anthropologists Susan L. Brown, Robbie Davis-Floyd, and Joseph Dumit, among others.

4. Although several of the books or authors discussed in part II appeared on a list of "top-40" New Age bestsellers that the manager of the New Age bookstore in Albany showed me, the list is still conspicuous by writers who are not mentioned, such as Jean Achtenberg, Fritjof Capra, Carlos Castaneda (although perhaps somewhat early), Ram Dass, Annie Dillard, Jane Roberts, David Spangler, Virginia Samdahl, Charlene Spretnak, and Starhawk. Davis-Floyd also informs me that *A Course in Miracles* (Foundation for Inner Peace, 1975, anonymous) is a key text for the Texas New Agers among whom she is doing fieldwork. I have come across that text in the Albany/Berkshires region, although I believe it is less prevalent here than in Texas.

5. I therefore place in a related category the work of Gilbert and Mulkay (1984), Latour and Woolgar (1979), Latour (1987:21–62), Lynch (1985), Mulkay (1985), Myers (1985, 1990), and to some extent Bazerman (1988). For a discussion of some of the important differences within this field, see the excellent review by Myers (1990:25–34).

6. Detienne also deserves mention in this context, for his work frequently achieves a clarity that Lévi-Strauss's project sometimes lacks due to its great complexity and formalism. In *Dionysius Slain*, Detienne provides a method for showing how opposing Greek cults form a system in terms of multiple codes, and in *The Gardens of Adonis* he provides a model for following out one code across multiple texts and contexts. Likewise, Jean-Paul Dumont's *Under the Rainbow* provides a model for articulating codes within one society. Some might also include the work of Lakoff and Johnson (1980) in this category, but I find the method of Detienne and Dumont more useful because their interpretations of codes are more sustained and culture-bound.

7. See, for example, Marcus and Fischer (1986:45), who draw on Dumont to problematize individualist assumptions in contemporary sociology and anthropology.

8. In a postscript to *Anthropology as Cultural Critique*, Fischer (1991) recognizes science and technology studies as one area of future growth for the cultural critique project. However, whereas, critical STS researchers such as Restivo have endorsed feminism, there have been more tensions in anthropology. I find feminist approaches to be very important in critical cultural studies, particularly for the question of paraculture, and thus it is important to pay close attention to feminist criticisms of the new ethnographers (e.g., Mascia-Lees, Sharpe, and Cohen 1989; Visweswaran 1988).

Bibliography

Abell, George, and Barry Singer (eds.)
1981   *Science and the Paranormal.* New York: Charles Scribner's Sons.
Achterberg, Jeanne
1990   *Woman as Healer.* Boston: Shambhala.
Adamenko, Victor G. et al.
1987   "Open Peer Commentary." *Behavioral and Brain Sciences* 10 (4): 566–618.
Adelman, George
1983   *"Frames of Meaning,* by Harry Collins and Trevor Pinch [book review]."
        Parapsychology Review 14 (3): 20–21.
Adler, Margot
1979   *Drawing Down the Moon: Witches, Druids, Goddess-Worshippers and
        Other Pagans in America Today.* New York: Viking.
Adolph, Jonathan, and Richard Smoley
1989   "Bevery Hills Shaman." *New Age Journal* March/April: 24.
Albanese, Catherine
1990   *Nature Religion in America.* Chicago: University of Chicago Press.
Alcock, James
1987   "Parapsychology: Science of the Anomalous or Search for the Soul?" *Be-
        havioral and Brain Sciences* 10 (4): 553–65.
1989   "Channeling: Brief History and Contemporary Context." *Skeptical In-
        quirer* 13 (4): 380–84.
Alvarado, Carlos S.
1987   "Comments on *Case Studies in Parapsychology* and on the Value of Re-
        search in this Area." *Journal of Parapsychology* 51:337–52.
1990   "The History of Women in Parapsychology." *Journal of Parapsychology*
        53:233–49.
Anderson, Ian
1987   "Taking Up the Sceptics' Burden." *New Scientist* April 16:51–52.
Anderson, Roger
1990   *"Channeling into the New Age,* by Henry Gordon [book review]." *Jour-
        nal of the American Society for Psychical Research* 84 (4):390–93.
Andrews, Lynn
1981   *Medicine Woman.* New York: Harper and Row.
1987   *Crystal Woman: Sisters of the Dreamtime.* New York: Warner Books.

213

Angoff, Allan, and Diana Barth
1974   *Parapsychology and Anthropology.* New York: Parapsychology Foun-
         dation.
Ardner, Edwin
1972   "Belief and the Problem of Women." In J. S. LaFontaine (ed.), *The Inter-
         pretation of Ritual.* London: Tavistock.
Argüelles, José
1987   *The Mayan Factor: The Path Beyond Technology.* Santa Fe, N.M.: Bear
         and Co.
Ashmore, Malcolm
1989   *The Reflexive Thesis.* Chicago: University of Chicago Press.
Ashmore, Malcolm, Michael Mulkay, and Trevor Pinch
1989   *Health and Efficiency: A Sociology of Health Economics.* Philadelphia:
         Open University Press.
Ashworth, C. E.
1980   "Flying Saucers, Spoon-Bending, and Atlantis: A Structural Analysis of
         New Mythologies." *Sociological Review* 28 (2): 353–76.
Asimov, Isaac
1981   "The Subtlest Difference." In George Abell and Barry Singer (eds.), *Science
         and the Paranormal.* New York: Charles Scribner's Sons.
1982   "Introduction: The Deadly Misinformation." In James Randi (ed.), *Flim-
         Flam! Psychics, ESP, Unicorns, and Other Delusions.* Buffalo: Prometheus
         Books.
1985–86 "The Perennial Fringe." *Skeptical Inquirer* 10 (2): 212–14.
1988   "Foreword." In Henry Gordon, *Channeling into the New Age.* Buffalo:
         Prometheus Books.
Badone, Ellen
1991   "Ethnography, Fiction, and the Meanings of the Past in Brittany." *American
         Ethnologist* 18 (3): 518–45.
Bailey, Alice A.
1954   *Education in the New Age.* New York: Lucis.
Barnes, Barry
1981   "On the 'Hows' and 'Whys' of Cultural Change." *Social Studies of Science*
         11:481–98.
1982   *Thomas Kuhn and Social Science.* London: MacMillan.
Barnes, Barry, and Donald MacKenzie
1979   "On the Role of Interests in Scientific Change." In Roy Wallis (ed.), *On
         the Margins of Science: The Social Construction of Rejected Knowledge.*
         Sociological Review Monograph No. 27. Keele, Staffordshire: University
         of Keele.
Barnouw, Victor
1946   "Paranormal Phenomena and Culture." *Journal of the American Society
         for Psychical Research* 40:1–21.
Basil, Robert (ed.)
1988   *Not Necessarily the New Age.* Buffalo: Prometheus Books.

Bastide, Roger
1967   "Le Spiritisme au Brésil." *Archives de Sociologie des Religions* 24:3–16.
Bateson, Gregory
1972   *Steps to an Ecology of Mind.* New York: Ballantine.
Baudrillard, Jean
1988   *America.* New York: Verso.
Bazerman, Charles
1988   *Shaping Written Knowledge: The Genre and Activity of the Experimental Article in Science.* Madison: University of Wisconsin Press.
Beer, Gillian
1983   *Darwin's Plots: Evolutionary Narrative in Darwin, George Eliot, and Nineteenth-Century Fiction.* London: Routledge.
Bellah, Robert
1975   *The Broken Covenant: American Civil Religion in Time of Trial.* New York: Seabury Press.
Bellah, Robert, et al.
1985   *Habits of the Heart: Individualism and Commitment in American Life.* Berkeley: University of California Press.
Bercovitch, Sacvan
1978   *The American Jeremiad.* Madison: University of Wisconsin Press.
Berger, Arthur
1985a   "The Early History of the ASPR: Origins to 1907." *Journal of the American Society for Psychical Research* 79 (1): 39–60.
1985b   "Problems of the ASPR Under J. H. Hyslop." *Journal of the American Society for Psychical Research* 79 (2): 205–19.
Berliner, H. S., and J. W. Salmon
1980   "The Holistic Alternative to Scientific Medicine: History and Analysis." *International Journal of Health Services* 10:133–47.
Blackmore, Susan
1982   *Beyond the Body: An Investigation of the Out-of-the-Body Experience.* London: Heinemann.
1983   "Comments." *Zetetic Scholar* 11:141–43.
1987   "Parapsychology's Choice." *Behavioral and Brain Sciences* 10 (4): 572–73.
1988   "Do We Need a New Psychical Research?" *Journal of the Society for Psychical Research* 55: 49–59.
Bleier, Ruth
1986   "Introduction." In Ruth Bleier (ed.), *Feminist Approaches to Science.* New York: Pergamon.
Boon, James A.
1982   *Other Tribes, Other Scribes.* Cambridge, U.K.: Cambridge University Press.
Bourdieu, Pierre
1977   *Outline of a Theory of Practice.* Cambridge, U.K.: Cambridge University Press.

Boyd, Doug
1974   *Rolling Thunder.* New York: Delta (Random House).
Braude, Ann
1989   *Radical Spirits: Spiritualism and Women's Rights in Nineteenth-Century America.* Boston: Beacon.
Braude, Stephen
1986   *The Limits of Influence: Psychokinesis and the Philosophy of Science.* New York: Methuen.
1991   "P.A. President's Message, 1991: Limping Toward the Millennium." *P. A. News and Annual Report.* Research Triangle Park, N.C.: Parapsychological Association.
Brown, Judith
1975   "Iroquois Women: An Ethnohistorical Note." In Rayna Reiter (ed.), *Toward an Anthropology of Women.* New York: Monthly Review Press.
Brown, Michael F.
1989   "Dark Side of the Shaman." *Natural History* November: 8–10.
Brown, Susan Love
1987   "Ananda Revisited: Values and Change in a Cooperative, Religious Community." M.A. Thesis, Anthropology Department, San Diego State University.
1989   "Babyboomers, American Character, and the New Age: A Synthesis." Paper presented at the 88th Annual Meeting of the American Anthropological Association, Washington, D.C.
Bruner, Edward
1990   "The Scientists Versus the Humanists." *Anthropology Newsletter* 31 (2): 28.
Burke, Kenneth
1966   *Language as Symbolic Action.* Berkeley: University of California Press.
1970   *The Rhetoric of Religion: Studies in Logology.* Berkeley: University of California Press.
Burton, John, and David Hicks
1976   "Chaos Triumphant: Archetypes and Symbols in *The Exorcist.*" In William Arens and Susan Montague (eds.), *The American Dimension: Cultural Myths and Social Realities.* Port Washington, N.Y.: Alfred Publishing Co.
Bush, Vannevar
1960   *Science: The Endless Frontier.* Washington, D.C.: National Science Foundation (orig. 1945).
Capra, Fritjof
1975   *The Tao of Physics.* New York: Bantam.
1982   *The Turning Point: Science, Society, and the Rising Culture.* New York: Simon and Schuster.
Carlson, Eugene
1990   "'New Age' Spawns New Businesses, but Not All Succeed." *The Wall Street Journal* April 13: B2.

Carroll, Noël
1990   *The Philosophy of Horror, or Paradoxes of the Heart.* London: Routledge.
Cayce, Edgar Evans
1968   *Edgar Cayce on Atlantis.* New York: Warner.
Cerullo, John
1982   *The Secularization of the Soul.* Philadelphia, ISHI.
Chevalier, Gérard
1986   "Parasciences et procédés de légitimation." *Revue française de sociologie* 27:205–19.
Chubin, Daryl E., and Sal Restivo
1983   "The 'Mooting' of Science Studies: Research Programmes and Science Policy." In Karin D. Knorr-Cetina and Michael Mulkay (eds.), *Science Observed: Perspectives on the Social Study of Science.* London: Sage.
Clark, Jerome
1990   "New Age Politics." In J. Gordon Melton, Jerome Clark, and Aidan A. Kelly (eds.), *New Age Encyclopedia.* Detroit: Gale Research Inc.
Clifford, James
1988   "On Ethnographic Authority." In James Clifford, *The Predicament of Culture.* Cambridge, Mass.: Harvard University Press.
Clifford, James, and George Marcus (eds.)
1986   *Writing Culture.* Berkeley: University of California Press.
Collins, Harry
1983   "An Empirical Relativist Programme in the Sociology of Scientific Knowledge." In Karin D. Knorr-Cetina and Michael Mulkay (eds.), *Science Observed: Perspectives on the Social Study of Science.* London: Sage.
1985   *Changing Order: Replication and Induction in Scientific Practice.* Beverly Hills, Cal.: Sage Publications.
1987   "Scientific Knowledge and Scientific Criticism." *Parapsychology Review* 18 (5): 1–8.
1991   "Captives and Victims: Comment on Scott, Richards, and Martin." *Science, Technology, and Human Values* 16 (2): 249–51.
Collins, Harry, and Trevor Pinch
1979   "The Construction of the Paranormal: Nothing Unscientific Is Happening." In R. Wallis (ed.), *On the Margins of Science: The Social Construction of Rejected Knowledge. Sociological Review Monograph No. 27.* Keele, Staffordshire: University of Keele.
1982   *Frames of Meaning. The Social Construction of Extra-Ordinary Science.* London: Routledge.
Coon, Deborah J.
1988   "Spiritualism and the 'New Psychology': Maintaining Public Interest While Fighting Its Demons." Paper presented at Cheiron.
1990   "Testing the Limits of Sense and Science: American Experimental Psychologists Combat Spiritualism, 1880–1920." Paper presented at the University of Wisconsin Symposium on the Secularization of Science.

Cox, Harvey
1977   *Turning East: The Promise and Peril of the New Orientalism.* New York: Simon and Schuster.
Cozzens, Susan, and Thomas Gieryn (eds.)
1990   *Theories of Science in Society.* Bloomington: Indiana University Press.
Crapanzano, Vincent, and Vivian Garrison
1977   *Case Studies in Spirit Possession.* New York: Wiley.
Culler, Jonathan
1982   *On Deconstruction.* Ithaca: Cornell University Press.
Curran, Douglas
1985   *In Advance of the Landing: Folk Concepts of Outer Space.* New York: Abbeville.
DaMatta, Roberto
1985   *A Casa e a Rua.* São Paulo: Brasiliense.
1991   *Carnivals, Rogues, and Heroes.* Notre Dame, Ind.: Notre Dame University Press.
Danforth, Loring
1989   *Firewalking and Religious Healing.* Princeton: Princeton University Press.
Davidson, Nicholas
1988   *The Failure of Feminism.* Buffalo: Prometheus Books.
Davis, Mike
1988   "Urban Renaissance and the Spirit of Postmodernism." In E. Ann Kaplan (ed.), *Postmodernism and Its Discontents.* New York: Verso.
David-Floyd, Robbie
in press "The Technocratic Body and the Organic Body: Cultural Models for Women's Birth Choices." In David Hess and Linda Layne (eds.), *Knowledge and Society Volume 9: The Anthropology of Science and Technology.* Greenwich, Conn.: JAI Press.
Degler, Carl
1986   *Neither Black Nor White.* Madison, Wisc.: University of Wisconsin Press.
Derrida, Jacques
1974   *Of Grammatology.* Baltimore: Johns Hopkins University Press.
Detienne, Marcel
1977   *The Gardens of Adonis.* Atlantic Highlands, N.J.: Humanities Press.
1979   *Dionysius Slain.* Baltimore: Johns Hopkins Press.
Douglas, Mary
1966   *Purity and Danger.* London: Routledge.
1975   "The Social Control of Cognition: Some Factors in Joke Perception." In *Implicit Meanings.* London: Routledge (orig. 1968).
1982   "The Effects of Modernization on Religious Change." *Daedalus* 111 (1): 1–19.
Downey, Gary L.
1986   "Ideology and the Clamshell Identity: Organizational Dilemmas in the Anti-Nuclear Power Movement." *Social Problems* 33 (5): 357–73.

1988   "Reproducing Cultural Identity in Negotiating Nuclear Power: The Union
            of Concerned Scientists and Emergency Core Cooling." *Social Studies
            of Science* 18 (2): 231–65.
in   "Agency and Structure in Negotiating Knowledge." In Mary Douglas and
press a   David Hull (eds.), *How Classification Works: Nelson Goodman among
            Social Scientists.* Edinburgh: Edinburgh University Press.
in   "CAD/CAM Saves the Nation? Toward an Anthropology of Technol-
press b   ogy." In David Hess and Linda Layne (eds.), *Knowledge and Society
            Volume 9: The Anthropology of Science and Technology.* Greenwich,
            Conn.: JAI Press.

Dubinskas, Frank
1988   *Making Time: Ethnographic Studies of High-Technology Organizations.*
            Philadelphia: Temple University Press.

Dumit, Joseph
1991   "Cyborg Anthropology: Brain-Mind Machines and Technological Nation-
            alism." Paper presented at the annual meeting of the American Anthro-
            pological Association, Chicago.

Dumont, Jean-Paul
1972   *Under the Rainbow.* Austin: University of Texas Press.

Dumont, Louis
1977   *From Mandeville to Marx,* Chicago: University of Chicago Press.
1980   *Homo Hierarchicus.* Chicago: University of Chicago Press.
1986   *Essays on Individualism.* Chicago: University of Chicago Press.

Durkheim, Émile
1965   *The Elementary Forms of the Religious Life.* New York: The Free Press
            (orig. 1912).

Dwyer, Kevin
1987   *Moroccan Dialogues: Anthropology in Question.* Prospect Heights, Ill.:
            Waveland Press.

Edge, Hoyt
1985   "The Dualist Tradition of Parapsychology." *European Journal of Para-
            psychology* 6:81–93.
1990   "Psi, Self, and the New Mentalism." In Linda Henkel and John Palmer
            (eds.), *Research in Parapsychology 1989.* Metuchen, N.J.: Scarecrow
            Press.

Edge, Hoyt, Joseph Rush, Robert Morris, and John Palmer
1986   *Foundations of Parapsychology.* London: Routledge.

Ehrenreich, Barbara
1991   "Teach Diversity—with a Smile." *Time* April 8:84.

Elkin, Adolphus
1977   *Aboriginal Men of High Degree.* New York: St. Martin's.

Ellwood Jr., Robert S.
1973   *Religious and Spiritual Groups in America.* Englewood, Cliffs, N.J.:
            Prentice-Hall.

1979   *Alternative Altars: Unconventional and Eastern Spirituality in America.*
          Chicago: University of Chicago Press.
1987   *Eastern Spirituality in America.* New York: Paulist Press.
Emmons, Charles
1982   *Chinese Ghosts and ESP.* Metuchen, N.J.: Scarecrow Press.
Fabian, Johannes
1983   *Time and the Other.* New York: Columbia University Press.
Feder, Kenneth
1980   "Psychic Archaeology: The Anatomy of Irrationalist Prehistoric Studies."
          Skeptical Inquirer 4 (4): 32–43.
1990   *Frauds, Myths, and Mysteries: Science and Pseudoscience in Archaeol-
          ogy.* Mountain View, Cal.: Mayfield Publishing Co.
Ferguson, Marilyn
1987   *The Aquarian Conspiracy.* New York: St. Martin's. (orig. 1980).
Fischer, Michael
1991   "*Anthropology as Cultural Critique:* Inserts for the 1990s. Cultural Studies
          of Science, Visual-Virtual Realities, and Post-Trauma Polities." *Cultural
          Anthropology* 6 (4): 525–37.
Fodor, Nandor
1948   "The Poltergeist Psychoanalyzed." *Psychiatric Quarterly* 22:195–203.
Forsythe, Diana
in press "Blaming the User in Medical Informatics: The Cultural Nature of Sci-
          entific Practice." In David Hess and Linda Layne (eds.), *Knowledge and
          Society Volume 9: The Anthropology of Science and Technology.* Green-
          wich, Conn.: JAI Press.
Foucault, Michel
1979   *Discipline and Punish.* New York: Vintage Books.
1980   *Power/Knowledge.* New York: Pantheon Books.
Frazier, Kendrick
1981   "Introduction." In Kendrick Frazier (ed.), *Paranormal Borderlands of
          Science.* Buffalo: Prometheus Books.
1986   "Introduction." In Kendrick Frazier (ed.), *Science Confronts the Para-
          normal.* Buffalo: Prometheus Books.
Gardner, Martin
1952   "Atlantis and Lemuria." In *In the Name of Science.* New York: Putnam's
          Sons.
1981a   "Parapsychology and Quantum Mechanics." In George Abell and Barry
          Singer (eds.), *Science and the Paranormal.* New York: Charles Scribner's
          Sons.
1981b   *Science: Good, Bad, and Bogus.* Buffalo: Prometheus Books.
1983   *The Whys of a Philosophical Scrivener.* Brighton, U.K.: Harvester Press.
1988   *The New Age: Notes of a Fringe Watcher.* Buffalo: Prometheus Books.
Gauld, Alan
1968   *The Founders of Psychical Research.* New York: Schocken.

Geertz, Clifford
1971   "Introduction." In C. Geertz (ed.), *Myth, Symbol, and Culture*. New York: W. W. Norton and Co.
1973   *The Interpretation of Cultures*. New York: Basic Books.
1983   *Local Knowledge*. New York: Basic Books.
Gieryn, Thomas
1983a   "Boundary-Work and the Demarcation of Science from Non-Science: Strains and Interests in Professional Ideologies of Scientists." *American Sociological Review* 48:781–95.
1983b   "Making the Demarcation of Science a Sociological Problem: Boundary-Work by John Tyndall, Victorian Scientist." In Rachel Lauden (ed.), *The Demarcation Between Science and Pseudo-Science*. Working Papers in Science and Technology 2 (1): 57–86.
Gieryn, Thomas, and Anne Figert
1990   "Ingredients for a Theory of Science in Society." In Susan Cozzens and Thomas Gieryn (eds.), *Theories of Science in Society*. Bloomington: Indiana University Press.
Gilbert, G. Nigel, and Michael Mulkay
1984   *Opening Pandora's Box*. Cambridge, U.K.: Cambridge University Press.
Goodrich, Lawrence J.
1990   "U.S. Religious Life Holds Steady." *Christian Science Monitor* 28 (Jan. 2): 12.
Gordon, Henry
1988   *Channeling into the New Age*. Buffalo: Prometheus Books.
Greeley, Andrew W.
1975   *The Sociology of the Paranormal: A Reconnaissance*. Beverly Hills: Sage Publications.
Griffin, David Ray (ed.)
1990   *The Reenchantment of Science*. Albany: State University of New York Press.
Grosso, Michael
1982   "*Out-of-Body Experiences: A Handbook*, by Janet Lee Mitchell [book review]." *Journal of the American Society for Psychical Research* 76 (2): 186–88.
Grove, J. W.
1988   "The Intellectual Revolt Against Science." *Skeptical Inquirer* 13 (Fall): 70–75.
Guralnik, David B. (ed.)
1986   *Webster's New World Dictionary of the American Language*, Englewood Cliffs, N.J.: Prentice-Hall.
Halifax, Joan
1979   *Shamanic Voices: A Survey of Visionary Narratives*. New York: E. P. Dutton.
1982   *Shaman: The Wounded Healer*. New York: Crossroad.

Hammond, William
1871   *The Physics and Philosophy of Spiritualism.* New York: Appleton and
        Co.
Hansel, C. E. M.
1989   *The Search for Psychic Power.* Buffalo: Prometheus Books.
Hansen, George
1987   "CSICOP and Skepticism: An Emerging Social Movement." *Proceedings
        of Presented Papers, the Thirtieth Annual Convention of the Parapsycho-
        logical Association.* Edinburgh, Scotland, Aug. 5–8.
1992   "CSICOP and the Skeptics: An Overview." *Journal of the American So-
        ciety for Psychical Research* 86:19–63.
Haraway, Donna
1989   *Primate Visions.* London: Routledge.
1991   "A Cyborg Manifesto." In *Simians, Cyborgs, and Women.* London:
        Routledge.
Harding, Sandra
1986   *The Science Question in Feminism.* Ithaca: Cornell University Press.
Harman, Willis
1976   "The Societal Implications and Social Impact of Psi Phenomena." In J. D.
        Morris, W. G. Roll, and R. L. Morris (eds.), *Research in Parapsychology
        1975.* Metuchen, N.J.: Scarecrow Press.
1990   "The Postmodern Heresy: Consciousness as Causal." In David Ray Griffin
        (ed.), *The Reenchantment of Science,* Albany: State University of New
        York Press.
Harner, Michael
1980   *The Way of the Shaman.* New York: Harper and Row.
Hess, David J.
1987a   "The Many Rooms of Spiritism in Brazil." *Luso-Brazilian Review* 24 (2):
        15–34.
1987b   "Religion, Heterodox Science, and Brazilian Culture." *Social Studies of
        Science* 17:465–77.
1988   "Gender, Hierarchy, and the Psychic: An Interpretation of the Culture
        of Parapsychology." Paper presented at the annual meeting of the Para-
        psychological Association, panel on women and gender in parapsychol-
        ogy. Forthcoming in *Controversial Scientists: The Women of Parapsy-
        chology,* Sally Drucker and Nancy Zingrone (eds.). Metuchen, N.J.:
        Scarecrow Press.
1989a   "Disobsessing Disobsession: Religion, Ritual, and the Social Sciences in
        Brazil." *Cultural Anthropology* 4 (2): 182–93.
1989b   "Psychical Research and Cultural Values." *Newsletter for the History and
        Sociology of Marginal Science* 1 (2): 1–4.
1989c   "Spirit Infestation of an Idiom of Distress." *Transcultural Psychiatric Re-
        search Review* 26:33–37.
1990   "Ghosts and Domestic Politics in Brazil." *Ethos* 18 (4): 407–38.
1991a   "On Earth as It Is in Heaven: Spiritist Other-Worldly Ethnographies."

In Roberto Reis (ed.), *Toward Socio-Criticism: "Luso-Brazilian Literatures."* Tempe, Arizona: Center for Latin American Studies, Arizona State University.

1991b   *Spirits and Scientists: Ideology, Spiritism, and Brazilian Culture.* University Park, Penn.: Pennsylvania State University Press.

in   "Disciplining Heterodoxy, Circumventing Discipline: Parapsychology,
press a Anthropologically." In David Hess and Linda Layne (eds.), *Knowledge and Society Volume 9: The Anthropology of Science and Technology.* Greenwich, Conn.: JAI Press.

in   "Introduction: The New Ethnography and the Anthropology of Science
press b and Technology." In David Hess and Linda Layne (eds.), *Knowledge and Society Volume 9: The Anthropology of Science and Technology.* Greenwich, Conn.: JAI Press.

Hoebens, Piet Hein
1986   "Sense and Nonsense in Parapsychology." In Kendrick Frazier (ed.), *Science Confronts the Paranormal.* Buffalo: Prometheus Books.

Holmberg, David
1983   "Shamanic Soundings: Femaleness in the Tamang Ritual Structure." *Signs* 9 (1): 40–58.

Honorton, Charles
1977   "Psi and Internal Attention States." In Benjamin Wolman (ed.), *Handbook of Parapsychology.* New York: Van Nostrand.

Houdini, Harry
1972   *A Magician Among Spirits.* New York: Arno Press (orig. 1924).

Hövelman, Gerd
1984   "Against Historicism: Critical Remarks on Thomas Kuhn's Conception of Science and Its Reception in Parapsychology." *Journal of Parapsychology* 48:101–19.

Hövelman, Gerd, and Stanley Krippner
1986   "Charting the Future of Parapsychology." *Parapsychology Review* 17 (6): 1–5.

Hsu, Francis
1972   "American Core Value and National Character." In Francis Hsu (ed.), *Psychological Anthropology.* Cambridge, Mass.: Schenkman Publishing Co.

Hyman, Ray
1982   "Pathological Science." In R. A. McConnell (ed.), *Encounters with Parapsychology.* Pittsburgh: Author.

1989   *The Elusive Quarry.* Buffalo: Prometheus Books.

Hyman, Ray, and Charles Honorton
1986   "A Joint Communique: The Psi-Ganzfeld Controversy." *Journal of Parapsychology* 50:351–64.

Hyman, Stanley Edgar
1974   *The Tangled Bank: Darwin, Marx, Frazer, and Freud as Imaginative Writers.* New York: Atheneum.

Hyslop, James Hervey
1908a   *Psychical Research and the Resurrection.* Boston: Small, Maynard, and Co.
1908b   "Professor Jastrow and Science." *Journal of the American Society for Psychical Research* 2:139–71.
1916   "Christianity and Psychical Research." *Journal of the American Society for Psychical Research* 10:253–74.
1918   "The Troubles of Psychical Research." *Journal of the American Society for Psychical Research* 12 (8): 469–76.
Irwin, Harvey
1985   *Flight of Mind: A Psychological Study of the Out-of-Body Experience.* Metuchen, N.J.: Scarecrow Press.
Jackson, Shirley
1959   *The Haunting of Hill House.* New York: Viking.
Jahn, Robert
1983   "On the Representation of Psi Research to the Community of Established Science." *Technical Note: Princeton Engineering Anomalies Research 83004.* Princeton: Princeton University School of Engineering. (Also in R. White and R. Broughton (eds.), *Research in Parapsychology 1983.* Metuchen, N.J.: Scarecrow Press, 1984).
James, William
1960   *William James on Psychical Research.* Edited and compiled by Gardner Murphy and Robert O. Ballou. New York: Viking.
Jameson, Fredric
1984a   "The Politics of Theory: Ideological Positions in the Postmodernism Debate." *New German Critique* 33:53–65.
1984b   "Postmodernism, or the Cultural Logic of Late Capitalism." *New Left Review* 146:53–93.
Jastrow, Joseph
1900   *Fact and Fable in Psychology.* Boston: Houghton-Mifflin.
Jones, Margaret
1989a   "'Convergence' at the Bookstore." *Publisher's Weekly* November 3:32–33.
1989b   "New Age on the Brink." *Publisher's Weekly* November 3:14–18.
1989c   "Sorting Out the Strata." *Publisher's Weekly* November 3:20–31.
Jordanova, Ludmilla
1980   "Natural Facts: A Historical Perspective on Science and Sexuality." In C. MacCormack and M. Strathern (eds.), *Nature, Culture, and Gender.* Cambridge, U.K.: Cambridge University Press.
1989   *Sexual Visions: Images of Gender in Science and Medicine between the Eighteenth and Twentieth Centuries.* Madison, Wisc.: University of Wisconsin Press.
Kant de Lima, Roberto
1985   *A Antropologia da Academia: Quando os Índios somos Nós.* Petrópolis: Vozes and Niterói: Universidade Federal Fluminense. Translation forthcoming in David Hess and Linda Layne (eds.), *Knowledge and Society*

    Volume 9: The Anthropology of Science and Technology. Greenwich, Conn.: JAI Press.

Keller, Evelyn Fox
1985   *Reflections on Gender and Science.* New Haven: Yale University Press.

Kelly, Edward F., and Ralph G. Locke
1981   *Altered States of Consciousness and Psi: An Historical Survey and Research Prospectus. Parapsychological Monographs No. 18.* New York: Parapsychology Foundation.

Kenny, Michael
1986   *The Passion of Ansel Bourne: Multiple Personality in American Culture.* Washington, D.C.: The Smithsonian Institution Press.

Kiev, Ari
1964   *Magic, Faith, and Healing.* New York: Free Press.

Knorr-Cetina, Karin
1981   *The Manufacture of Knowledge: An Essay on the Constructivist and Contextual Nature of Science.* New York: Pergamon.

Kofman, Sarah
1985   *The Enigma of Woman: Woman in Freud's Writings.* Ithaca: Cornell University Press.

Krippner, Stanley
1975   *Song of the Siren: A Parapsychological Odyssey.* New York: Harper and Row.
1990   "Parapsychology and Postmodern Science." In David Ray Griffin (ed.), *The Reenchantment of Science.* Albany: State University of New York Press.

Kroker, Arthur, and David Cook
1986   *The Postmodern Scene: Excremental Culture and Hyper-Aesthetics.* New York: St. Martin's Press.

Kuhn, Thomas
1962   *The Structure of Scientific Revolutions.* Chicago: University of Chicago Press.

Kurtz, Paul
1969a   "An Invitation to Repression." *Humanist* 29 (5): 33–34.
1969b   "Notes from the Editor: Counter-Culture." *Humanist* 29 (4): 1.
1970   "The Radical Center." *Humanist* 30 (3): 5–7.
1974   "Humanism and Religion: A Reply to Critics of Humanist Manifesto II." *Humanist* January/February: 4–5.
1976a   "Committee to Scientifically Investigate Claims of Paranormal and Other Phenomena." *Humanist* May/June: 28.
1976b   "The Scientific Attitude vs. Antiscience and Pseudoscience." *Humanist* July/August: 27–31.
1981   "Believing the Unbelievable: The Scientific Response." A Foreword. In George Abell and Barry Singer (eds.), *Science and the Paranormal.* New York: Charles Scribner's Sons.

1983a   *In Defense of Secular Humanism.* Buffalo: Prometheus Books.
1983b   *Sidney Hook: Philosopher of Democracy and Humanism.* Buffalo: Prometheus Books.
1985–86 "CSICOP After Ten Years: Reflections on the 'Transcendental Temptation.'" *Skeptical Inquirer* 10 (2): 229–32.
1986   "Debunking, Neutrality, and Skepticism in Science." In Kendrick Frazier (ed.), *Science Confronts the Paranormal.* Buffalo: Prometheus Books.
1988   *Forbidden Fruit: The Ethics of Humanism.* Buffalo: Prometheus Books.
1989a   *Eupraxophy: Living without Religion.* Buffalo: Prometheus Books.
1989b   "The New Age in Perspective." *The Skeptical Inquirer* 13 (4): 365–367.

Lakoff, George, and Mark Johnson
1980   *Metaphors We Live By.* Chicago: University of Chicago Press.

Lamont, Corliss
1975   "Highlights of the Humanist Movement." *Humanist* January/February: 52–53.

Langmuir, Irving
1953   "Colloquium on Pathological Science." Paper presented at the Knolls Research Laboratory, December 18, 1953.

Latour, Bruno
1987   *Science in Action.* Cambridge, Mass.: Harvard University Press.
1988   "The Politics of Explanation: An Alternative." In Steve Woolgar (ed.), *Knowledge and Reflexivity.* Beverly Hills: Sage.

Latour, Bruno, and Steve Woolgar
1979   *Laboratory Life: The Social Construction of Scientific Facts.* Beverly Hills: Sage.

Layne, Linda
in   *Home and Homeland: The Dialogics of Tribal and National Identities*
press a *in Jordan.* Princeton: Princeton University Press.
in   "Of Fetuses and Angels: Fragmentation and Integration in Narratives
press b of Pregnancy Loss." In David Hess and Linda Layne (eds.), *Knowledge and Society Volume 9: The Anthropology of Science and Technology.* Greenwich, Conn.: JAI Press.

Lee, Raymond
1987   "Amulets and Anthropology: A Paranormal Encounter with Malay Magic." *Anthropology and Humanism Quarterly* 12 (3–4): 69–74.

Levine, George (ed.)
1987   *One Culture: Essays in Science and Literature.* Madison: University of Wisconsin Press.

Lévi-Strauss, Claude
1963   *Totemism.* Boston: Beacon.
1966   *The Savage Mind.* Chicago: University of Chicago Press.
1973   *From Honey to Ashes.* New York: Harper.
1975   *The Raw and the Cooked.* New York: Harper.
1978a   *Myth and Meaning.* New York: Schocken Books.

1978b   *The Origin of Table Manners.* New York: Harper.
1981   *The Naked Man.* New York: Harper.
1985   *The View from Afar.* New York: Basic Books.
Lewis, I. M.
1971   *Ecstatic Religion.* New York: Penguin.
Linton, Ralph
1927   "The Witches of Andilamena." *Atlantic Monthly* 13:191–96.
Long, Joseph
1977   *Extrasensory Ecology.* Metuchen, N.J.: Scarecrow Press.
Luhrmann, Tanya
1989   *Persuasions of the Witch's Craft: Ritual Magic—Contemporary England.*
         Cambridge, Mass.: Harvard University Press.
Lynch, Michael
1985   *Art and Artifact in Laboratory Science.* London: Routledge.
McClenon, James
1984   *Deviant Science: The Case of Parapsychology.* Philadelphia: University
         of Pennsylvania Press.
McConnell, Robert A.
1983a   *An Introduction to Parapsychology in the Context of Science.* Pittsburgh:
         Author.
1983b   *Parapsychology and Self-Deception in Science.* Pittsburgh: Author.
1987   *Parapsychology in Retrospect. My Search for the Unicorn.* Pittsburgh:
         Author.
MacCormack, Carol, and Marilyn Strathern (eds.)
1980   *Nature, Culture, and Gender.* Cambridge, U.K.: Cambridge University
         Press.
McDannell, Colleen, and Bernhard Lang
1988   *Heaven: A History.* New Haven: Yale University Press.
McGuire, Meredith
1988   *Ritual Healing in Suburban America.* New Brunswick, N.J.: Rutgers Uni-
         versity Press.
MacKenzie, Donald
1978   "Statistical Theory and Social Interests: A Case Study." *Social Studies
         of Science* 8:35–83.
1981   "Interests, Positivism, and History." *Social Studies of Science* 11:498–504.
1983   *Statistics in Britain.* Edinburgh: Edinburgh University Press.
McKusick, Marshall
1981   "Deciphering Ancient America." *Skeptical Inquirer* 5 (3): 44–50.
MacLaine, Shirley
1983   *Out on a Limb.* New York: Bantam Books.
Marcus, George, and Michael Fischer
1986   *Anthropology as Cultural Critique.* Chicago: University of Chicago Press.
Marcuse, Herbert
1969   *An Essay on Liberation.* Boston: Beacon.

Markley, O. W., and Willis Harman
1982   *Changing Images of Man.* New York: Pergamon.

Marks, David, and Richard Kammann
1980   *The Psychology of the Psychic.* Buffalo: Prometheus Books.

Martin, Brian, Evelleen Richards, and Pam Scott
1991   "Who's a Captive? Who's a Victim? Response to Collins's Method Talk."
         Science, Technology, and Human Values 16 (2): 252–55.

Martin, David
1990   *Tongues of Fire: The Explosion of Protestantism in Latin America.* Ox-
         ford: Basil Blackwell.

Martin, Emily
1987   *The Woman in the Body.* Boston: Beacon Press.
1990   "Toward an Anthropology of Immunology: The Body as Nation-State."
         Medical Anthropology Quarterly 4 (4): 410–26.
1991   "The Egg and the Sperm: How Science Has Constructed a Romance Based
         on Stereotypical Male-Female Roles." *Signs* 16 (3): 485–501.
1992   "The End of the Body?" *American Ethnologist* 19 (1): 121–40.

Mascia-Lees, Frances, Patricia Sharpe, and Colleen Cohen
1989   "The Postmodernist Turn in Anthropology: Cautions from a Feminist
         Perspective." *Signs* 15 (11): 7–33.

Mauskopf, Seymour
1989   "The History of the American Society for Psychical Research: An Inter-
         pretation." *Journal of the American Society for Psychical Research* 83
         (1): 7–29.

Mauskopf, Seymour, and Michael McVaugh
1980   *The Elusive Science: Origins of Experimental Psychical Research.* Balti-
         more: Johns Hopkins University Press.

Mauss, Marcel
1967   *The Gift.* New York: W. W. Norton.

Melton, J. Gordon
1986   *Biographical Dictionary of American Cult and Sect Leaders.* New York:
         Garland.
1988   "A History of the New Age Movement." In Robert Basil (ed.), *Not Nec-
         essarily the New Age.* Buffalo: Prometheus Books.

Melton, J. Gordon, Jerome Clark, and Aidan A. Kelly
1990   *New Age Encyclopedia.* Detroit: Gale Research Inc.

Merchant, Carolyn
1980   *The Death of Nature: Women, Ecology, and the Scientific Revolution.*
         New York: Harper and Row.

Merton, Robert
1970   *Science, Technology, and Society in Seventeenth Century England.* New
         York: Howard Fertig.

Mishlove, Jeffrey
1983   *Psi Development Systems.* Jefferson, N.C., and London: McFarland.

1985   "Correspondence." *Journal of Parapsychology* 49:205–7.

Mitchell, Janet Lee

1981   *Out-of-Body Experiences: A Handbook*. New York: Ballantine.

Montgomery, Ruth

1965   *A Gift of Prophecy: The Phenomenal Jeane Dixon*. New York: Morrow.

1971   *A World Beyond*. Greenwich, Conn.: Fawcett.

Moore, R. Laurence

1977   *In Search of White Crows: Spiritualism, Parapsychology, and American Culture*. New York: Oxford University Press.

Morris, Robert L.

1981   "The Case of the Amityville Horror." In Kendrick Frazier (ed.), *Paranormal Borderlands of Science*. Buffalo: Prometheus Books.

Mulkay, Michael

1985   *The Word and the World: Explorations in the Form of Sociological Analysis*. Boston: George Allen and Unwin.

1988   *On Humor: Its Nature and Its Place in Modern Society*. Oxford and New York: Basil Blackwell.

1991   *Sociology of Science: A Sociological Pilgrimage*. Bloomington: Indiana University Press.

Mulkay, Michael, Jonathan Potter, and Steven Yearley

1983   "Why an Analysis of Scientific Discourse Is Needed." In Karin D. Knorr-Cetina and Michael Mulkay (eds.), *Science Observed: Perspectives on the Social Study of Science*. London: Sage.

Murphy, Lois

1990   *Gardner Murphy: Integrating, Expanding, and Humanizing Psychology*. Jefferson, N.C.: McFarland.

Myers, Greg

1985   "Texts as Knowledge Claims: The Social Construction of Two Biology Articles." *Social Studies of Science* 15:593–630.

1990   *Writing Biology: Texts in the Social Construction of Scientific Knowledge*. Madison: University of Wisconsin Press.

Namenworth, Marion

1986   "Science Seen Through a Feminist Prism." In R. Bleier (ed.), *Feminist Approaches to Science*. New York: Pergamon Press.

Nelkin, Dorothy

1982   *The Creation Controversy: Science or Scripture in the Schools*. New York: W. W. Norton.

Nickell, Joe

1986   "The Nazca Drawings Revisited: Creation of a Full-Sized Duplicate." In Kendrick Frazier (ed.), *Science Confronts the Paranormal*. Buffalo: Prometheus Books.

O'Hara, Maureen

1989   "A New Age Reflection in the Magic Mirror of Science." *Skeptical Inquirer* 13 (4): 368–74.

Ortner, Sherry
1974   "Is Female to Male as Nature Is to Culture?" In Michelle Zimbalist Ro-
          saldo and Louise Lamphere (eds.), *Woman, Culture, and Society.* Stan-
          ford: Stanford University Press.
Owen, Alex
1989   *The Darkened Room: Women, Power, and Spiritualism in Late Victorian
          England.* London: Virago.
Owen, Nancy
1981   "Witchcraft in the West Indies: The Anthropologist as Victim." *Anthro-
          pology and Humanism Quarterly* 6 (2–3): 15–21.
Palmer, John
1980   "Parapsychology as a Probabilistic Science." In William Roll (ed.), *Re-
          search in Parapsychology 1979.* Metuchen, N.J.: Scarecrow Press.
1988   "Conceptualizing the Psi Controversy." *Parapsychology Review* 19 (1): 1–5.
Palmer, John, Charles Honorton, and Jessica Utts
1989   "Reply to the National Research Council on Parapsychology." *Journal
          of the American Society for Psychical Research* 83 (1): 31–49.
Pamplin, Brian, and Harry Collins
1975   "Spoon Bending: An Experimental Approach." *Nature* 257 (September
          4): 8.
Pinch, Trevor
1979   "Normal Explanations of the Paranormal: The Demarcation Problem and
          Fraud in Parapsychology." *Social Studies of Science* 9:329–48.
1987   "Some Suggestions from the Sociology of Science to Advance the Psi De-
          bate." *Behavioral and Brain Sciences* 10 (4): 603–5.
Pinch, Trevor, and Harry Collins
1984   "Private Science and Public Knowledge: The Committee for the Scien-
          tific Investigation of the [sic] Claims of the Paranormal and Its Use of
          the Literature." *Social Studies of Science* 14:521–46.
Podmore, Frank
1898–9   "Andrew Lang, *The Making of Religion* [book review]." *Proceedings of
          the Society for Psychical Research* XIV: 128–38.
Pratt, J. Gaither
1964   *Parapsychology: An Insider's View of ESP.* New York: Doubleday.
1979   "Parapsychology, Normal Science, and Paradigm Change." *Journal of
          the American Society for Psychical Research* 73 (1): 17–28.
Prelli, Lawrence
1989   *A Rhetoric of Science: Inventing Scientific Discourse.* Columbia, S.C.:
          University of South Carolina Press.
Rabinow, Paul
1990   "From Sociobiology to Biosociality: Artificiality and Enlightenment."
          Paper presented at the annual meeting of the American Anthropological
          Association. Forthcoming in *Zone 6: Incorporations,* Jonathan Crary and
          Sanford Kwinter (eds.). New York: Zone Books.

in press "Severing the Ties: Fragmentation and Dignity in Late Modernity." In
          David Hess and Linda Layne (eds.), *Knowledge and Society Volume 9:
          The Anthropology of Science and Technology.* Greenwich, Conn.: JAI
          Press.
Radcliffe-Brown, A. R.
1952   *Structure and Function in Primitive Society.* New York: Free Press.
Radin, Dean
1989   "The Tao of Psi." In Linda Henkel and Rick Berger (eds.), *Research in
          Parapsychology 1988.* Metuchen, N.J.: Scarecrow Press.
Randi, James
1982   *Flim-Flam! Psychics, ESP, Unicorns and Other Delusions.* Buffalo: Pro-
          metheus Books.
1986   "The Columbus Poltergeist Case." In Kendrick Frazier (ed.), *Science Con-
          fronts the Paranormal.* Buffalo: Prometheus Books.
1992   "Help Stamp Out Absurd Beliefs." *Time* April 13:80.
Rao, K. Ramakrishna
1979   "Psi: Its Place in Nature." In William Roll (ed.), *Research in Parapsychol-
          ogy 1978.* Metuchen, N.J.: Scarecrow Press. Pp. 157–73.
Rao, K. Ramakrishna (ed.)
1986   *Case Studies in Parapsychology.* Jefferson, N.C.: McFarland.
Rao, K. Ramakrishna, and John Palmer
1987   "The Anomaly Called Psi." *Behavioral and Brain Sciences* 10 (4): 539–
          51.
Raphaell, Katrina
1985   *Crystal Enlightenment. Volume 1.* Santa Fe, N.M.: Aurora Press.
1987   *Crystal Healing. Volume 2.* Santa Fe, N.M.: Aurora Press.
1990   *The Crystalline Transmission. Volume 3.* Santa Fe, N.M.: Aurora Press.
Rapp, Rayna
1991   "Moral Pioneers: Women, Men, and Fetuses on a Frontier of Reproduc-
          tive Technology." In Micaela di Leonardo (ed.), *Gender at the Crossroads
          of Knowledge.* Berkeley and Los Angeles: University of California Press.
Raschke, Carl
1988   "New Age Economics." In Robert Basil (ed.), *Not Necessarily the New
          Age.* Buffalo: Prometheus Books.
Rawlins, Dennis
1981   "sTARBABY [sic]." *Fate* 34 (10): 67–99.
Reed, Graham
1989   "The Psychology of Channelling." *Skeptical Inquirer* 13 (4): 385–90.
Reingold, Nathan
1991   *Science, American Style.* New Brunswick: Rutgers University Press.
Restivo, Sal
1985   *The Social Relations of Physics, Mysticism, and Mathematics.* Boston/
          Dordrecht: D. Reidel.
1988   "Modern Science as a Social Problem." *Social Problems* 35 (3): 206–25.

Restivo, Sal, and Julia Loughlin
1987   "Critical Sociology of Science and Scientific Validity." *Knowledge: Creation, Diffusion, Utilization* 8 (3): 486–508.
Rhine, Joseph Banks
1934   *Extra-Sensory Perception.* Boston: Boston Society for Psychical Research.
1953   *New World of the Mind.* New York: William Sloane Associates.
1982   "Psychology and Parapsychology." In R. A. McConnell (ed.), *Encounters with Parapsychology.* Pittsburgh: Author (orig. 1967).
Rhine, Joseph Banks, and Associates
1965   *Parapsychology from Duke to FRNM.* Durham, N.C.: Parapsychology Press.
Rhine, Joseph Banks, and J. Gaither Pratt
1957   *Parapsychology: Frontier Science of the Mind.* Springfield, Ill.: Thomas.
Rhine, Louisa E.
1961   *Hidden Channels of the Mind.* New York: William Morrow and Co.
1967   *ESP in Life and Lab.* New York: MacMillan.
1975   *Psi, What Is It?* New York: Harper and Row.
1977   "Research Methods with Spontaneous Cases." In Benjamin B. Wolman (ed.), *Handbook of Parapsychology.* New York: Van Nostrand.
1983   *Something Hidden.* Jefferson, N.C.: McFarland.
Rockwell, Theodore, Robert Rockwell, and W. Teed Rockwell
1978   "Irrational Rationalists: A Critique of *The Humanist's* Crusade Against Parapsychology." *Journal of the American Society for Psychical Research* 72 (1): 23–34.
Rogo, D. Scott
1976   *In Search of the Unknown: The Odyssey of a Psychical Investigator.* New York: Taplinger Publishing Co.
1983   *Leaving the Body: A Complete Guide to Astral Projection.* New York: Prentice-Hall.
Roll, William
1972   *The Poltergeist.* New York: New American Library.
1986   "Introduction. Symposium on Clinical Parapsychology." *Research in Parapsychology* 1985:168–77.
Romanucci-Ross, Lola
1980   "On the Researching of Lost Images." *Anthropology and Humanism Quarterly* 5 (1): 14–20.
Rosaldo, Renato
1989   *Culture and Truth.* Stanford: Stanford University Press.
Rosen, Jay
1989   "Consumer Culture and the New Age." *Skeptical Inquirer* 13 (4): 401–4.
Ross, Andrew
1991   *Strange Weather: Culture, Science, and Technology in the Age of Limits.* New York: Verso.
Rossman, Michael
1979   *New Age Blues.* New York: Dutton.

Roszak, Theodore
1969   *The Making of a Counter Culture.* New York: Doubleday/Anchor.
Rushing, Janice Hocker
1986   "Reagan's 'Star Wars' Address: Mythic Containment of Technical Reasoning." *Quarterly Journal of Speech* 72:415–33.
Sabbagh, Karl
1985–86   "The Psychopathology of Fringe Medicine." *Skeptical Inquirer* 10 (2): 154–64.
Sahlins, Marshall
1976   *Culture and Practical Reason.* Chicago: University of Chicago Press.
1981   *Historical Metaphors and Mythical Realities.* Ann Arbor, Mich.: University of Michigan Press.
Said, Edward
1978   *Orientalism.* New York: Pantheon.
Sargent, Epes
1869   *Planchette, or the Despair of Science.* Boston: Roberts Brothers.
Satin, Mark
1978   *New Age Politics.* West Vancouver, B.C.: Whitecap Books.
Schultz, Ted
1989   "The New Age: The Need for Myth in an Age of Science." *Skeptical Inquirer* 13 (4): 375–79.
Schumacher, John, and Robert Anderson
1970   "In Defense of Mystical Science." *Philosophy East and West* 29 (1): 73–90.
Scott, Pam, Evelleen Richards, and Brian Martin
1990   "Captives of Controversy: The Myth of the Neutral Social Researcher in Contemporary Scientific Controversies." *Science, Technology, and Human Values* 15 (4): 474–94.
Seckel, Al
1986   "Explaining Rather Than Debunking." *Skeptical Inquirer* 11 (1): 6.
Shames, Laurence
1990   "Has the Thirty- and Fortysomething Generation Passed its Peak?" *Utne Reader* January/February: 78–82.
Shapin, Betty, and Lisette Coly
1977   *The Philosophy of Parapsychology.* New York: Parapsychology Foundation.
Sheaffer, Robert
1989   "Guerrilla Ontology and Factoids in Action [book review of *The New Inquisition*, by Robert Anton Wilson]." *Skeptical Inquirer* 14 (1): 78–82.
Shore, Lys Ann
1989   "New Light on the New Age." *Skeptical Inquirer* 13:226–40.
Siegel, Bernard S.
1986   *Love, Medicine, and Miracles.* New York: Harper and Row.
Smith, Adam (George Jerome Waldo Goodman)
1975   *Powers of Mind.* New York: Random House.

Snow, C. P.
1959   *The Cultures and the Scientific Revolution.* New York and Cambridge, U.K.: Cambridge University Press.
Spraggett, Allen, with William Rauscher
1973   *Arthur Ford: The Man Who Talked with the Dead.* New York: W. W. Norton and Co.
Stalker, Douglas, and Clark Glymour
1985   *Examining Holistic Medicine.* Buffalo: Prometheus Books.
Stanford, Rex
1977   "The Application of Learning Theory to ESP Performance: A Review of Dr. C. T. Tart's Monograph." *Journal of the American Society for Psychical Research* 71 (1): 55–80.
1978   "Toward Reinterpreting Psi Events." *Journal of the American Society for Psychical Research* 72 (3): 197–214.
1984   "A Walk Among the Trees in Search of the Forest." *Journal of Parapsychology* 48:333–51.
1985   "Correspondence." *Journal of Parapsychology* 49:207.
Starhawk (sic)
1979   *The Spiral Dance.* San Francisco: Harper and Row.
1982   *Dreaming the Dark.* Boston: Beacon.
1987   *Truth or Dare.* San Francisco: Harper and Row.
Stein, Diane
1985   *The Kwan Yin Book of Changes.* St. Paul, Minn.: Llewellyn.
1986   *The Women's Spirituality Book.* St. Paul, Minn.: Llewellyn.
1988   *Stroking the Python: Women's Psychic Lives.* St. Paul, Minn.: Llewellyn.
Stevenson, Ian
1980   "Gaither Pratt—An Appreciation." *Journal of the American Society for Psychical Research* 74 (3): 277–93.
1981   "Can We Describe the Mind?" In William Roll and John Beloff (eds.), *Research in Parapsychology 1980.* Metuchen, N.J.: Scarecrow Press.
1984   "Guest Editorial: Are Parapsychology Journals Good for Parapsychology?" *Journal of the American Society for Psychical Research* 78 (2): 97–104.
1987a   "Guest Editorial: Changing Fashions in the Study of Spontaneous Cases." *Journal of the American Society for Psychical Research* 81 (1): 1–10.
1987b   "Guest Editorial: Why Investigate Spontaneous Cases?" *Journal of the American Society for Psychical Research* 81 (2): 101–9.
1988   "Guest Editorial: Was the Attempt to Identify Parapsychology as a Separate Field of Science Misguided?" *Journal of the American Society for Psychical Research* 82 (4): 309–18.
Stewart, Jeannie, William Roll, and Steve Baumann
1987   "Hypnotic Suggestion and RSPK." In Debra Weiner and Roger Nelson (eds.), *Research in Parapsychology 1986.* Metuchen, N.J.: Scarecrow Press.
Still, Alfred
1950   *Borderlands of Science.* New York: Philosophical Library.

Stocking, George, Jr.
1971   "Animism in Theory and Practice: E. B. Tylor's Unpublished 'Notes on
        "Spiritualism.""" *Man* 6:88–104.
1987   *Victorian Anthropology.* New York: Free Press.
Stokes, Douglas
1983   *"Frames of Meaning,* by H. M. Collins and T. J. Pinch [book review."
        Journal of the American Society for Psychical Research 77 (1): 83–92.
1984   *"Science, Good, Bad, and Bogus,* by Martin Gardner [book review]."
        Journal of the American Society for Psychical Research 78 (1): 87–95.
Stoller, Paul, and Cheryl Olkes
1987   *In Sorcery's Shadow.* Chicago: University of Chicago Press.
Story, Ronald
1980   *Guardians of the Universe?* New York: St. Martin's Press.
Strauss, Linda
1991   "Stage-Magic and Spiritualism as Discourses on Natural Science." Paper
        presented at the annual meeting of the Society for Literature and Sci-
        ence, Montreal.
Suchman, Lucy
1987   *Plans and Situated Actions: The Problem of Human-Machine Communi-
        cation.* Cambridge: Cambridge University Press.
Tanner, Amy
1910   *Studies in Spiritism.* New York and London: D. Appleton.
Tarcher, Jeremy P.
1989   "Here's to the End of 'New Age' Publishing." *Publisher's Weekly* Novem-
        ber 3:36.
Targ, Russell, and Harold E. Puthoff
1977   *Mind Reach: Scientists Look at Psychic Ability.* New York: Delacorte
        Press.
Tart, Charles
1969   *Altered States of Consciousness.* New York: John Wiley and Sons,
        Inc.
1976   *Learning to Use Extrasensory Perception.* Chicago: University of Chi-
        cago Press.
1977   *Psi: Scientific Studies of the Psychic Realm.* New York: E. P. Dutton.
Taussig, Michael
1980   "Reification and the Consciousness of the Patient." *Social Science and
        Medicine* 14B:3–13.
1987   *Shamanism, Colonialism, and the Wild Man.* Chicago: University of
        Chicago Press.
Taylor, Joan Kennedy
1992   *Reclaiming the Mainstream: Individualist Feminism Rediscovered.* Buf-
        falo: Prometheus Books.
Thomas, Keith
1971   *Religion and the Decline of Magic.* New York: Scribner's.

Thouless, Robert
1972   *From Anecdote to Experiment in Psychical Research.* London: Routledge.
Tipton, Stephen
1982   *Getting Saved from the Sixties.* Berkeley: University of California Press.
Tiryakin, Edward
1972   "Toward a Sociology of Esoteric Culture." *American Journal of Sociology*
         78:401–12.
Toumey, Christopher
in press "Evolution and Secular Humanism." *Journal of the American Academy*
         of Religion.
Travers, Peter, and Stephanie Reiff
1974   *The Story Behind the Exorcist.* New York: Crown.
Traweek, Sharon
1988   *Beamtimes and Lifetimes: The World of High Energy Physicists.* Cam-
         bridge, Mass.: Harvard University Press.
1990   "Law and Order, Sexy Machines, and the Erotics of Fieldwork." Paper
         presented at the annual meeting of the Society for Social Studies of Sci-
         ence. Forthcoming in *Anthropology Today.*
Truzzi, Marcello
1982   "Analysis and Discussion of Rawlins." *Zetetic Scholar* 9:33–83 and 10:
         43–81.
Turner, Frank Miller
1974   *Between Science and Religion.* New Haven: Yale University Press.
Turner, Victor
1967   *The Forest of Symbols.* Ithaca: Cornell University Press.
1974   *Dramas, Fields, and Metaphors.* Ithaca: Cornell University Press.
Visweswaran, Kamala
1988   "Defining Feminist Ethnography." *Inscriptions* 3/4:27–46.
Walker, Gregory
1986   *The Living and the Undead.* Urbana and Chicago: University of Illinois
         Press.
Wallace, Anthony F. C.
1956   "Revitalization Movements." *American Anthropologist* 58:264–81.
Wallis, Roy
1985   "Science and Pseudo-Science." *Social Science Information* 24 (3): 585–601.
Walzer, Michael
1965   *The Revolution of the Saints.* Cambridge, Mass.: Harvard University
         Press.
Weber, Max
1958   *The Protestant Ethic and the Spirit of Capitalism.* New York: Charles
         Scribner's Sons (orig. 1904–5).
Webster, Paula
1975   "Matriarchy: A Vision of Power." In Rayna Reiter (ed.), *Toward an An-*
         thropology of Women. New York: Monthly Review Press.

Weeks, Priscilla, and Jane Packard
1991   "Parkman and the Mullet Marshall: Science and Power Plays in Natural
        Resource Management." Paper presented at the annual meeting of the
        Society for Social Studies of Science.
White, Rhea
1985   "The Spontaneous, the Imaginal, and Psi: Foundations for a Depth Para-
        psychology." In Rhea White and Jerry Solfvin (eds.), *Research in Para-
        psychology 1984.* Metuchen, N.J.: Scarecrow Press.
1990   "An Experience-Centered Approach to Parapsychology." *Exceptional Hu-
        man Experience* 8 (1–2): 7–36.
1991   "Feminist Science, Postmodern Views, and Exceptional Human Experi-
        ence: An Editorial." *Exceptional Human Experience* 9 (1): 1–9.
Williams, Rosalind
1990   *Notes on Underground: An Essay on Technology, Society, and the Imagi-
        nation.* Cambridge, Mass.: MIT Press.
Wilson, Robert Anton
1986   *The New Inquisition: Irrational Rationalism and the Citadel of Science.*
        Phoenix: Falcon Press.
Winkelman, Michael
1980a   "Science and Parapsychology: An Ideological Revolution." (Abstract.)
        In William Roll (ed.), *Research in Parapsychology 1979.* Metuchen, N.J.:
        Scarecrow Press.
1980b   "Science and Parapsychology: An Ideological Revolution." *Revision* 3 (1):
        59–64.
1982   "Magic: A Theoretical Reassessment." *Current Anthropology* 23 (1):
        37–66.
Winner, Langdon
1977   *Autonomous Technology.* Cambridge, Mass.: MIT Press.
1986   *The Whale and the Reactor.* Chicago: University of Chicago Press.
1989   "Technological Frontiers and Human Integrity." Steven L. Goldman (ed.),
        *Science, Technology, and Social Progress: Research in Technology Studies,
        Vol. 2.* Bethlehem: Lehigh University Press and London and Toronto: Asso-
        ciated University Presses.
Woolgar, Steve
1981a   "Critique and Criticism: Two Readings of Ethnomethodology." *Social
        Studies of Science* 11:504–14.
1981b   "Interests and Explanation in the Social Study of Science." *Social Studies
        of Science* 11:365–94.
Woolgar, Steve (ed.)
1988   *Knowledge and Reflexivity: New Frontiers in the Sociology of Knowl-
        edge.* Beverly Hills: Sage.
Yates, Frances
1972   *The Rosicrucian Enlightenment.* London: Routledge (U.S. edition: Boulder,
        Colo.: Shambhala).

Zabusky, Stacia
in press   "Multiple Contexts, Multiple Meanings: Scientists in the European Space
            Agency." In David Hess and Linda Layne (eds.), *Knowledge and Society
            Volume 9: The Anthropology of Science and Technology*. Greenwich,
            Conn.: JAI Press.
Zingrone, Nancy
1988   "A Study of Authorship and Gender in American Parapsychology." *Jour-
            nal of Parapsychology* 52:321–43.
Zukav, Gary
1984   *The Dancing Wu Li Masters: An Overview of the New Physics*. New
            York: Bantam.
Zusne, Leonard
1985   "Magical Thinking and Parapsychology." In Paul Kurtz (ed.), *A Skep-
            tic's Handbook of Parapsychology*. Buffalo: Prometheus.
Zusne, Leonard, and W. H. Jones
1982   *Anomalistic Psychology*. Hillsdale, N.J.: Erlbaum.

Index

Adler, Margot, 194n7, 209n18
Alcock, James, 199n13
Alvarado, Carlos, 102, 201n8
American culture, x, 46, 69, 71, 88–93, 137–41, 153, 159, 197n25. *See also* Body; Frontier; Individualism; Materialism; New World; Puritans; Revolutionary
American Society for Psychical Research (ASPR), 7–9, 22–25, 83, 149, 166, 190n6
Andrews, Lynn, 6, 48–49, 96, 194n7
Anthropology and anthropologists: actors in the ideological area, 15–16, 36–37, 149–50, 203n5, 205nn8–11; perspective of, 14, 113–14, 148–59, 203n5, 205n9; theories and methods, 180–86; viewed by nonanthropologists, 66, 86, 131
Aquarian conspiracy. *See* Ferguson, Marilyn
Aquarius, Age of, 21, 44, 47, 70, 116
Argüelles, José, 6, 72–73, 92
Asia and Asian religions, 3–4, 19–22, 36, 45–46, 52, 65, 72, 117, 175, 195n15. *See also* Tao and Taoism
Asimov, Isaac, 12, 86, 112, 118, 191n11, 196n22
ASPR. *See* American Society for Psychical Research
Astral projection. *See* Out-of-body experience
Atlantis, 21, 46–48, 51, 92, 194n6, 194n10

Baby boomers, 5–6, 36, 86, 201–2n12
Bailey, Alice, 20–21
Barnes, Barry, 3, 183–84, 203ch.7n1

Bellah, Robert, 90–91, 115
Bercovitch, Sacvan, 91, 200n15
Blavatsky, Madame, 19–20
Bleier, Ruth, 113–14
Body, and cultural representations of, 115–19
Boon, James, 43, 180, 185, 193n4
Boundary-work, 17–18, 25, 29, 31, 40, 51, 100, 141, 145–48, 153, 170. *See also* Gieryn, Thomas
Bourdieu, Pierre, 15, 184–85
Boyd, Doug, 173
Braude, Ann, 95
Braude, Stephen, 104, 164–65, 201n8
Brazilian parapsychology and religion, x, 18, 28, 74, 111, 154, 160, 165–66, 169, 179–80, 198n5
Brown, Susan Love, 5
Burke, Kenneth, 55, 185, 195n12

California, 3, 45, 48, 50–51, 65
Capra, Fritjof, 46, 200n1, 201n10
Catholic church, 124, 131, 166, 190n10
Cayce, Edgar Evans, 194n6
Channelers. *See* Mediums
Collins, Harry, 33, 88, 150–55, 165, 204n4, 205n12, 205n13
Committee for the Scientific Investigation of Claims of the Paranormal. *See* CSICOP
Communism, 77, 173, 207n6. *See also* Marx, Karl; New Left; Revolutionary
Community, 189n2. *See also* Movement
Consumer culture, 14, 81, 88–89
Coon, Deborah J., 27–28, 192n9
Crystals, 3, 46–48, 159, 172, 193–94n5, 209n17. *See also* Raphaell, Katrina

239

SCIENCE AND LITERATURE
A series edited by George Levine

One Culture: Essays in Science and Literature
Edited by George Levine

In Pursuit of a Scientific Culture: Science, Art, and Society in the Victorian Age
Peter Allan Dale

Sexual Visions: Images of Gender in Science and Medicine between the Eighteenth and Twentieth Centuries
Ludmilla Jordanova

Writing Biology: Texts in the Social Construction of Scientific Knowledge
Greg Myers

Gaston Bachelard, Subversive Humanist: Texts and Readings
Mary McAllester Jones

Science in the New Age: The Paranormal, Its Defenders and Debunkers, and American Culture
David J. Hess

Realism and Representation: Essays on the Problem of Realism in Relation to Science, Literature, and Culture
Edited by George Levine

DATE DUE

JUN 4 '9			
JUL 2 5 1999			
AG 30 00			
JE 3 '02			
		WITHDRAWN	

| GAYLORD | | | PRINTED IN U.S.A |